IZMIR AND THE LEVANTINE WORLD, 1550–1650

PUBLICATIONS ON THE NEAR EAST
UNIVERSITY OF WASHINGTON
NUMBER 5

IZMIR AND THE

Daniel Goffman

Levantine World, 1550–1650

UNIVERSITY OF WASHINGTON PRESS
Seattle and London

Sponsored by
the Department of
Near Eastern Languages and Civilization
and the
Middle East Center
of the Henry M. Jackson
School of International Studies
University of Washington

The Library of Congress Cataloging-in-Publication Data
will be found at the back of this book.

UNIVERSITY OF WASHINGTON PRESS
Seattle and London

*Publication of this book
has been made possible
by grants from the*

Institute of Turkish Studies

*Maurice D. and Lois Schwartz
International Studies Endowment*

Seattle–Izmir Sister City Association

For Carolyn

CONTENTS

ILLUSTRATIONS

Audience of the Consul of Smyrna with the Kadı, from du Mont, *Voyages*

The *beylerbeyi* of Anadolu, from Happel, *Thesaurus exoticorum*

An Ottoman official, from *Turkische Chronica* (1577)

Portrait of Murat IV, from Happel, *Thesaurus exoticorum*

A *kazasker*, from Nicolas de Nicolay, *The Navigations, Peregrinations and Voyages, Made into Turkie* (1585)

Armenian, Greek, and Jewish merchants, from de Nicolay, *The Navigations*

TABLES

ACKNOWLEDGMENTS

This work has reached fruition through support from many individuals and institutions. At the University of Chicago, the late Arcadius Kahan's unyielding yet kind guidance led to a reassessment of my beliefs and assumptions about Jewish history, Donald F. Lach's suggestion that I consider Ottoman studies at a time of doubts was decisive, and Halil İnalcık's enthusiasm for and willingness to share his unrivaled knowledge of Ottoman history and paleography inspired me to change course midway through graduate school and devote my endeavors to the Ottoman empire.

Most of the research for this volume was undertaken in the Prime Ministry's archives in Istanbul, and I thank my hosts, the Turkish government and the staff of that archive. In my first months there, Zeliha Argon was most patient with a novice. Over the course of several sojourns in Istanbul, William M. Blair, Selim Deringil, Suraiya Faroqhi, Caroline Ballingal Finkel, Mehmet Genç, Nejat Göyünç, Antony M. Greenwood, Douglas A. Howard, Rhoads Murphey, William Peachey, Donald Quataert, Halil Sahillioğlu, and many others willingly shared their knowledge and ideas, and warmed cold and often frustrating hours in that depot. In West Lafayette, my parents, Eve and Casper, gave my family a critical one-and-a-half years of haven, and Robert A. McDaniel, of Purdue University, moderated for me the despair of jobless writing. The history faculty of Emory

University—particularly Ralph S. Hattox, Kermit E. McKenzie, Kenneth W. Stein, and Thomas E. Williams—were encouraging as I completed early drafts of this work; and the history faculty of Ball State University has provided a stimulating environment in which to complete it. I must single out my colleagues Richard Aquila, Andrew R. L. Cayton, Mark Charles Fissel, Susan C. Lawrence, and John M. Glen for lively conversations, acute critiques, and benign cajolings.

The Commission for Educational Exchange between the United States and Turkey, the American Research Institute in Turkey, the Center for Middle Eastern Studies at the University of Chicago, and the offices of the Provost and Research, and the Publications Committee at Ball State University provided financial support for travel, research, and writing; the staffs of the Library of Congress in Washington, D.C. (especially Christopher M. Murphy), the Public Record Office in London, the Regenstein Library at the University of Chicago (particularly Gary Van Zante), the Lilly Library at Indiana University, and the James Ford Bell Library at the University of Minnesota were consistently courteous and helpful; and John E. Weakland and Anthony O. Edmonds of Ball State University worked hard to help me find the time to complete this book. No one, however, can share responsibility for its deficiencies.

I wish finally to thank my editor, Felicia J. Hecker, who made delightful the process of turning a dissertation into a book; my children, Samuel and Laura, who may have slowed down production of this volume but more importantly increased immeasurably the joy of its creation; and most of all my wife, Carolyn.

Izmir and the Levantine World, 1550–1650

ABBREVIATIONS

BBA: Başbakanlık Arşivi (Prime Ministry's Archives, Istanbul)

CSP,
Venice: Calendar of State Papers and Manuscripts Relating to English Affairs in the Archives and Collections of Venice, and in Other Libraries of Northern Italy

ED: Ecnebi Defterleri, Registers Dealing with Foreigners (Prime Ministry's Archives, Istanbul)

EI²: *Encyclopaedia of Islam*. New ed. Leiden: E.J. Brill, 1960–

HD: Hadariye Defterleri, Registers Dealing with the Salaries and Appointments of Dervishes (Prime Ministry's Archives, Istanbul)

İE: İbnülemin Catalogue of Documents (Prime Ministry's Archives, Istanbul)

MD: Mühimme Defterleri, Registers Dealing with a Variety of Matters (Prime Ministry's Archives, Istanbul)

MM: Maliyeden Müdevver, Materials Transferred from the Office of Finance (Prime Ministry's Archives, Istanbul)

MZD: Mühimme Zeyli Defterleri, Supplementary Registers Dealing with a Variety of Matters (Prime Ministry's Archives, Istanbul)

PRO: Public Record Office, London

SP: State Papers (Public Record Office, London)

TKS: Topkapı Sarayı, Istanbul

TT: Tapu-Tahrir Defterleri, Registrations of Peoples and Produce in the Ottoman Empire (Prime Ministry's Archives, Istanbul)

NOTE ON USAGE

When Turkish appears in the text, modern orthography is adopted. Such terms are contextually defined in the glossary. Ottoman spellings can be found in the *New Redhouse Turkish-English Dictionary* (Istanbul: Yayınevi, 1968). Village names pose a particular problem, for some sites have vanished and others have changed names. The names of such villages have been transliterated as carefully as possible. Except when English provides its own spelling (the initial *I* of neither Istanbul nor Izmir is dotted), Ottoman place names appear in their Turkish forms (Dubrovnik rather than Ragusa).

1

Izmir before the Seventeenth Century

History is riddled with clouded times and unexplained changes. Sometimes a paucity of sources deepens the mystery. At other times, it is an inaccessibility of sources or an indifference toward or ignorance of a particular subject that beget historical lacunae. Fernand Braudel, in one of his last major works, cites such a gap in Ottoman commercial history.[1] He remarks, quite rightly, that "the major axes of trade running through the empire themselves gave it a certain coherence," and insists that while "these axes might shift, . . . they remained in existence." Braudel specifies that "in the fifteenth century, the major crossroads of trade was probably . . . Bursa," and that "the Turkish advance into Syria and Egypt then moved the centre of the Ottoman economy towards Aleppo and Alexandria." This transfer is generally accepted; murkiness descends in the subsequent period. "It is known," Braudel continues, "that the centre moved yet again in the seventeenth century, this time to Smyrna [Izmir], though it has never been satisfactorily explained."

The emergence of Izmir as a commercial center in the critical century during which the Ottoman empire stopped expanding and began to contract still remains an unexplained phenomenon. Curiously, this birth of an entrepôt in the Ottoman heartland has only recently been linked to axes of international commerce and never to the empire's administrative, social, and economic distress. Viewing Izmir's emergence as an outgrowth of a convergence between internal events and structural changes in world trade can satisfactorily fill this gap in eastern Mediterranean commercial history.

Since about 1650 Izmir has rivaled and at times surpassed other entrepôts in the Mediterranean world; as recently as 1600, however, fewer than five-thousand souls inhabited the town. Throughout the ancient and medieval periods of history, Izmir competed for commerce, not always successfully, with several other ports in western Anatolia, including Foça (Phocaea), Ayasoluğ (which replaced the silted-up Ephesus), Kuşadası (Scala Nuova), and Balat (Miletus). The region's rich diversity of valleys, plains, isthmuses, deltas, and rivers emptying into bays and inlets, assured that while centers occasionally emerged to dominate commerce, their periods of hegemony remained brief, they never emerged as "major crossroads," and they soon faded back into obscurity. At the same time, the subcontinent's ragged coastline, broken by innumerable gulfs and harbors, has allowed merchants and pirates to trade and smuggle through a number of relatively small ports, thereby reducing the often prohibitive costs of overland transport and customs duties.

The commercial fortunes of Izmir and its sister ports varied according to time and circumstance. During the brief period of Constantinople's bondage to the Latins (1204–61), Izmir experienced a renascence. Michael Paleologus, the Byzantine emperor who in 1261 returned to the capital city from exile in Nicaea (İznik), and his predecessors strove to consolidate their positions in Asia Minor and shore up their defenses against Crusader and Turk. During those years the Byzantines with Genoese assistance cultivated the port of Izmir as a commercial and cultural center. In the following century, the Turkoman principalities of Aydın and Menteşe wrested control of the region from the Genoese. Commerce through the two main ports of the emirates of Aydın and Menteşe—Kuşadası and Balat— overtook and surpassed Byzantine Izmir.[2] Then, after the Ottoman sultan Bayezid I conquered most of the region in 1390, trade through these ports also subsided. While political and military confrontation did not smother all trade, commerce became evenly distributed among Foça, Ayasoluğ, Balat, Urla, Çeşme, Seferihisar, Kuşadası and other regional port towns.

Alone among these ports, Izmir remained outside Bayezid's empire in 1390; it was the last bastion of Christendom along the Anatolian littoral. The Christians had not, however, enjoyed a continuous occupation. Between 1076 and 1117 the Seljuk empire briefly controlled the port, and in 1329 Aydınoğlu Umur, a Turkoman bey, expelled the Genoese from the harbor's fortress before relinquishing it in 1344 to a Christian league organized by Pope Clement VI. Forty-six years later, Bayezid was unable to pry the castle from Christian hands, and it sat like a festering and embarrassing sore at the edge of the conquering ghazi's subcontinent.

THE GREAT OTTOMAN PEACE

It was left not to an Ottoman, but to the Turco-Mongol warrior Timur (Tamerlane), to seize the outpost. Timur's goal as he marched westward across Anatolia in 1402 was the dissolution of the Ottoman empire, which, under Bayezid I, had come to encompass much of Anatolia and the Balkans. Bayezid fueled a growing rivalry with Timur by annexing several Turkoman principalities in southwestern and central Anatolia. Timur considered these emirates his protectorates and several of the vanquished emirs sought his assistance against Bayezid. He responded in 1402 and, after a fierce battle, routed the Ottoman army at Ankara.[3] Timur then proceeded across Anatolia to Izmir, which he swiftly crushed and depopulated in December of that same year. The great conqueror wintered in Ephesus before wheeling back toward Central Asia to begin planning an invasion of China. Prior to leaving Anatolia, he reestablished those Turkoman states that Bayezid had annexed, including the emirate of Aydınoğlu and the town of Izmir within it.

Timur's abrupt departure left a political vacuum in western Anatolia, and Bayezid's sons—most prominently İsa, Süleyman, Musa, and Mehmet—struggled among themselves and against the emperor of Byzantium, the reconstituted Turkoman principalities, and various Latin lords and Latin states for control of the territory, which had been their father's empire.[4] After considerable turmoil, Mehmet emerged victorious from this internecine war and in 1421 handed over a weakened but intact realm to his son Murat II.

Political anarchy plagued Anatolia in the first years of the fifteenth century. During Timur's campaigns many Turks and Christians fled to the Balkans or Aegean islands such as Samos and elsewhere in order to escape the turmoil in which the entire region including Izmir was fully embroiled.[5] In 1402 Timur turned the port over to Aydınoğlu Cüneyd bey, Umur bey's grandson, and not until 1414 did the Ottomans under Mehmet I finally regain possession of it. For the next ten years, Cüneyd bey engaged in intricate diplomatic and political maneuvering with the Ottomans, the Byzantines, and others in his endeavor to regain autonomy in his forefathers' domain. He ruled again in 1422, but only briefly, for in 1424 the Ottomans annexed all of Aydın, including Izmir, and soon thereafter had Cüneyd bey executed.[6]

It is unlikely that Izmir prospered while Cüneyd grappled with the Ottomans, and the port and its hinterland must have been in a desolate state when they fell into Ottoman hands. A region with such rich agricultural resources enhanced by its proximity to the sea, however, would not remain undeveloped for long. The consolidation of Ottoman rule in western Anatolia spawned conditions under which prosperity again could be realized.

While Ottoman power expunged land-based opposition, conquest did not end the threat from the sea. In the first decades of the fifteenth century, Venice was the dominant maritime force in the eastern Mediterranean and in 1424 Murat II could not adequately defend his coasts from naval attacks. Between 1423 and 1430, the Ottoman and Venetian empires battled each other to a stalemate, with the Muslim army governing the land and the Christian navy the sea. For the next several decades, Izmir and other ports in western Anatolia suffered seaborne depredation. Even though the Gulf of Izmir provided some natural protection, as late as 1472 a Venetian fleet penetrated the gulf and attacked and pillaged the port.[7] Mehmet II responded by rebuilding the disused castle at the entrance to the port of Izmir, thereby protecting the port on both land and sea.

BYPASSING WESTERN ANATOLIA

Although any demographic and commercial resurgence in Izmir required such a *pax ottomanica*, the port did not at once evolve into a center for international trade. Izmir for the fifteenth and much of the sixteenth centuries retained its small-town characteristics.[8] In part, the configuration of international trade and the types of goods that flowed along commercial arteries determined this underdevelopment. Silks and spices dominated trade from east to west, while textiles and bullion were given in return. The principal exchanges for these commodities were to the south in Aleppo and Alexandria. While some luxury goods crossed the Anatolian peninsula, their terminus was not Izmir. Because of geography and geopolitics, the Tabriz-Bursa caravan route monopolized trade.

Under the first emirs, Bursa had been the capital of the Ottoman principality and when Murat I moved his court to Edirne (Adrianople), Bursa remained the capital city of the Asian half of the empire. After 1453, when Mehmet II settled in Istanbul, Bursa became the closest Anatolian city to the new capital and boats regularly plied the waters between the Golden Horn and Bursa's port of Mudanya.[9] Bursa's strategic position determined the conquering sultan's subsequent campaigns in Anatolia. The Ottomans sought to secure the overland routes stretching north-south between Bursa and Antalya and east-west between Tabriz and Bursa.[10] Mehmet II's thrust southward toward Konya in 1468 secured the overland route from Antalya, to Konya, to Bursa, and finally to Istanbul. While this route was costlier and slower than the sea route around Anatolia, it also was safer than the hazardous circuit through Venetian- and Genoese- held islands. Many merchants preferred transporting their valuable goods along the caravan roads of Anatolia. It was

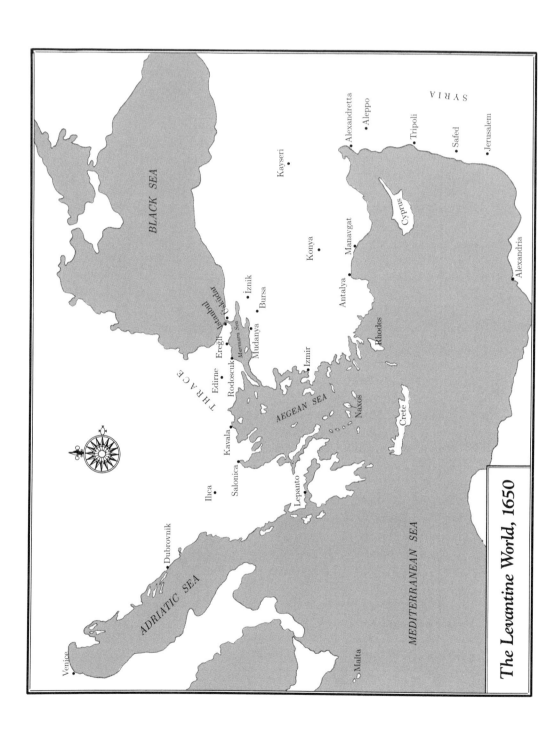

The Levantine World, 1650

not until the Ottoman conquests of the Fertile Crescent and Egypt in 1516–17 and Rhodes in 1522 that the sea lanes from the south became reasonably secure.

The conquests of Arab lands opened the rich ports of the eastern Mediterranean to Ottoman trade and engendered a commercial shift southward that bypassed western Anatolia. While this circumvention of Izmir and its hinterland occurred because of geo-economic considerations beyond Ottoman control, Istanbul welcomed and even encouraged it. Authorities funneled the modest quantities of luxury goods that found their way to the region through the nearby port of Çeşme to the Genoese-controlled island of Chios.[11] This exclusion of Izmir stemmed directly from the Ottoman theory of government. The sultan's principal duty was to guarantee the well-being of his subjects, which resulted in the creation of a relatively closed economic system. The foremost consideration of the state was to ensure adequate supplies of food and other goods for the needs of subjects and the perquisites of government and army.[12] In pursuing this goal, the Ottomans worked to revitalize western-Anatolian agriculture and directed the flow of produce through Izmir and other ports to desired destinations within the empire. Istanbul discouraged commercial development that might divert goods outside the empire.

The region's geography lent itself well to the Ottomans' chosen economy. The mountain ranges of Anatolia extend east to west and, whereas the northern coastline is barren and rocky, innumerable gulfs and fertile valleys break the western littoral.[13] The Ottomans exploited this configuration by developing a number of small ports, each containing several hundred inhabitants and serving as the distribution center for produce from its immediate hinterland. Istanbul, demanding a monopoly over locally produced goods in exchange for the protection that Ottoman military might provided, directed the marketing of western Anatolia's surplus according to its needs and desires.[14] In this regional lattice, Izmir's principal function was as a point of embarkation for goods bound for Istanbul and Ottoman Europe.

While this carefully regulated economy left little room for commercial expansion, it did not totally exclude international trade in local produce. The geography of the Aegean basin not only expedited the seaborne transport of bulky goods, but also lent itself to smuggling, a situation that audacious seamen chronically exploited. Ottoman officials often ignored or even abetted the carriage of nonessential goods westward. In the fifteenth and sixteenth centuries, much western-Anatolian cotton, dried fruits, grains, and leathers found their way into the hands of European merchants. The Ottomans endeavored however to restrict this trade to commodities that would not damage their military machine and to a scale that would not disrupt their provisioning network. As a result, international trade had little effect on western Anatolia.

Although Izmir in the early sixteenth century was part of a large and stable empire, the Ottoman peace did not appreciably hasten its commercial growth and the port remained economically insignificant. Moreover, as long as the Ottomans monopolized the produce of western Anatolia and merchants continued to circumvent the region and were uninterested in its indigenous commodities, the port languished.

IZMIR IN THE 1520S

This Ottoman regulation of trade, and its dispersal among Anatolian ports, continued until the end of the sixteenth century, and western Anatolia benefited little from ongoing commerce between the Ottoman empire and Christian Europe. Although Italian ships navigated the Gulf of Izmir in search of fibers and fruits, neither Latins nor other westerners established permanent residences in Izmir or other coastal towns. European disinterest suited Istanbul, which consumed western Anatolia's fruits, nuts, rice, leathers, and other goods and insisted upon preserving the provisioning network linking the region to the empire's capital city. Seeking a steady flow of foodstuffs, the Sublime Porte secured the sea lanes between Istanbul and the littoral, regulated prices, restricted commerce in commodities deemed essential or strategic, and discouraged the enlargement of western-Anatolian ports. Istanbul neither cared to exploit Izmir in other ways nor, because of the devastation that preceded Ottoman hegemony over the region, even envisioned its potential as an international entrepôt.

In the half century before Timur despoiled the town in 1402, Izmir's Turkish population had confined itself to Kadifekale, the castle on the hill, and its immediate surroundings because of the Christian menace ensconced in Aşağıkale, the castle guarding the divided settlement's inner harbor. As the site became repopulated during the *pax ottomanica* following Timur's decisive victory, the Turks gradually drifted down the hill from the quarter (*mahalle*) of Faikpaşa, to Mescid-i Selâtinzade, Han-Bey (Pazar), and Liman-i Izmir until by 1528–29 a solid band of Muslim settlement extended from castle to castle and obliterated the ancient partition between Crusader and Turk (see table 1).[15] While these four quarters formed the heart of the renascent town, this downward movement did not envelop its

TABLE 1

Population of Izmir, 1528 29
(*In* hane*s and* nefer*s*)

Quarter (*mahalle*)	*Hanes*	*Nefers*
Faikpaşa	45	70
Mescid-i Selâtinzade	38	61
Han-bey (Pazar)	27	39
Liman-i Izmir	17	33
Boynuzseküsü	50	61
Cemaat-i Gebran	29	43
Total	206	307

SOURCE: BBA, TT 148, pp. 8–10. A *hane* is a household, a *nefer* is a taxable adult male. The problem of interpreting these terms is perplexing. Barkan uses a flat multiplier of five for a *hane*, believing that the typical household consisted of five individuals. Leila Erder in "Measurement of Preindustrial Population Changes: The Ottoman Empire from the 15th to the 17th Century," *Middle Eastern Studies* 11 (1975): 294–99 espouses a male to total population rather than a household approach and suggests a multiplier of three or four. The issue revolves around the meanings of the relevant terms—*hane*, *nefer*, *mücerred*, *bive*, and so on. For more details see Halil İnalcık, "Impact of the *Annales* School on Ottoman Studies and New Findings," *Review* 1 (1978): 71–80, especially p. 80n41.

other two quarters, Boynuzseküsü and Cemaat-i Gebran. The
first was a largely autonomous village near Izmir and linked
only administratively to it. The second, a "community of Christians" (*cemaat-i gebran*), constituted a Greek Orthodox enclave adjoining the harbor.[16] Its twenty-nine households, whose
members rebuilt their quarter in the decades after Timur's onslaught, comprised approximately 14 percent of the town's inhabitants.

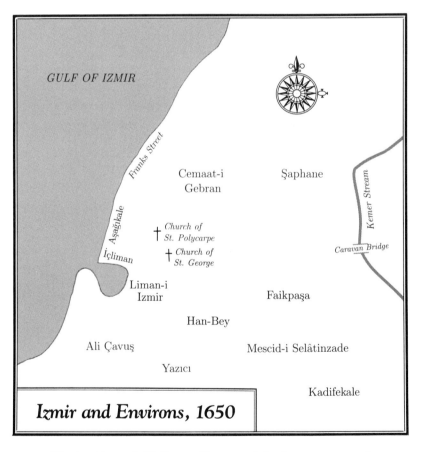

Izmir and Environs, 1650

NOTE: The locations of Ali Çavuş, Yazıcı, and Şaphane are approximate.

In the early sixteenth century, Izmir's Turkish inhabitants cultivated most of the crops congenial to the region's climate and terrain, although the quantities, somewhat smaller per capita than in other towns and villages within the *kaza* (administrative district), indicate that farming was not the only employment open to the town's inhabitants (see Appendix 2). Governmental collection in Izmir of 22,000 *akçes* per year from market dues, taxes on sheep, the transport of broad beans, rush mats, beeswax and honey, fines, and marriage registration signals service as a market for the surrounding villages.[17] Other commercial activities confirm an economy diversifying around agriculture. Authorities centralized at Izmir the customs revenue on locally produced commodities and weighing dues for the entire gulf other than Urla.[18] Istanbul, however, placed "silk and similar goods coming through Chios and Europe under the jurisdiction of the agents and collectors of the port of Çeşme," thereby stifling Izmir's potential by restricting it to the export of goods native to its hinterland and earmarked for domestic distribution.[19] In other words, while Izmir provisioned the Ottoman capital and army with fruits, grains, and fibers, Çeşme acted as the western-Anatolian conduit for luxury goods brought by ship from Istanbul and Bursa, and Antalya and other southern ports, or from the Genoese stronghold of Chios on vessels, which cast anchor at Çeşme without ever entering the gulf. Izmir's economy was largely agricultural (customs revenue generated a relatively meagre eighty-thousand *akçes* annually), thus discouraging either Armenians or Jews, who employed themselves largely in commerce-related activities, from residing there.[20] In the early sixteenth century international trade routes simply passed Izmir by, leaving it an exclusively Greek and Turkish town.

INDIGENOUS GROWTH IN A
WESTERN-ANATOLIAN TOWN

As the sixteenth century progressed Izmir became more tightly bound to Istanbul and insulated from the states surrounding the Ottoman empire. While piracy was endemic on the Aegean, corsairs rarely penetrated the narrow mouth of Izmir's gulf; while

Christian navies ranged the eastern Mediterranean, Ottoman naval superiority until well after the battle of Lepanto (1571) protected the western-Anatolian coast.[21] The Muslim power vanquished Genoese Chios, the last Christian outpost in the Aegean, in 1566 and Venetian Cyprus in 1570. In the final few decades of the century the Aegean, to all intents and purposes, became an Ottoman lake.

Although sheltered from the non-Ottoman world, Izmir did not remain unaltered. The secure stability of the mid-sixteenth century benefited the port and between 1528–29 and 1575–76 its population grew from 307 to 658 taxpayers, an impressive increase during a period when in all of western Anatolia only Bursa boasted a population of more than 3,000 households (see tables 1 and 2).[22] All of the established quarters other than Mescid-i Selâtinzade swelled past the bursting point, compelling the creation of three small spill-over neighborhoods—Ali Çavuş, Yazıcı, and Şaphane.

TABLE 2

Population of Izmir, 1575–76

(*In* nefer*s*)

Quarter (*mahalle*)	*Nefers*	Change from 1528–29
Faikpaşa	83	+13 (19%)
Mescid-i Selâtinzade	56	–5 (9%)
Han-Bey (Pazar)	92	+53 (235%)
Ali Çavuş	35	new quarter
Yazıcı	32	new quarter
Liman-i Izmir	54	+21 (64%)
Şaphane	30	new quarter
Boynuzseküsü	166	+105 (272%)
Cemaat-i Gebran	110	+67 (256%)
Total	658	+351 (215%)

SOURCE: BBA, TT 537, pp. 8–13.

Natural growth, while certainly a factor, cannot alone explain this doubling of Izmir's population. Turkish migrants pressing westward across Anatolia and fleeing the rural unrest that infested the subcontinent's interior even in Süleyman's time gravitated to the port, as did Greeks displaced from Thrace and the Aegean islands, particularly Chios whose recently conquered inhabitants slipped away to the more secure and thriving mainland town. While this growth lured neither Armenian nor Jew to Izmir, Christians and Muslims trickled into the port at about the same relative rates and although the absolute number of Greeks in Izmir increased two and a half times between 1527–28 and 1575–76, the percentage of the town that was Greek increased only marginally and Izmir retained a substantial Turco-Muslim majority.[23]

In a purely agricultural economy, such a demographic thrust would portend a division and redivision of land, soil exhaustion, and a consequent plummet in the quality of life. Although the fields of Izmir yielded half as much grain per capita in 1575–76 as they had fifty years earlier, the populace avoided such a crisis because recent settlers did not till the soil (see table 3). The presence of twenty-eight inhabitants who had taken the pilgrimage to Mecca, twenty-one ex-slaves, fifteen mariners (or perhaps Arabs), six dervishes, fifty-seven salt-pan workers, and other nonagriculturalists as well as workers in leather tanning and sesame oil industries signals a bustling market town (see table 4).[24] Also indicative of Izmir's rejection of the peasant's life was the lack of functioning flour mills and olive presses in the port, although the *kaza* boasted 232 of them.[25] Flour mills, clustered around grain-rich villages such as Özeroğlu, Kıyas, and Karacadağ, ground flour; and olive presses, crowded in villages with substantial olive groves such as Timurcilu, Denizliburnu, and Çamlu, squeezed olive oil before the peasantry brought the yield to market in Izmir. The presence in the town of four of the *kaza*'s five disused mills further attests to its repudiated agrarian past. As it shifted from rural to market economy, Izmir more and more induced the peasantry in its hinterlands—the rich valleys and alluvial plains whose rivers fed into the gulf—to nourish its inhabitants, who cultivated onions, garlic, and other culinary vegetables in gardens and small vegetable plots and neglected the grains, raisins, nuts,

TABLE 3

Tithe Dues in Izmir

(*In* akçes)

Commodity	1528–29	1575–76
Wheat	6,000/75 *kile*[a]	3,920/35 *kile*
Barley	1,500/30 *kile*	3,200/50 *kile*
Raisins and nuts	10,000	9,605
Cotton	800	800
Olives	1,500	1,500
Onions and garlic	1,500	3,000
Citrus fruit	200	250

SOURCE: BBA, TT 148, p. 11 and TT 537, p. 13. The table lists only those commodities for which direct comparison is possible. Much of the produce is lumped together in varying groupings. For example, the scribe in the earlier register assigned the chickpea, the broad bean, and the kidney bean each a separate heading; the scribe working on the later survey lumped all legumes together. These differences make direct comparison of these goods impossible.

[a] A *kile* is a bushel. Because weights and measures in the Ottoman empire were not standardized, it is difficult to assess its exact metric equivalent (see in particular scattered references in Ömer-Lütfi Barkan, *XV. ve XVI. asırlarda Osmanlı imparatorluğunda ziraî ekonominin hukukî ve malî esasları (kanunlar)* [Istanbul: Bürhaneddin Matbaası, 1943]; and Halil İnalcık, "Rice Cultivation and the *Çeltükçi-reâyâ* System in the Ottoman Empire," *Turcica* 14 [1982]: 119–20).

cotton, olives, and citrus fruits of subsistent and cash-producing agriculture, which they now habitually purchased in the market.

Although hindsight discloses that this drift away from tillage marked the genesis of a trading capital, Ottoman authorities did not perceive this progression. In the 1570s, the imperial treasury gleaned from Izmir's market and customs house the same returns as it had fifty years earlier, and continued to reserve its port facilities for the transfer of foodstuffs—dried fruits, nuts, and grains—from its hinterland to Istanbul and elsewhere within the empire. Not only were luxury goods still routed through Chios ten years after the conquest of that island, but a growing population and consequent burgeoning demand for food without a con-

TABLE 4

Sample Occupations/Titles in Izmir, 1575–76

Occupation	Faikpaşa	Mescid-i Selâtinzade	Han Bey	Ali Çavuş	Yazıcı	Liman-i Izmir	Şaphane	Boynuz-seküsü	Total
Salt-pan workers (Tuzcu)	16	5	8	3	7	9		9	57
Pilgrims (Hacı)	2	3	2	2	1	4	2	12	28
Ex-slaves (Mut'ak)	3	3	3	2	2		6	2	21
Mariners/Arabs (Azeb/Arab)		1	3		4	1	6		15
Dervishes	1							2	3
Imams	1								1
Teachers (Müderris)		1		1					2
Spiritual leaders (Dede)			2						2
Assistants to dedes			1	1					2
Bath attendants (Hamamcı)				1					1
Spiritual guides (Mevlana)					2			1	3
Sheiks							1		1
Bachelors (Mücerred)	4								4

SOURCE: BBA, TT 537, pp. 8–13. The system under which these Muslim quarters were administered did not apply to the non-Muslim community in Izmir.

current agricultural revolution in western Anatolia constricted the amount of food in Izmir available for export.[26]

Despite Istanbul's objections, Izmir in the late sixteenth century blossomed into a regional market and commercial hub. Its population, while remaining predominantly Turco-Muslim, unquestionably had increased. The reasons for this demographic expansion remain hazy, but likely relate in part to a similar urban expansion occurring thoughout Anatolia and the Mediterranean basin, in part to rural insecurities in Izmir's hinterland, in part to a continuing nomadic drift westward across the plateau, and in part to a superb geographic position.[27] While the inhabitants of the town in the 1570s had lost agricultural self-sufficiency, a combination of commercial and industrial developments transformed Izmir into a regional market capable of generating ample cash for essential foodstuffs. Although these changes did not set it apart from other ports along the western-Anatolian seaboard, which also developed during the century, Izmir's evolving economic infrastructure would allow it to adapt with relative ease to further commercial and industrial expansion.[28]

IZMIR AND ITS HINTERLAND

While the limits of agricultural production around Izmir and the ability of the *kaza*'s inhabitants to feed themselves are uncertain, by the 1570s Izmir itself undeniably had lost self-sufficiency.[29] Among the many characteristics distinguishing the port as a town were dietary dependency upon its hinterland and the ability to recompense in cash and services. This maturing symbiosis between town and country, together with Izmir's function as a funnel for the region's fruits and grains, bespoke a commercial network linking the port to surrounding villages and the outside world.

Despite wide variations in the sizes of the 44 documented villages within the *kaza* of Izmir, from the 413 taxpayers of Mande to the 2 of Palamud, virtually all cultivated certain foodstuffs in common—wheat and barley, legumes, cotton, garden vegetables, culinary vegetables, fruits and nuts, olives, honey and beeswax, and figs. They also produced more selectively citrus fruits, mohair, hemp, clover, mulberry and sumac leaves, acorns, turnips, radishes, pears, and chestnuts. Istanbul imposed not only a graduated head tax upon holders of farms (*çift*s) and half farms (*nimçift*s), landless married men and bachelors within these villages, but also a tithe upon all of these commodities, fines for unlawfulness, and dues on sheep, wells, marriage, registration of lands and houses, flour mills, olive oil presses, wind mills, fisheries, and grazing and enclosed areas.[30]

The *kaza*'s villages in the 1570s seemed to be land poor and suffering, with only 2 percent of its peasantry possessing farms and 32 percent plunged into often destitute (sometimes signaling the inability to support a family) bachelorhood. This appearance, however, was deceptive, for although the meager landholdings suggest a land squeeze and the dispossession and underemployment of peasants who wandered the province and inundated Izmir and other towns (as in southern France and elsewhere in the Mediterranean basin during that time), the division and redivision of land did not affect each village equally.[31] Some villages such as Burunak, Rub' Kordan, Dere, Hasırlar, and Balihun enjoyed no farms. Others such as Timurcilar, Gümüldere, Palamud, and Oğlanas not only boasted many farms, but also produced far more grain per household and were burdened with fewer bachelors than other villages.

Administrative restraints and societal conditions in part caused these variations from village to village. Even though endemic brigandage tormented the villagers of western Anatolia, Istanbul, striving to preserve order and maintain yields, forbade peasants from fleeing to towns, or to safer or more prosperous villages.[32] A more important factor in the apparent disparities between the prosperity of villages was western Anatolia's diverse terrain. On the one hand, there were villages like Palamud, nestled on the rich plain surrounding Buca and producing no fruits or nuts; instead, bountiful harvests of wheat and barley and three free-hold (*hassa*) farms sustained its inhabitants. On the other hand, there were peasants like those of Malkoç who possessed almost no grain fields, but cultivated fruits and nuts. The first of these villages boasted many farms and the second, although land poor, enjoyed lush orchards. While Palamud and Malkoç contrasted strikingly in production, both paid heavy tithes to Istanbul. Other villages, Bayraklu among them, suffered greatly from the land squeeze of overpopulation and the government's reluctance to condone migration.

Products and incomes varied more widely in the environs of Izmir than elsewhere in the empire. On the isolated and monocultural central-Anatolian plateau grains typically devoured over 90 percent of peasant holdings and in much of the interior of the Balkans grains and livestock consumed an equally large proportion of land.[33] In Izmir's hinterland, however, grains constituted barely 40 percent of production. Consequently, ownership and productivity of land could not accurately reflect subsistence and income levels as it did in the grain-dominated economies of the Anatolian and Balkan interiors. Peasants in fruit-producing villages like Goğulca and Özeroğlu, who frequented markets in Izmir and elsewhere, did not suffer from shortfalls in staples. Not only grains and fruits but also cotton, wool, fish, legumes, and other produce denoted affluence and market flexibility in the *kaza* of Izmir.[34] Even villagers without ample grains and fruits often could convert other cash-crops and purchase essentials at local markets. This structural diversity not only lessened the risk of starvation, but also enabled peddlers and merchants to respond flexibly and lucratively to market disparities.

In the 1500s Ottoman, Venetian, and Genoese vessels exported not only grains and fruits but also nuts, legumes, cotton, and beeswax through the port of Izmir. Even in the first decades of the century, when the population of the empire was relatively small and the state still engaged in vigorous expansion, the Ottomans through tariffs strove to regulate this commerce. In western Anatolia, commodities from Europe were "assessed at 5 percent, both for Muslim and for tribute-paying misbeliever. If foodstuffs [came], with the exception of sugar which is assessed at 5 percent for all, the assessment is 2 percent for Muslims and 5 percent for misbelievers."[35] Istanbul intended such statutes both to abet the import by Muslim merchants of precious foodstuffs (particularly grains), and to discourage the export by Christian traders of staples.[36]

Despite such regulations, in the last decades of the century even the grain-poor *kaza* of Izmir at times provided this necessity of life to foreign traders. At other times, Izmir resorted to importing grains to fend off famine. In November 1574, Istanbul suffered shortages in part because Ottoman vessels with "provisions en route to Istanbul . . . from Egypt and other places" anchored at Izmir and sold their cargoes there.[37] A century and a half later the inhabitants of the Aegean island of Samos exported contraband "corn" to the west and, in order to offset the loss, imported grains from Anatolia.[38] Ottoman and foreign ship captains plying the sea lanes between the granaries of Egypt and Istanbul or simply seeking profitable price imbalances marketed their cargoes in Izmir and other ports along the route rather than resign themselves to the fixed prices of the capital. These traders, exploiting the Ottoman peace, which calmed Aegean waters, made the basin sensitive to price discrepancies and diversified markets.[39] Izmir, secure in its gulf and fed by its hinterland, shared in this commerce.

ECONOMIC, ETHNIC, AND SOCIAL DIVERSITY
IN THE *KAZA* OF IZMIR

Izmir's environs consisted of more than villages. The peasant population of the port's hinterland were also fishermen, mountain pass guards, and rice cultivators who confronted Turkoman nomads, migrants from the coastal town of Manavgat near Antalya, Arab camel drivers, and of course the vagrants and outlaws who infested the western-Anatolian upcountry wilds. These persons, all of whom contributed to the variety and economic elasticity of the region, also upset the stable and static peasant society, which Ottoman surveyors and tax collectors strove to preserve.

The terrain of western Anatolia with its rugged mountains and temperate valleys accommodated transhumant groups, such as the fourteen Turkoman families seasonally settled near Gökçe-karı.[40] Such nomads, who represented the Ottoman past and frustrated many of the empire's sixteenth-century social goals, received no exemptions from taxes, performed no special duties, and formed autonomous entities quite separate from the peasantry, with whom they uneasily coexisted. The villagers, who did not herd sheep, provided winter pasturage for pastoralists in return for meats, fibers, leather, and woven cloth.[41] At the same time, the encroachments of sedentary farmers upon traditional pasture lands and the free-spirited lawlessness of roaming nomads ensured mutual wariness.

Peddlers, merchants, and caravaners who frequented mountain and valley roads were a favorite prey of Turkomans and outlaws. A network of caravansarays fed, boarded, and protected these travelers while specially appointed villagers guarded the dangerous fords and passes they had to traverse. The inhabitants of the town of Gökyaka, in the district of Kızılcadağ, "received a decree that after giving their tithes, . . . they were exempted from all extraordinary taxes. They guarded [the mountain pass of Karıyolu] from thieves and wrongdoings."[42] In 1575-76 "only two of the original forty" guards still lived and the other thirty-eight had to be replaced, with sons if possible. Such posts were held ad infinitum and much coveted because, while authorities rarely exempted subjects from taxes based in sultanic laws and never from tithes, which were Islamic in origin, Istanbul often released them from onerous extraordinary dues in return for services.[43]

While available villagers could secure roads, Arab camel-drivers provided the more specialized service of transport. These men probably were deported from Arab lands after 1516–17 in order to distribute salt from western-Anatolian pans.[44] Although they retained their communal structure, they soon stopped hauling salt for the state and instead leased their camels to merchants transporting goods to and from the interior. As Izmir developed into a commercial hub, these same communities found a secure economic niche in the lively caravan trade linking the port with the east.[45]

Rice growers and fishermen furthered the commercial options of merchants using the roads secured by mountain pass guards and traveled by camel-drivers. In the delta village of Deryanda and elsewhere, peasants cultivated the bounty of rice fields and gave an extortionary two-thirds of the harvest to the government.[46] In return, the workers received drastic reductions in taxes and the right to vend one-third of this eminently marketable crop, for which the palace in Istanbul had developed an appetite. Along the shores of streams and rivers and on deltas, villagers who labored over rice funneled much of it through Izmir to Istanbul.[47] At Urba, Malkoç, Deryanda, and elsewhere along the coast, meanwhile, fishermen farmed the waters of streams, rivers, deltas, inlets, and gulfs.

● ● ●

Turkomans, guards, and camel-drivers exemplified the diversity of the region's population, while rice growers and fish farmers reveal the variety and intensity of land use. The region's inhabitants were sensitive not only to which crops best suited their soils, but also to their marketability. This attunement to the demands of the market reflected the region's proximity to the major shipping lanes of the Levant. While the Ottomans provided the security that nurtured Izmir's birth as a hub of international commerce, they also carefully regulated trade and gave priority to internal provisioning needs, particularly Istanbul's. This largely static and self-contained network began to crumble in the decades after the 1570s. Even as internal threats forced the central administration to relinquish some of its authority first to local officials and later to "notables" (*ayan*), precipitous changes in patterns of world commerce made foreign traders more aggressive in their efforts to exploit the agricultural production of western Anatolia. Quite suddenly, western-Anatolian trade began to expand and consolidate itself at Izmir. Curiously, this stimulation and convergence of commerce occurred despite

Ottoman opposition and during a time of stagnation in trade and industry throughout the empire. Odder still, as brigands freely roamed the countryside and threatened towns and cities, as peasants abandoned their exposed and sometimes overworked lands in despair, and as the populations of other settlements diminished, the port town of Izmir emerged as the principal warehouse of Levantine trade. Izmir's economy boomed even as social and economic disaster struck in western Anatolia.

2

Catalysts of Change in Western Anatolia

Despite the Sublime Porte's efforts to retain western Anatolia as a provisioning zone for Istanbul, the region's social, economic, and commercial position in the Ottoman empire changed dramatically during the early seventeenth century. During this period, a series of severe and prolonged wars, first with the Austrian empire (1593–1606) and then with the Safavids of Persia (1603–18), wracked the empire. These wars and all wars in which the Ottomans subsequently were engaged demanded enormous outlays in men and matériels and brought sudden and prodigious demands on the treasury. The land-based cavalry forces of the empire were unable to adjust to the exigencies of seventeenth-century warfare, and a grave need for musket-carrying infantry forced the government to expand the janissary corps and to draft into the army subjects who were not members of the military class. Istanbul recruited companies of peasants and landless persons who during their military service acquired a working knowledge of firearms and the martial arts, but who subsequently had difficulty finding employment.[1] Many ex-soldiers, particularly in the period 1598–1607, roamed through Anatolia in numerous small bands and armies, stripping the countryside of provisions and property, driving the peasantry from their lands, and threatening even the largest cities with ransacking and destruction.

In the face of these *"celâli* rebellions" and the resulting uprooting of peasants throughout Anatolia, the Sublime Porte struggled to maintain the fabric of Anatolian society. The uprisings, which recurred sporadically for decades, eventually forced the government to authorize, or at least tolerate, the emergence of local notables who, as representatives in the provinces, at times usurped the authority of the state.[2] The breakdown in central control also necessitated the stationing of permanent garrisons of janissary troops in troubled regions. These infantrymen gradually associated themselves with local interests and became an additional centrifugal force within the empire. One incident occurred in the town of Seferihisar near Izmir, where the troops refused to join the military campaign on the eastern front in 1617–18 because they had become butchers, bakers, and market people.[3] The garrison's insubordination not only threatened the campaign, but its abuses also undermined the guild system in Seferihisar. The janissaries ignored official market prices and overcharged for their merchandise.

Another catalyst toward change was the urgent need for ready cash during the long wars against Habsburgs and Safavids, which, exacerbated by the inflation of Ottoman currency, led the government more and more to relinquish its privileges of taxation to tax farmers, state officials, or religious and social communities. All of these factors contributed to an evolving decentralization and eventually a fragmentation of authority in Anatolia, which Istanbul was never fully able to arrest.[4]

BRIGANDAGE AND AUTHORITY IN WESTERN ANATOLIA

Before the end of the sixteenth century, incidents of violence and lawlessness occurred regularly in Izmir and its environs. In 1577–78, Ottoman authorities were sufficiently alarmed to condemn to the oars of the imperial fleet those brigands in western Anatolia who were not summarily executed.[5] Yet, the situation worsened. From 1592 until well into the seventeenth century, vagrancy, lawlessness, even organized bands of rebellious soldiery plagued the countryside and often the towns as well within the western-Anatolian provinces of Aydın, Hamid, Teke, Menteşe, Saruhan, and Suğla.

Distinctions between protectors and destroyers of the social order became blurred as members of the Ottoman military class veered into banditry. In 1592, several soldiers assigned to the defense of the channel of water separating the island of Rhodes from the Anatolian mainland each recruited groups of ruffians and drifted northward into the environs of Tire, Izmir, and Çeşme. This band of one- or two-hundred men ambushed cara-vans, plundering provisions and merchandise and even raided villages, leaving Muslim families homeless.[6] In the following year, a certain Kısrak oğlu Hamza from the coastal town of Urla "donned the felt-cap" emblem of the janissaries and terrorized his community.[7] Soon thereafter corsairs disrupted Urla's tran-quility when, disembarking in the town, they ostensibly "became drunk and rowdy" and stole merchandise.[8] In 1596, another in-habitant of Urla, Ali, claiming to be a military chief, gathered under his command the brigands of several *kaza*s, then perpe-trated outrages in the province of Suğla.[9] Ali collected money from the peasantry, and punished and even executed them ac-cording to his own interpretation of Islamic law. This military man co-opted state prerogatives, thereby threatening the Ot-toman state as well as its subjects.

Local administrative officials in western Anatolia also abused their privileges, especially in the collection of taxes. In 1616, the villagers of Boynuzsekiz near Izmir accused the revenue collector for castle upkeep in the port of Izmir, Mehmet oğlu Mahmut, of taking unauthorized monies.[10] Mahmut's abuses included the yearly seizure of five-hundred *akçe*s for each *kantar* of olive oil, sixty *akçe*s for each head of sheep, twenty for each servant, ten to pay his personal scribe, one-half *guruş* per ox, and one *guruş* per camel. These impositions were far in excess of the norm, which rarely rose above one or two *akçe*s per *kantar* of olive oil or per camel load.[11]

In response to this breakdown in fiscal and military con-trol within the province, local notables assumed a role in main-taining order and authority. As early as 1592, the local elite in the province of Suğla was involved in administering govern-mental affairs and quashing the anarchy that tormented the

countryside.[12] It complained to Istanbul that brigands within
the province made life intolerable and warned that "if they are
not conquered, all of us shall be scattered." In this seemingly
desperate situation, influential subjects appealed to the government for succor. They did so again in 1605 when the notables
and local preachers in the *kaza* of Izmir joined the inhabitants of
the village of Burun Abar (Bornova) in complaining to Istanbul
about a janissary, Hasan Osman, and his sons who broke into
houses in the village, plundered properties and provisions, and
raped women—all this while claiming to be representatives of a
kadı. The villagers threatened to disband the community if the
government did not suppress the marauders, and the provincial
notables contended that many of the villagers already had fled.[13]
The Sublime Porte, while acknowledging the seriousness of the
charges, meted out an inappropriately weak response:

It is commanded to Mehmet, son of Üveys Paşa, the *beylerbeyi* of Anatolia
and to the *kadı* of Izmir that the people of the village of Burun Abar
presented a petition while we were on campaign. Some people from the class
of foot soldiers (*piyade taifesi*) . . . living in this village are brigands. While
[assisting a *kadı* from the region], besides tearing down [someone's] house
and plundering his property and provisions, four people also took his female
slave [or wife] carnally into their possession. Upon [their] also possessing the
wife of someone named Abu Bekr, she killed herself. In addition, they tied
a certain Tuzcu to a tree and raped his daughter in front of him. . . . If
these men are not subjugated, the villagers tell us that all the people of the
village will scatter. The income of Hasan Osman, who is a janissary, should
be discontinued.[14]

The Ottoman government reacted ineffectually to such anarchic
behavior by men attached to—or recently released from—the
Ottoman army who undertook villainy in the name of Ottoman
officialdom.[15] Later in the seventeenth century, as the Sublime
Porte became increasingly unable to quell provincial disorders,
local notables began to generate responses and power structures
of their own.[16]

It was not always Ottoman officials—*beylerbeyi*s and *kadı*s—
who suppressed disturbances. These were crisis years on both the
northwestern and eastern military fronts, and *kaymakam*s often

substituted for official appointees during the campaign season and became responsible for maintaining order in the provinces. The requirement of beys to wage war against the Safavids in August 1607 left only a *kaymakam* in Suğla to subdue lawlessness within the province.[17] Without adequate protection, the *reâyâ* were increasingly exposed to depredation and were compelled to choose between abandoning land and livelihood or procuring alternate means of defense.

Disorders within the *kaza* of Izmir recurred with regularity. In 1590–91, after clearing Suğla of brigandage, the beys boarded ships to protect merchants from Rhodes and to transport broadcloth from Salonica to Istanbul, but left the province open to renewed disturbances. Four years later, bandits infested the mountainous terrain between Izmir and Çeşme. The year 1607–8 was crisis-ridden, with brigands in Kızılhisar plundering the house of a campaigning janissary, fifteen or twenty natives of Seferihisar stealing six-hundred head of cattle and oxen from the villagers of Barçınlı, groups of irregular soldiery choking off the roads around Izmir, rebels pillaging a *sipahi*'s home near Izmir, other outlaws channeling illegal goods through Seferihisar, and bands of brigands fortifying against the state castles near Manisa. In 1615–16, mariners disembarking from light and maneuverable coastal vessels terrorized the inhabitants of Suğla and in 1630–31 killings and plunderings plagued the countryside around Urla.[18]

Despite frequent and urgent appeals, the government took no decisive action against the disturbances. Istanbul asserted the authority of the state in condemning the roving bands but did not provide the requisite monies and manpower to subdue them. Instead, it contented itself with administrative actions— striking off the payrolls rebellious janissaries and *sipahi*s or ordering convicted brigands to the oars, to the local courts, or to Istanbul for trial and punishment. Whoever happened to be on the scene—a *kadı*, a *kaymakam*, or even agents appointed to unrelated tasks—undertook the actual prosecution of brigands.[19] In the past, the government's cavalier approach had been sufficient. The erosion of central control over provincial organs of administration, however, now rendered these measures inadequate. Although the government several times bypassed local officials and organized its own operations against rebels in Anatolia, pressing concerns elsewhere often forced Istanbul to ignore internal unrest.[20]

MUSKETS DISTRIBUTED, BRIGANDAGE TRANSFORMED

While the Ottomans took a casual attitude toward brigandage, the Sublime Porte viewed with urgency the related dissemination of firearms, which, more directly than rural or urban agitation, threatened its authority in the provinces. The military lost its monopoly over the newly introduced musket in the early sixteenth century and, by the 1570s, guns were cheaply and easily obtained throughout the empire. At the same time, in order to fight their wars the Ottomans needed ever-larger armies, yet they lacked the funds to maintain them. Thus, particularly in Anatolia, groups of irregular soldiers, who had been conscripted or otherwise induced into the Ottoman army and subsequently released, hired themselves out to beys and notables as mercenaries or, muskets in hand, terrorized the countryside in roving bands.[21] By the end of the century, musket-wielding outlaws infested the peninsula and exacerbated, or even precipitated, the *celâli* uprisings and social upheavals that followed.

Throughout the sixteenth century, the government endeavored, at times successfully, to restrain the unauthorized use of firearms. In the district of Kayseri it implemented registration in order to systematically disarm the *reâyâ* and restrict gun ownership to the military class.[22] The region's landlocked isolation enabled Istanbul to apply this policy of control; in the coastal zones of Anatolia, the Sublime Porte was less successful. As early as 1568–69, the government warned *kadı*s around Kocaeli, across the Marmara from Istanbul, not to allow the *reâyâ* to possess firearms.[23] This line of action was to no avail, and by 1592 the state had utterly lost control of firearms. Private armies, equipped with muskets, roamed through Suğla and other coastal provinces. When the government attempted to seize these men, the outlaws "fortified themselves in rocky country" where no one could dislodge them. The authorities next confiscated the firearms of all the *reâyâ* in Suğla in order to choke off the outlaws' supplies and replenish government arsenals. This strategy also had only limited success, for alternative supply routes quickly materialized.[24]

Although outlawry was a nuisance, the Sublime Porte did not view it per se as a distinct threat. It did, however, fear the power, demonstrated by the capacity of brigands to repulse troops, that the musket gave to rebellious forces. The military also proved unable to disarm the *reâyâ*, whom it deemed responsible for the proliferation of firearms. Although the authorities scoured the coastal provinces, fining the inhabitants and confiscating their firearms, suppliers cheaply and quickly replaced the weapons through native manufacture or through smuggling along the serpentine Anatolian seaboard.[25] Istanbul, through this policy of confiscation, was not merely trying to rid the countryside of banditry, but was taking the opportunity to restock imperial armories with seized muskets.[26] In 1587–88, a strongly worded decree ordered the bey of Suğla and the *kadı* of Ayasoluğ to deliver to Istanbul one-thousand firearms confiscated from brigands and temporarily secured in the castle of Ayasoluğ; another specifically warned the bey against destroying such weapons.[27]

All firearms could not arbitrarily be confiscated by the Sublime Porte. The Ottoman military class carried weapons, and governmental functionaries took pains not to infringe upon this privilege.[28] The blurring of distinctions between soldier and outlaw during the period, however, complicated this task; it was no easy matter to differentiate between upholders and abusers of the system. Further confusion arose because others enjoyed exemption from confiscation. Foreign traders journeying along caravan routes feared attack and obtained permission to carry firearms.[29]

Far more threatening to the policy of confiscation were exemptions granted to *reâyâ* who felt exposed to brigands, pirates, or foreign invaders. Authorities in the town of Kayseri routinely took inhabitants' muskets. In 1609, however, the townsmen only had to prove their right to possess and register their firearms; the weapons were not seized.[30] This policy change not only reflected the inability of the authorities to safeguard the community, it also readmitted social disorder to the district. With the increased ownership of firearms came the greater likelihood that criminals would possess them.

The Ottomans often confronted the difficult choice between a universal ban upon firearms and selective license to own them. In 1593, Istanbul first ordered the bey of Suğla to seize all firearms from *reâyâ*, but then added that

> in the town of Urla situated on the edge of the sea in the *kaza* of Izmir the *reâyâ* pleaded "we live on the frontier and the ships of the misbelievers have come many times and plundered our province. It is likely that they will come again. We need firearms in order to protect our property." This situation is confirmed. It seems both useful and good that the *reâyâ* in Urla and its surrounding villages retain their firearms. . . . As for the rest, you should take their firearms for the state. But repeat the warning to the inhabitants of Urla that they must not give their firearms to outlaws.[31]

The residents of Urla did not fabricate this threat; the western-Anatolian littoral *was* exposed to sea raiders. In 1559–60, thirty pirates plundered Çeşme.[32] A naval captain from the town of Kavala finally apprehended their ship off the island of İpsala.[33] In 1565–66, men from four or five corsair vessels repeatedly assaulted villages in the *kaza* of Balat.[34] Istanbul's principal anxiety was that representatives of hostile states piloted these ships. Finally, in 1567–68 pirates maneuvered coastal boats in lightning forays against Aegean islands in order to capture *zimmi*s and plunder vessels, and then found refuge in villages near Manisa.[35] In the following decades, coastal raiding intensified. In 1592–93, the year the townsmen of Urla demanded exemption from gun control, ten men from the castle of Çeşme and twenty from the castle of Chios joined a fleet being outfitted to patrol the region against piracy.[36]

The government understood the function of muskets in civil defense and realized that if Istanbul proved unable to protect its subjects, they would demand the right to defend themselves, which in turn would bring more outlawry and foster provincial centers of power. Because of Urla's exposed location near the mouth of the Gulf of Izmir, the Sublime Porte allowed its inhabitants to own firearms to shield them from sea raiders. Relinquishing gun control in Urla and other exposed towns and villages along the coasts of Anatolia, however, encouraged the smuggling and distribution of guns, and threatened Ottoman dominion in this and other outlying regions of the empire.[37]

PROVISIONING ISTANBUL

Although always concerned with the well-being and security of the empire's subjects, the Sublime Porte was equally absorbed in keeping foodstuffs flowing to the capital city from Egypt, western Anatolia, and elsewhere. Every city in the pre-modern world strove to moderate inevitable shortages of necessities and each depended upon either hinterland or seaborne access to fruits and grains, fibers, and fuels in order to fend off starvation. The fecundity of provisioning regions together with cities' strategic locations along major land and sea routes determined the sizes and importance of urban centers. Within the Mediterranean basin, Genoa, Marseilles, Dubrovnik, Venice, and other ports owed their dominance to these factors.[38] An imperial capital such as Istanbul, which served not only a commercial function but also as the administrative nucleus of a vast provisioning and military network, particularly relied upon adequate harvests and dependable supply routes. During the sixteenth century, when neither food and fiber production nor shipping and caravan capacities kept up with expanding populations in the Ottoman empire, resources became strained.[39]

In order to relieve shortages in Istanbul, authorities fostered trading lanes linking the capital to its hinterlands while discouraging improvements in intraregional systems of transport within western Anatolia, which might have helped supplies meet local demand. Officials feared that free movement of grains would undermine governmental controls and make unpredictable both the

availability and the price of this precious staple in Istanbul. In 1565–66, the authorities reluctantly licensed transport of a limited quantity of grain from Izmir to the famished inhabitants of Urla; without such authorization merchants could not transfer wheat and barley even between adjacent *kazas*.[40] The Ottomans realized that harvests varied and were not indifferent to pleas for grain outside the capital, or even outside the empire. When in 1564–65 famine struck the Genoese-controlled island of Chios, the Sublime Porte dispatched relief grain from Üsküdar.[41] More typically, however, Istanbul remained impervious to shortages in the provinces; it was too sorely pressed securing adequate food supplies for itself.

Western Anatolia was not a principal source for grains, but the region yielded other foodstuffs. The sultan's household in the 1630s annually consumed fifteen camel loads of honey, sixteen of sultanas, five of wild apricots, four of figs, fifty of rice, and thirty-three of raisins, all of which were plentiful in Izmir's surroundings.[42] The appetite of the sultan's retinue was voracious. In May 1609 the imperial larder demanded from the *kadıs* of Izmir, Manisa, Chios, Menemen, Nif, Foça, Güzelhisar, Ayasoluğ, Marmara, İlica, Birgi, Nazlı, and Karaburun 2,000 *kantars* of sultanas, 1,500 of raisins, 150 of almonds, 150 of beeswax, 200 of olive oil, 200 of Urla soap, 500 of figs, 15 of pressed and spiced meat, 200 of wild apricots, 300 of honey, and 100 of dried pears, as well as 200 boxes of figs, 200 of honeycombs, and 500 *kiles* of black-eyed peas.[43] Most of these commodities originated in the coastal regions of western Anatolia, many in Izmir's hinterland (see table 5). The *kaza* of Izmir provided almost half of the 1,500 *kantars* of raisins the imperial retinue consumed in 1626–27. The remainder came from the adjoining districts of Nif, Menemen, and Foça. Virtually all the imperial larder's honey flowed out of Izmir, and over half of its sultanas were imported from Manisa, with Izmir as their point of embarkation. The peasantry also cultivated substantial quantities of olive oil, figs, and almonds a short distance from the port. Obviously, any disruptions along Anatolian and Aegean commercial arteries threatened intolerably the palace's stock of these foodstuffs.

TABLE 5
Provisions for the Imperial Larder, 1620
(*In* kantars)

Commodity	Izmir	Ayasoluğ	Gördos	Manisa	Mendehorya	Menemen	Nif	Foça	Marmara	Total
Raisins	700					400	500	100		1,700
Beeswax	30									30
Olive oil	40		100					5		145
Dried beans	100									100
Figs	200					150				350
Honey	200[a]									200
Almonds	40					10	10			60
Sultanas				1,000	100				500	1,600
Wild apricots		100				20				120
Meviz kelter								200		200

SOURCE: M. Çağatay Uluçay, *XVIIınci yüzyılda Manisa'da ziraat, ticaret, ve esnaf teşkilâtı* (Istanbul: Manisa Halkevi Yayınlarından, 1942), p. 48.

[a] Calculated in boxes.

ISTANBUL'S PROVISIONS DIVERTED

Yet, in the 1560s, 70s, and 80s the Ottoman provisioning network in western Anatolia sporadically failed as local merchants redirected fruits and grains destined for Istanbul. When in 1564–65 the government ordered raisins and sultanas from the region around Izmir, merchants complained of uncompetitive prices and marketed their fruits elsewhere.[44] Such action displeased the authorities, who the following year quashed the buying and hoarding of dried fruit by the peddlers and merchants of Izmir and Foça, by ripping down storehouses and confiscating fruits, and then selling them at the current market rate to ships embarking for the capital city.[45] Three years later, the government repeated these drastic measures.[46] This struggle between private merchants and governmental supervisors became perennial.[47] While ambitious entrepreneurs, given sufficient capital, could store these non-perishables almost indefinitely and make great profits when the inevitable shortages arrived, the government perceived the choking off of its provisioning network and manipulation of its price controls as a menace to Istanbul and other heavily populated or infertile regions.

Grains

The growing number of European merchants along the western-Anatolian coast and their adept smuggling increased the fluidity of the market in fruits, fabrics, and especially grains by providing an alternative outlet. In 1559–60, *kadıs* along the Mediterranean coasts sought to smother the sale of grain to infidels; in 1565–66, Frankish vessels sailed furtively into the port of Foça to buy provisions; and in 1567–68 and the following year, townsmen of Izmir and Foça smuggled grain and dried fruits onto Venetian ships.[48] This trickle of goods westward from Anatolia, though inconvenient, was not disastrous to the Ottoman provisioning network.

In the last years of the century, the trickle became a torrent as European merchants increased their business within the Aegean basin. Even before the 1550s, Venetian and other Latin vessels had scoured Ottoman coastal regions for grains and other provisions to compensate for deficits in Italian production. Near the end of the century crop failures and population growth inflicted a series of famines on various parts of Europe. The Venetians particularly experienced difficulties in feeding their subjects; until 1594, when grain merchants opened the Baltic region, Ottoman granaries subsidized such domestic shortfalls.[49] In 1592–93, just before exploitation of the rich Baltic granaries commenced, European ambassadors in Istanbul sought to have rescinded Ottoman restrictions on grain exports. Commercial organizations from England, France, Dubrovnik, and Venice initiated an urgent scramble for the right to export "corn" freely to the famished south of France, where they expected to reap tremendous profits, and elsewhere.[50] The Ottomans, who strictly regulated sale of staples to foreigners, required the sultan to authorize exportation of grains, and Christian states issued their appeals at this lofty level. Queen Elizabeth herself petitioned Murat III to allow the English to partake in the grain trade. He replied in January 1592 that "as you have requested permission for the export of corn into France, we have given orders to the Beglierbeys [*sic*] of Algiers, Tunis, and Tripoli in Barbary, to take the necessary steps."[51] Imperial intervention on behalf of the queen and other European rulers, however, proved futile. Western ambassadors still sought to export grains in the following year.[52] In 1594 the Ottomans imposed a blanket prohibition on such commerce, causing the Italian city-states to begin large-scale importation of grains from the Baltic.[53]

The combined Ottoman prohibition and Baltic penetration did not halt international commerce in Levantine grains. It simply forced business underground. During the late sixteenth and early seventeenth centuries, disruptions along commercial routes and diversions from the capital city occurred with alarming regularity. Because the market in Europe was almost insatiable, Ottoman consent to the export of some grains and other restricted goods merely sharpened western cravings. In 1609, everywhere along the Mediterranean littoral provisions found their way not only into the holds of "enemy infidel," probably Venetian, vessels, but even into friendly Dubrovnik and French bottoms in quantities greater than consented to in capitulatory agreements.[54] Both the merchants of the city-state of Dubrovnik, which enjoyed a singular trading arrangement with the Ottomans because of its tributary status, and France, which, despite Dutch and English pretensions, retained its most-favored-nation status due principally to its longstanding and acrimonious opposition to the Habsburgs, strained Ottoman relations by routinely abusing their privileges.[55] Istanbul complained bitterly against French and Dubrovnik ship captains who attempted an assortment of artifices in order to procure grains and, with assistance from high-ranking Ottoman dignitaries who sold to foreigners foodstuffs from their own estates, secured rescripts countermanding capitulatory restrictions. Ottoman authorities, ascribing the "great scarcity and disorder" within the empire to these doings, threatened unscrupulous French and Dubrovnik merchants with loss of commerce and ordered implicated Ottoman officials and subjects punished.

Between 1590 and 1610, grain smuggling intensified throughout the eastern Mediterranean. The protestations of the beys of Egypt and notables of Alexandria against an Alexandrian merchant, Hacı Osman, who in 1607 sold enormous quantities of grain to western merchants denote one site for this illegal trafficking.[56] Even along the Anatolian littoral and in the Gulf of Izmir, however, where grain was more precious than elsewhere in the empire, interstate smuggling intensified.[57] The concurrence between the incursions of European traders into the hinterland around the port of Izmir and throughout the Aegean, where infidel ship captains sought to satisfy a growing need for grains in the Venetian empire, France, and elsewhere, and the social and administrative turmoil plaguing the Anatolian peninsula upset the carefully sustained provisioning network in that region.

Ottoman administrators, from obscure bureaucrats to grand vezirs, conspired in this unauthorized extraction of grains.[58] In 1592, Ottoman pilots stowed grains in small boats at the ports of Ayazmend, Çandarlı, the two Foças, Izmir, Kuşadası, Samos, Kökova, and Acısu, all situated upon or near the western-

Anatolian coast, and embarked for the multitudinous islands of the Aegean basin where they sold their cargoes to European ship captains.[59] The bey of Suğla, striving to contain the westward flow of grains, inspected vessels, confiscated grains, and apprehended smugglers, especially members of the military class. His efforts were unavailing. Not only was it difficult to pursue crafts upon the labyrinthine Aegean, but a cornered vessel could be deadly. Ottoman galleys, while effective near the shore, were ill-equipped to confront in open waters the three-masted, broad, sturdy, twenty- or thirty-cannoned *bertone* introduced by Dutch and English merchantmen and widely piloted by pirates frequenting those waters.[60] Through the seventeenth century, the admirals of the Ottoman navy increasingly relied on the Barbary states for naval defense against Christian incursions into Ottoman waters, which during the winter months left them almost powerless.[61]

The technological imbalance with the Atlantic states that facilitated the movement of contraband at sea did not exist on land and the Ottomans thus seemed better positioned to curb grain smuggling in this arena. The state had constructed an intricate and rigid collection system through which grains and other goods moved from regions of production, to points of distribution, markets, and consumers.[62] These safeguards were meant to ensure the adequate and continuous flow of basic goods to the populace, capital, and army of the empire; but flagrant abuse of regulations in western Anatolia during the 1590s and well into the seventeenth century crippled the government's endeavors. Just as with trafficking upon the seas, the brigandage that concurrently ravaged western Anatolia ensnared members of the Ottoman military class. Artillerymen, grain officials, janissaries and their sons, and those feigning membership in these privileged groups took advantage of a preoccupied government and the consequent slackened regulations. In 1592, Fırıncı oğlu Reis, a "rogue and robber" from the *kaza* of Ahırlı (Karaburun), wandered about the province claiming to be the captain of a royal galleon commissioned to procure grains for Istanbul and, counterfeit sanction in hand, purchased the regulated commodity.[63]

He then profitably diverted the grain to western traders. Pretending to represent the state, he abused Ottoman regulations by purchasing grain at fixed rates and selling it at market prices.

Fırıncı oğlu Reis was not alone in undertaking this lucrative yet dangerous business. A host of Ottoman subjects—military and non-military, Muslim and non-Muslim—illicitly sold grains and other foods to Europeans at prices exceeding those offered by the Sublime Porte. In 1592–93, the government appointed Abu Bekr to procure grapes and beeswax for Istanbul from state-run lands around Izmir.[64] He embezzled dues from the *reâyâ* without forwarding to the capital the required provisions. In the following year, the government denounced Yoma Niko, a Greek subject, as a smuggler who utilized his merchant status in order to pass grains to foreign traders.[65] Even religious figures participated in this profitable commerce. The authorities required priests living on the island of Kesendere to grind wheat into flour and send it to the *evkaf* of Gazanfer Ağa in Istanbul. Instead, in 1613 they dispatched it to the monks of Mount Athos and allegedly sold it to western merchants disembarking at their island.[66] The Ottomans' inability to subdue brigandage, establish gun control, suppress corruption, or restrain social upheaval in western Anatolia foretold their failure to arrest the flow of grains westward, in which the same outlaws and officials were involved.

Even in the major ports of western Anatolia, where the Ottomans supervised distribution most closely, unauthorized vessels stowed grains and other provisions. Ships from within the empire and Europe stealthily anchored in the ports of Urla, Izmir, Seferihisar, Kuşadası, and Balat. Able to pay prices exceeding those offered by the janissaries and pursuivants from Istanbul, they spirited away grain, barley, kidney beans, sesame seeds and other provisions.[67] Because of prohibitive conveying costs, Ottoman price regulations and internal transport restrictions, and the region's specialized agriculture, which left little land for the cultivation of staples, western Anatolia could ill afford losses in locally produced grain and barley. Thus, these grain runners not only upset the empire's provisioning network, but also brought "scarcity and dearth" to the province. The system of rigid price fixing meant to guarantee a contented and flourishing population no longer sufficed even locally.

Fruits

In the last years of the 1500s, Venetians dominated the band of sea peddlers who roamed the eastern Aegean sniffing out deals and markets. In the first years of the next century, however, Dutch, English, and French merchants supplanted Venetian traders and began systematizing commerce by organizing themselves into companies and concentrating their energies upon certain goods and localities. In western Anatolia, Izmir emerged from the throng of port towns and by 1610, Ottoman authorities, becoming increasingly aware of it, endeavored through the *kadı* to halt particularly French trafficking in weapons and merchandise there. In that year, the market inspector in the town not only examined weights, measures, and provisions in Izmir's market, but also checked the holds of merchant vessels for contraband. French captains circumvented this inspection with counterfeit or purchased rescripts from Istanbul, thereby enabling them to move forbidden goods, most alarmingly muskets, with impunity. The authorities, although eager to stay this stream of arms to brigands, had to proceed cautiously because of the treaty of friendship between the French and Ottoman states, which induced the *kadı* and other officials not to "injure, seize, and threaten [the French] with the pretext of inspection."[68]

This incident suggests that grain was not the only, or even the principal, magnet that lured smugglers to Izmir. Indeed, in March 1605 Musa, an imperial agent striving ineffectually to procure dried fruit for the sultan's larder, complained that every French vessel anchoring at Izmir loaded over twelve-thousand pounds of beeswax.[69] He did not mention grains. Although in their most recent commercial agreements the Ottomans had assented to French export of beeswax, they acted quickly, if unavailingly, to seal this gaping breach in their closed economy.

The Sublime Porte for some time restricted the export of neither beeswax, nor figs, grapes, and other fruits abundant in Izmir's hinterland. Indeed, the government's unusual laissez-faireism may have helped draw merchants to this port. Europeans also found these goods, which could be dried (and in the case of grapes, fermented) and shipped particularly suitable to long-distance commerce. Although not as profitable and manageable as the "spices" of traditional Middle Eastern trade, whose route through the Levant the Dutch choked off in the first decades of the seventeenth century, fruits were more precious and less bulky than grains, cottons or woolens.[70] The warnings of officials endeavoring to secure sufficient dried fruits for the prodigious requirements of the sultan's table, retinue, capital city, and army, however, soon jarred Istanbul into initiating a barrage of directives limiting amounts and stipulating prices of fruits sold to European buyers.

Regulations governing fruits were similar to those ruling grains. In theory, government officials assembled fruits at strategically located stations where they were weighed, taxed, and, after the state had skimmed off its portion, sold to consumers.[71] In western Anatolia during the 1590s, government representatives then routed the state's share to the port of Izmir where the *kadı* twice registered the quantities loaded into ships, once for the judicial records (*sicil*s) of his *kaza* and a second time for the captain of the conveying vessel, who was responsible for the document's safe delivery, together with the fruits, to Istanbul. Thus checked and double checked, it was hoped these provisions would reach the Ottoman capital.[72] In practice, hoarding and direct selling to merchants and consumers in order to bypass official weighing stations and artificially controlled and often depressed prices during the late sixteenth and early seventeenth centuries sabotaged these efforts.

Grapes especially were subjected to the manipulations of hoarders, peddlers, and merchants both domestic and foreign. Christian and Jewish merchants sought grapes for wine-making; after bottling, the product could be stored for later consumption, vended in the taverns of port cities (in Izmir in 1649–50 there were at least three such establishments), or shipped to Christian lands.[73] In 1584 Christians and Jews, gathering grapes in the environs of Mytilene, Ayazmend, and the two Foças in order to manufacture wine, rendered them unavailable for consumption while fresh, or as raisins, syrup or vinegar.[74] Muslims also partook in this commerce. In 1591, they joined Christians in selling grapes to infidels along the eastern Aegean and Marmara coasts.[75]

Although the government protested that wine production caused grave shortages in the capital, it suppressed this trade no more successfully than it had put down brigandage, or curbed the movements of peasants, guns, and grains. In 1605, sailors supplying grapes for Istanbul in Mudanya, an easy day's crossing of the Marmara, could find none because of Jewish "speculators and hoarders" who bought them even as they were harvested in order to produce wine, probably for local consumption.[76] Such native consumers no less than foreign purchasers contributed to grape shortages. In 1593 Istanbul, noting the diversion of black grapes in the environs of Izmir, Çeşme, Foça, and Çandarlı, protested that Christians, Jews, and Muslims in Izmir were converting these grapes into wine and raki, and insisted instead that they produce grape syrup and vinegar, to be delivered to the capital together with sultanas, almonds, and figs.[77]

Even merchants uninvolved in wine marketing preferred to hoard preserved fruits and await the soaring prices induced by seasonal shortages, sudden demand, foreign buyers, and that period's inflation, rather than haul them to the weighing stations established in Ottoman ports where marketers had to pay taxes and accept controlled pricing. They stubbornly "made pretexts and remained obstinate" against complying with governmental directives. In response, janissaries garrisoning castles in Izmir, Ayazmend, Çeşme, Foça, Ayasoluğ, and elsewhere along the coasts trekked from garden to garden and village to village confiscating stocks and stripping the offenders of their livelihoods.[78]

The lessening of state power in western Anatolia during these years prevented such severe measures from impeding the stockpiling and wholesaling of dried fruits and nuts. The result was an amorphous yet extensive peddling network that thrived conjointly with and at the expense of the Ottomans' regulated economy. In 1593, speculators scoured the *kaza* of Izmir for black grapes, figs, almonds, and sundry dried fruits.[79] These itinerant peddlers, disregarding every regulation and acting as black-market middlemen, bought directly from the peasantry and sold to merchants in Izmir and other ports.[80] Local officials ineffectually registered all provisions in transit and dispatched detachments of janissaries to patrol the perilous countryside.

Violent seasonal fluctuations in the market values of the perishable produce of Izmir's hinterland helped convince merchants to challenge the state's monopoly and peddle fruits independently, supplying even Istanbul.[81] In April 1593, provisioners from the capital paid profiteers 125 *akçes* per *kantar* of raisins and figs, even though the fixed price was only 50 or 60 *akçes*.[82] In December of the same year, with raisins swamping the market in Izmir, Istanbul strove to maintain a minimum price for them.[83] While changing seasons and speculating peddlers certainly orchestrated these wild fluctuations, the palace's prodigious appetite also promoted them. Topkapı's urgent appeals for fruits compelled desperate imperial agents, from whom speculators reaped huge profits, to purchase out-of-season produce. In the spring of 1593, with the imperial larder impatiently signaling its agent Bekr to bring grapes and beeswax from the environs of Izmir, the Sublime Porte querulously inquired of the *kadı* in that town, "What is the cause of the delay? Is it the negligence of Bekr? Or does it originate from your lack of attention to these matters?" In the following passage, implying shortages within the palace itself, the authorities demanded that "if any of the ordered grapes and beeswax are available, you should acquire them immediately and deliver them quickly to Istanbul."[84] Three years later, the palace first dispatched a pursuivant, Hacı Receb, to Izmir in order to procure grapes, figs, almonds, and other provisions, and then two *kapıcı*s, Hasan and Umur, in order to hurry Hacı Receb along.[85] When even this maneuver failed, Istanbul urged the *kadı* of Izmir to spur Hasan and Umur to return to the capital "with all haste," hauling "whatever quantity of ready provisions Hacı Receb had been able to gather." With the palace oblivious to seasonal availability, frantic provisioners often turned to the very "hoarders and speculators" whom the Sublime Porte strove to suppress.

The empire's indeterminate metrology also crippled governmental regulations. With no standardized weights and measures, each region (and often every town) within the realm possessed its own measurements for grains, fruits, and finished goods such as textiles.[86] As sailors disembarking in Izmir to procure figs and raisins for the imperial larder learned in 1581, a *kantar* in Istanbul was not the same as a *kantar* in Izmir, Aleppo, or Alexandria. Their funds, estimated according to Istanbul's measures, were insufficient to purchase their allotments of figs and raisins.[87]

Exploiting their privileges and personal holdings, members of the Ottoman military class rapaciously helped undermine the state provisioning network. In 1609, guardsmen, janissaries, *sipahi*s, and others, shunning the official weighing station in Nif, had their peasants patronize scales in their own villages of Öksüzce, Yetmiş, Kızılca, Karabuk, Emirdedeler, Sarişeh, Dere, and Vıran.[88] The government had farmed out the scales of Nif to a scribe named Süleyman, who was authorized to collect an in-kind weighing charge on cereals and dried vegetables and an in-cash duty on other goods.[89] Not only did Süleyman lose revenue because of the refusal of military men to transport goods to Nif, but the evasion freed them to market unregistered goods elsewhere.

SMUGGLING CENTERS: THE CASE OF RODOSCUK

Along the entire supply line linking Izmir to its hinterland—from peasant and *timar*-holder, to peddler and middleman, distribution point, and vessel—Ottoman subjects fiercely opposed regulations governing grapes and other fruits. In the persons of pirates and smugglers, this resistance existed also on the sea lanes and beyond. Vessels that successfully navigated the pirate-infested Aegean often found their cargo spirited away when at anchorages along the route to Istanbul. The town of Rodoscuk (Tekirdağ), on the northern coast of the Marmara, was such a spot, serving not only as a point of embarkation for the grains of Thrace en route to Istanbul, but also as an entrepôt for the wheat, cotton, dried fruits, hemp, and other goods of Egypt and the Aegean coasts.[90] These commodities drew to Rodoscuk both Ottoman and foreign exporters, who smuggled provisions into the Ottoman Balkans and Christian Europe, often with the connivance of local functionaries.

In the late sixteenth and early seventeenth centuries, Istanbul grew particularly anxious about grains from Egypt and fruits from Izmir vanishing at Rodoscuk. In July 1593, vessels from Egypt, Izmir, and other places dispensed their rice, broad beans, chickpeas, lentils, grains and cereals, and grapes at the Marmaran ports of Rodoscuk, Ereğli, and Ibrıca rather than at the capital city.[91] These ports became favorite haunts for provisioning ships that "unloaded their goods . . . and sold them on the wharves or sent them to Edirne, Hoyrabolu, and other towns and villages," and for infidels, who slunk in from the islands of the Marmara and Aegean and took away precious wheat, bulgur, *tarhana* (a dough made from dried curd and flour), and other provisions.

Although in an insistent flurry of decrees in late 1593 and early 1594, the Sublime Porte forbade vessels from Izmir even to approach Rodoscuk for fear of losing the oil, tallow, rice, raisins, sultanas, figs, almonds and other dried fruits, iron, and hemp stowed in their holds, the smugglers persevered.[92] Three years later, infidel traders conveyed from Rodoscuk to other European ports wool in the fleece, iron, onions, clarified butter, black grapes, soap, leathers, olive oil, olives, beeswax, cotton, black oak, and linen cloth from Izmir; rice, lentils, pepper, cloves, and other goods from Egypt; and wheat and barley from Thrace.[93] By way of Egypt, Rodoscuk drew goods from as far away as southeast Asia, a full century after the Portuguese circumnavigation of Africa.[94]

The Sublime Porte, hard pressed to break so extensive and elaborate a smuggling network, even assigned janissaries to sail with ships bound for Istanbul. In the winter of 1593–94, one janissary from the castle of Foça accompanied each vessel loading black grapes, sultanas, almonds, figs, and other fruits "at the port of Izmir for the provisioning of Istanbul."[95] Probably because of janissary connivance, this ploy was no more successful than others. Fifteen years later, in November 1609, Istanbul protested to the *kadı* of Rodoscuk that forty or fifty ships en route from Izmir to Istanbul anchored at that port and there discharged their cargoes.[96]

The diversion of goods at Rodoscuk shows the wide range of exportable, sometimes strategically important, commodities provided by western Anatolia. Cotton sails and hemp rigging from the environs of Izmir propelled the imperial fleet, morocco leather and sheepskin clothed the empire's subjects, and the acorn from the valonia tree was needed by the tanning industry. In 1565–66 Istanbul sent two-thousand florins to the *sancak* of Saruhan in order to procure cotton sailcloths.[97] Several weeks later, the imperial shipyard in Galata urgently requested five-thousand sailcloths and four-thousand lengths of cotton cloth for a campaign.[98] In 1576–77, Istanbul demanded from the *kadı* of Izmir five-hundred *kantar*s of hemp rope from the region of Tire for the *beylerbeyi* of Egypt to outfit a great galley, nine years later reprimanded the superintendents of tax farms (*mukataas*) in western Anatolia for not financing the purchase of hemp, linen cloth, and beeswax for the imperial shipyard, and in 1593 directed officials in Izmir, Aydın, Saruhan, and Menteşe speedily to dispatch to the capital hemp, linen cloth, cotton thread, and beeswax.[99] Directives regarding leathers and acorns encompassed a greater region. In 1591, the *sancakbeyi*s and *kadı*s of the entire eastern Mediterranean shoreline prohibited European merchants from purchasing morocco leather and sheepskin and in 1609–10 the *kadı*s of Çeşme, Mytilene, Ayazmend, and Tuzlu, answering shortages in Istanbul's tanning industry, forbade the hoarding and sale to foreigners of acorns.[100]

Scarcities in cotton and hemp, leathers and acorns in the Ottoman empire during the late sixteenth century derived more from bureaucratic snafus and disruptions of the flow of money than from western competition. Although in the seventeenth century and thereafter, Izmir was to flourish principally because of the town's access to the cottons, wools, and tobacco of western Anatolia, in the previous century merchant vessels plying Aegean waters sought Izmir's abundant and succulent fruits.

● ● ●

Ottoman authorities at the turn of the seventeenth century concerned themselves with Izmir's hinterland not only because of fruits and other foodstuffs. The sultan's entourage, who realized the importance of a happy and prosperous people in cementing the social fabric of its empire and pursuing its expansionist goals, fought also to suppress the brigandage and smuggling that threatened not only the empire's well-being, but its very existence. Thus, in 1609 the bey of Suğla and the *kadı* of Çeşme arrested Muslih al-Din of Seferihisar, who was

in league with brigands and pirates who bring to his house property plundered from Muslims and furthermore send these goods to other lands and have them sold there. . . . This treatment brings about the dispersal of the households of the province.[101]

The futility of Istanbul's demands that brigandage be suppressed, guns confiscated, smuggling controlled, foods provided, and populations maintained reveals deep rifts within Ottoman political, economic, and social life and indicates an economic network within western Anatolia devoted to the buying and movement of contraband, expedited through the distribution of firearms and dispersals of people, and nourished by market imbalances within the empire and abroad. There was a tension, displayed in an escalating governmental nervousness, between Istanbul's obsession with provisioning, and the Ottomans' growing inability to control the situation in western Anatolia and elsewhere. This disjuncture between official Ottoman policy and internal realities constituted a wedge through which traders, officials, and locals could ignore Istanbul's directives. Westerners scouring the Levantine coasts in search of markets and goods to replace the spice trade lost to the Horn of Africa, found in western Anatolia not only cottons and wools to fuel their nascent industries, and potential consumers for their textiles, but also a malleable environment in which to ply their commercial craft. The Dutch, English, and French initiators of the seventeenth-century revolution in commerce discovered, developed, and exploited this embryonic commercial structure.

3

The Atlantic Seaboard Discovers Izmir

Izmir's rise as a commercial center usually is linked to a silk shortage in Aleppo. The resumption of the Ottoman-Safavid conflict in the 1620s, it is argued, severed a caravan trade, which already was threatened by corrupt officials who presided over a bewildering assortment of extraordinary payments. According to this view, frustrated European and Ottoman merchants escaped to Izmir as a surer and less expensive silk mart.[1] Such a dating, however, is too narrow and the analysis of causes too specific. Even before the crisis in Aleppo and more so after the city's recovery, Izmir asserted itself in international commerce as a distribution center not only for silks, but also for the produce of western Anatolia. Confusion over Izmir's development has arisen because of reliance on portrayals by western travelers, who booked passage on merchant vessels, followed well-worn commercial corridors, and consequently failed to "discover" Izmir until it had attained stature as a center for international trade.[2] Their accounts not only serve as a barometer of western interest in Izmir—demonstrating that whereas sixteenth-century wanderers rarely even mentioned the town, seventeenth-century travelers almost always visited and described it—but also reveal the genesis of misconceptions concerning the town's evolution into a city.

There are no descriptions of Izmir in sixteenth-century travel books. While Nicolas de Nicolay, writing in the mid-1500s, recorded the island of Chios in some detail, thanking the French consul there and remarking that the island's Genoese overlords gave the "Turks" every year a ten-thousand-ducat tribute, he did not journey to Izmir.[3] In 1596 Fynes Moryson, en route from Palestine to Istanbul, sailed from Crete to Naxos, skirted Chios, and disembarked at Mytilene. Although he records the commercial vigor of Aleppo and Alexandria, Izmir escapes his notice.[4] Thomas Dallam, touching port at Chios in 1599 on his way to Istanbul, describes the resident English consul, William Aldridge, but does not mention Izmir in the pages of his diary.[5] For two decades at the end of the sixteenth century, John Sanderson wandered through the Levant, usually as a factor for merchants of the English Levant Company. Although in 1601 one of his ship companions was a "Jew, merchant and a dweller in Sio [Chios] and Smirna [Izmir]" and in May of the same year he wrote to Thomas Smythe in London that some merchants on the ship the *Mermaid* paid 1 percent consulage at Chios and Izmir on their goods, Sanderson himself never set foot in Izmir.[6] Finally, Henry de Beauvau, whose work appeared in 1615, stopped at Chios on his way to Istanbul. Neither on this voyage nor on his subsequent pilgrimage to Jerusalem did his vessel anchor at Izmir.[7]

In the first years of the seventeenth century, Izmir suddenly jumped vividly into travelers' imaginations and writings. George Sandys, who left Venice in August 1610, touched port briefly in Chios (where the English consul entertained him) and then sailed on to the town of Izmir, much preferred the latter site. With his inquisitive eye, Sandys declared that "some silk they make [on Chios], and some cottons here grow, but short in worth unto those of Smyrna."[8] His wonder at Izmir's rich hinterland led him to exclaim: "the principall commoditie of Smyrna is Cotton wooll, which there groweth in great quantity. With the seeds thereof they do sow their fields as we ours with corn." His thoroughness directed him to add that "you would think it strange, that so small a shell should containe such a quantitie: [of cotton] but admire, if you saw them stive it in their ships: enforcing a sacke as big as a wool-packe, into a room at the first too narrow for your arme."[9] While valuing Izmir as a distributor of goods of local origin, remarking on the abundance of its environs, and praising the packaging of its principal export crop, Sandys scarcely reports on silk or other commodities from the east.

William Lithgow set forth from Paris in 1610 and four years later arrived in Izmir after a twelve-day sailing from Istanbul. The port impressed him no less than Sandys as a rich and lively commercial town, which had "great trafficke with all Nations, especially for fine Silke, Cotten wooll, and Dimmety, brought to it by the Countrey Peasants, which strangers buy from them." He enthused of Izmir's surroundings that "neare unto this city, I saw a long continuing plaine, abounding in Cornes, Wines, all sorts of fruitfull herbage, and so infinitely peopled, that me thought Nature seemed, with the peoples [sic] industry to contend, the one by propagating creatures, the other by admirable agriculture."[10] Lithgow speaks of the abundance and fertility of Izmir's hinterland and the industry of local inhabitants who transported cottons, fabrics, grains, wines, even silks to the port's market. He makes no mention of a caravan connection to the east.

Subsequent European travelers, who either considered a stop in Izmir de rigueur or else were forced to enter the town's gulf by their vessels' itineraries, subtly revised descriptions of trade there. In 1621 Louis Deshayes, baron de Courmenin, disembarked at Foça and Izmir en route from Istanbul to Jerusalem and, after describing how Christian merchants in Izmir had crowded the shore road with houses facing the sea and relegated the town's Greeks, Jews, and Turks to inland dwellings, wrote that

at present, Izmir has a great traffick in wool, beeswax, cotton, and silk, which the Armenians bring there instead of going to Aleppo. It is more advantageous for them to go there because they do not pay as many dues. There are several merchants, more French than Venetian, English, or Dutch, who live in great freedom.[11]

While produce of local provenance remains paramount in this account, the author also observes that in 1621 Armenian silk merchants invigorated Izmir's commerce. Courmenin ascribes their presence to relatively light duties. Indeed charges exacted on the caravan road linking Izmir to the east and in the port itself were infrequent, and less onerous than similar impositions in Aleppo.[12]

Well into the 1630s, some merchants still understood that local products lay at the core of Izmir's vigor. Lewes Roberts, whose guide to commerce appeared in 1638, relates that "the *trade* of this port it [*sic*] is most noted for the abundance of *cottons* which hence is [*sic*] transported to *England*, *France*, *Holland*, and *Italie*, estimated yearly to be about 20000 *quintall*, and is found here to grow in the adjoyning plaines, which they doe sow as wee doe Corne."[13] The author writes enthusiastically also of an abundance of "*Galles* for Diers, *aniseeds*, *cordovants*, *wax*, *cotton* and *grogram yarne*, *cute*, *carpets*, *grograms*, *mohers*, *chamblets*, and some *fruits* and *drugges*," but dismisses Persian silks as a supplemental commodity.

After the 1620s, such observations were exceptional. Most western agents and travelers routinely emphasized the silks available in Izmir, analyzed its position in international commerce, and ascribed its vigor to Aleppo's woes. Two years after Courmenin's journey, the Venetian bailo noted that "many Persian merchants have begun to arrive in Smyrna with silk and other commodities" and in 1626 the Venetian consul in Aleppo complained that "many big caravans with silk and other costly goods expected from Emit, Erzurum and Basra have now already dispersed, and most of them have made for Smyrna."[14] Jacob Spon and George Wheler, writing in 1675, devoted over ten pages to Izmir; Cornelis de Bruyn three years later asserted that "for commerce, Smyrna is the premier city in all the Levant" and included in his account a detailed map of the port; and Joseph Pitton de Tournefort, traveling fourteen years after the destructive earthquake of 1688, described daily life in the city at length.[15] These observers marveled at Izmir's size, diversity, and vigor; their analyses of Izmir's rise, concentrating on the ancient and diverted Persian silk trade, have rarely been questioned.

INTERNAL VERSUS MARITIME GROWTH
IN WESTERN ANATOLIA

The foundation for Izmir's dramatic growth, however, lay not
in silks, but in a surging European desire for the produce of
western Anatolia, in a transforming Ottoman society, economy,
and political policy, and in an altered role for western merchants.
The Ottomans perceived western trade in local products as a
threat both to their provisioning network and to the well-being
of western Anatolia's inhabitants, and labored to curb European
intrusions into the eastern Aegean. For much of the sixteenth
century Istanbul succeeded and foreign trade through Izmir and
other western-Anatolian ports was inconsiderable. Although the
town's population slowly rose throughout the century, Izmir in
the 1570s was no major population or commercial center and
still lagged far behind the busy entrepôts of Alexandria, Aleppo,
and Bursa. The settlement did not even dominate the urban network within the province of Aydın: Tire to the southeast was the
largest town in the region, and Bergama to the north, Denizli to
the southeast, and Manisa and Demirci to the northeast all supported relatively large populations. Nor was seaborne commerce
routed exclusively through Izmir; Çeşme, Urla, Kuşadası, Balat,
Foça, and Seferihisar shared the vigorous intrastate trade that
dominated the province.[16]

Between the 1520s and the 1570s Izmir participated in the
gradual demographic growth and increasing economic complexity that characterized Asia Minor. While the emergence of small
market towns in inaccessible interior provinces as well as along
its open coasts indicates that urban expansion and increasing
market sophistication owed as much to indigenous growth as
to international trade, maritime commerce along the western-
Anatolian coast was lively.[17] The Ottomans not only recognized
in the region's coastal plains and valleys an exploitable provisioning zone, but, endeavoring to overcome the prohibitive expenses of transporting bulky fruits, cottons, and grains overland
and striving to guarantee prompt, plentiful, and affordable delivery of provisions to Istanbul, they also directed commodities

to the nearest ports along the twisting western-Anatolian coastline. In the 1520s Urla and Menemen were the only coastal towns in western Anatolia. As the century progressed, however, an elaborate lattice of regional ports that drew only upon their immediate hinterlands emerged and by the 1570s Edremid, Ayazmend, Foça, Seferihisar, Balat, and Izmir had joined Urla and Menemen.[18] Provisions en route to Istanbul passed through all of them.

A CRITICAL DECADE, 1600-1610

In the last decades of the sixteenth century, Ottoman authorities began to lose their grasp of western-Anatolian commerce. In face of competition from both domestic and foreign buyers, the largely self-contained imperial system disintegrated. Initially, traders who roamed the Aegean did not converge upon Izmir. These merchant-corsairs prowled about haphazardly, buying and selling as opportunity arose. By the beginning of the seventeenth century, however, these meanderings had ceased and many traders labored both legitimately and illicitly at Izmir. As Courmenin observed, the French were particularly active. In 1605, French vessels touching port in Izmir each smuggled out over one-hundred *kantar*s of beeswax and by 1610 the French also trafficked in weapons and other contraband.[19] French dominance in this trade derived from the merchants of Marseilles' ability briefly to wrest most-favored-status from their English arch-rivals. In 1604 François Savari, Seigneur de Brèves, the French ambassador in Istanbul, elicited capitulations from the Sublime Porte that not only directed all trading states without ambassadors in Istanbul to sail under French banner and protection, but also permitted French merchants to purchase formerly forbidden leathers, cottons, and beeswax.[20] Istanbul soon regretted this capitulatory concession and sought futilely to seal the inadvertent breach of western Anatolia's economy, particularly at Izmir where French traders congregated.

Not only the French, but also the Dutch, English, and Venetians flocked to Izmir, and a redistributed Ottoman cus-

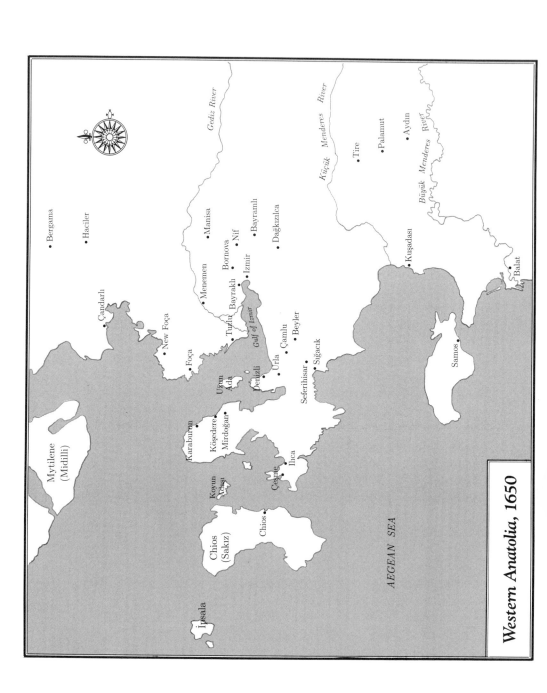

Gediz River

Küçük Menderes River

Büyük Menderes River

•Tire

•Palamut

•Aydın

•Bergama

•Haciler

•Manisa

•Bayramlı

•Nif

•Dağkızılca

•Kuşadası

•Menemen

•Bornova

•İzmir

•Balat

•Çandarlı

•New Foça

•Bayraklı

•Tuzlu

Gulf of İzmir

•Çamlu

•Beyler

•Foça

•Urla

•Sığacık

•Samos

Uzun
Ada

•Denizli

•Seferihisar

Mytilene
(Midilli)

Karaburun

•Köşedere

•Mirdoğan

•Ilıca

•Çeşme

Koyun
Adası

Chios
(Sakız)

•Chios

AEGEAN SEA

İpsala

Western Anatolia, 1650

toms revenue reflects their presence. The Ottomans, envisaging the western-Anatolian littoral as a single economic unit whose climate and geography fit the cultivation and marketing of fruits and fibers, farmed out to a single tax collector the revenue of the entire east-central Aegean region. While this consolidation obscured the contours of commerce within western Anatolia, the rising annual "bid for the customs farms of Sakız, Izmir, Çeşme, Balat, and associated payments" indicated a commercial change.[21] Between 1589 and 1626 revenue from this source almost doubled, from 3,603,334 to 6,469,140 *akçe*s.

A summary of monies collected between 3 May 1604 and 3 May 1607, when two Jews named İbrahim veled-i Davud and Davud veled-i İbrahim administered the tax farm for the western-Anatolian economic zone, divides this lump payment into its constituent components. The agents' gross returns on an approximately 6,000,000 *akçe*s' annual investment was 6,586,037 *akçe*s in 1604–5, 6,405,210 in 1605–6, and 6,177,956 in 1606–7 (see tables 6 and 7).[22] Individual entries for duties collected from raw silk, lumber, mastic, and the minting of money, and for customs procured at the ports of Chios/Çeşme, Izmir, Urla, Kuşadası, Balat, the two Foças, Sığacık/Seferihisar, Sant, Mîrdoğan, İpsala, Musabey, Koyun, Köşedere, and Haydarlı—all within the natural economic district of western Anatolia and most clustered in and around the Gulf of Izmir—document an abrupt regional redistribution of commerce.[23] Whereas in an earlier epoch Izmir, Urla, the two Foças, Ayasoluğ, Kuşadası, and Chios had vied for commercial prominence along the Anatolian coastline, by 1604 only Izmir and Chios, each generating approximately one-million *akçe*s per annum, remained in the fray (see figure , page 60). The other ports on the littoral, none of which brought in more than 150,000 *akçe*s, now lagged far behind.

In some cases, a port's geography precluded commercial expansion. Neither the small island of Koyun, nestled between Chios and the entranceway to the Gulf of Izmir, nor the mainland ports of Mîrdoğan and Köşedere possessed spacious natural harbors or uniquely marketable commodities. Other ports were better situated to rival Chios and Izmir, and had done so in the past. In the fourteenth century, Italian ship captains piloted much cotton out of Ayasoluğ; in the 1570s Urla boasted a population twice Izmir's; and in the fifteenth and sixteenth centuries Genoese and Venetian vessels frequently anchored at Balat.[24] Foça, which had been a bustling Genoese colony before the Ottomans definitively incorporated it into their state in 1455, derived its vitality from alum mining.[25] Although the district continued to produce alum after the capture of Foça, the domestic market gradually dominated sales.[26] By 1606 Izmir and Chios each contributed to the imperial treasury almost eight times as much customs revenue as Urla and Foça and twenty times as much as Kuşadası; Balat's contribution had become negligible.

TABLE 6

Customs Revenue in Central-Western Anatolia

(*In* akçes)

Port	3 May 1604– 3 May 1605	3 May 1605– 3 May 1606	3 May 1606– 3 May 1607
Chios/Çeşme	1,064,025	859,005	600,192
Izmir	981,854	1,171,958	1,332,733
Urla	112,523	105,500	103,423
Kuşadası	33,402	55,458	48,012
Balat	6,000	5,200	6,000
Foça	135,434	155,378	158,434
Sığacık/Seferihisar	34,575	33,300	9,102
Sant	12,500	17,500	17,500
Mîrdoğan	4,000	4,000	4,000
İpsara[a]	35,000	30,000	60,000
Musabey[a]	102	102	102
Koyun[a]	1,200	1,200	1,200
Köşedere	4,000	4,000	4,000
Haydarlı	canceled	canceled	canceled
Total	2,424,615	2,442,601	2,344,698

SOURCE: BBA, İE (Maliye) 640.

[a] These towns or islands were registered as single *mukataas* or *resims*. The customs revenue was not tabulated separately.

TABLE 7

Revenue Other Than Customs Collected in
Central-Western Anatolia

(*In* akçes)

Dues	3 May 1604– 3 May 1605	3 May 1605– 3 May 1606	3 May 1606– 3 May 1607
Cizye[a]	910,000	971,418	971,418
Inheritance	83,959	30,200	44,470
Fines[a]	146,462	59,341	53,370
Mastic[a]	2,292,000	2,195,650	2,035,000
İhtisab[a]	130,000	115,000	113,000
Raw silk	180,000	180,000	200,000
Lumber	110,000	110,000	110,000
Land and sheep	85,000	80,000	80,000
Evkaf of Piyale Paşa	3,000	3,000	3,000
Beans	6,000	10,000	8,000
Total	3,946,421	3,754,609	3,618,258

SOURCE: BBA, İE (Maliye) 640.

[a] The *cizye* or head tax on non-Muslims, the *cera'im* or fines, the mastic, and the *ihtisab* or market revenue all refer to Chios alone. The source does not specify from which port or ports the other dues were gathered.

Within the short span between 1604 and 1607, Izmir's commerce boomed. Customs revenue in the town rose from 981,854 to 1,332,733 *akçes*, whereas income at other regional ports either remained constant or declined. Urla's revenue dropped from 112,523 to 103,423 *akçes* and Seferihisar's plummeted from 34,575 to 9,102 *akçes*. Foça experienced a slight rise in customs revenue, from 135,434 to 158,434 *akçes*, not as a rival to other ports, but because it guarded the mouth of Izmir's gulf. Vessels that enemy ships or corsairs menaced en route to and from Izmir fled to Foça's fortress and guns, and traded while at anchor. As commerce through the gulf increased, so did the threat of piracy and the significance of this refuge's walls and cannon.[27]

While in 1604 Izmir and Chios shared western-Anatolian commerce and generated approximately the same customs revenue, the advantage soon shifted to the mainland port. Although in the intervening two years the volume of trade through western Anatolia remained virtually constant, in 1606 Chios supplied less than one-half as much revenue as Izmir (see table 6). Izmir, whose customs swelled by 350,879 *akçes* in three years, swiftly consumed the commerce of Chios, where customs contracted by 463,834 *akçes*.

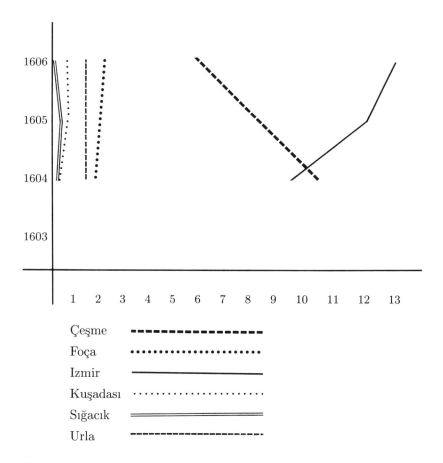

Comparison of customs revenue in selected western-Anatolian ports (in 100,000 *akçes*)

WHY CHIOS FALTERED

Chios's turbulent history during the fifty years prior to 1604 explains the island's commercial swoon. With the Ottomans conquering the Aegean islands of Mytilene in 1462, Negroponte in 1470, and Samos in 1550, Chios became for fifteen years the only Christian outpost on an Ottoman sea. It retained its political autonomy for so long not because of military prowess or impregnable walls, but initially because of an ancient Genoese-Ottoman friendship: a relationship, which in 1512 was buoyed by a treaty between Selim I and the Genoese rulers of Chios granting commercial privileges similar to those of the Latin city-states.[28] After 1528, when a Genoese-Habsburg alliance disrupted Genoese-Ottoman relations, the Genoese rulers of Chios severed political ties with their mother state and increased Ottoman tribute in order to appease the sultan.[29] These careful diplomatic maneuvers allowed Chios to function as a "middle island" and the slender waterway between it and the port of Çeşme acted as both cultural barrier and commercial bridge between Christian Europe and Muslim Anatolia.

The island's unusual autonomy ended abruptly in 1566 when Admiral Piyale Paşa led a virtually unopposed and instantly triumphant Ottoman naval invasion of Chios under pretext that the island had failed to pay its thirty-thousand ducat tribute. A deep economic malaise that afflicted the island in the 1550s and 1560s had persuaded the Chians not only to petition for postponement of tributary payments, but also to plead for Ottoman grain for the famine-stricken islanders.[30] Although Istanbul complied with both requests, Ottoman authorities gradually grew impatient with the Chians' persistent crisis and in 1566 annexed the island.

Istanbul and Piyale Paşa had been seeking an excuse to occupy Chios, whose Genoese rulers had in recent years angered Ottoman authorities. Chians fighting alongside the Knights of St. John on Malta helped thwart Piyale Paşa's investment of that crusading bastion in 1565 and Chios itself had become a refuge for escaped Ottoman slaves.[31] Such betrayals convinced the aged and invalided Süleyman, who sought to reclaim the stature of his youth, to resolve, however reluctantly, to reopen hostilities against the Habsburgs, and to perceive the island less as a convenient commercial hub than as an avenue for easy victory over a potent foe.

The Ottomans granted their new Chian subjects a number of requests, which indicates not only that the Sublime Porte's administration was benign, but also that Istanbul believed that nurturing the island's commerce would benefit the imperial treasury. Sultan Selim II agreed in 1567 to exempt Chian children from the slave corps, to confirm prior legal decisions, and to permit (with the *kadı*'s consent) the repair of damaged and disused churches. He also retained and strove to broaden the established Genoese commercial system.[32] Istanbul made wheat, barley, and luxury goods, especially silks, duty free; imposed no new charges upon other goods imported from the mainland; and exempted from duty vessels in transit from the Black Sea unless their merchandise was marketed on the island. Finally, authorities endorsed Çeşme's special commercial relationship with the island.

Despite these precautions, Chios lost to Izmir its commercial hegemony in the eastern Aegean. In part, the island's vulnerability to seaborne invasion precipitated this change. In 1599 a small Florentine naval expedition consisting of 5 ships and 350 men captured and occupied for 9 hours the town and castle of Chios.[33] This fleeting victory so alarmed recent Muslim settlers on the island that Istanbul immediately dispossessed the 350 Christian families dwelling within the fortress and removed them to the suburbs. Five years later the Sublime Porte had all churches within the town walls razed in order to halt the "accursed infidels'" ritualized and regular Sunday passage into town.[34] Muslim inhabitants tried also to expel the town's Jews, petitioning Istanbul in 1613 that "some Jews have a quarter within the castle. If the enemy invades, [the actions these Jews may undertake] frightens [the Muslim inhabitants]. The Jews should sell their houses at a fair price."[35] Although the town's struggling Jewish community proclaimed its loyalty and convinced Istanbul to allow it to remain, the domestic backlash from the Florentine invasion crippled the economic and social vitality of the old commercial town since European consuls and merchants now had to travel outside the town walls under the suspicious eyes of Muslim subjects and Ottoman officials in order to deal with Greek middlemen and translators.

Venetian merchants had much at stake on Chios. They had participated in Chian commerce under Genoese rule and continued to do so after 1566, and their long domicile on the island raised questions about their status. As a conquered people, Chios's non-Muslim inhabitants became liable to a head tax (*cizye*) and the Ottomans' first action as conquerors was to compile a population register and begin collecting *cizye* from the 406 Greek and 49 Jewish households residing in the town of Chios as well as from the island's 7,000 Greek villagers.[36] In order to encourage commerce, Istanbul accepted the Latins' spurious argument that they constituted a community of temporary residents and exempted the 140 Venetian and Genoese households living in the town from these dues.[37] Local officials and *cizye* collectors, questioning the claims of individuals whose families had dwelled in the town for generations, sought to divest Venetians of their foreigner status. The dispute, which continued for decades, exacerbated tensions between Turk and Latin and helped drive Venetians from this important entrepôt.[38]

Even as Ottoman authorities squelched Chian commerce after the 1599 fiasco, merchants from Christian Europe hit upon a route that circumvented the island. Before the turn of the century the Ottomans had directed to Çeşme the modest quantities of goods in transit through western Anatolia. From there they shipped them to the island of Chios and on to Europe. This passage made sense as long as international trade was in silks and spices and Chios remained a Christian outpost. When Chios lost its autonomy and as western traders began seeking commodities native to Anatolia, the island lost its advantages as an entrepôt. It became more convenient and less expensive to bring commodities to Izmir and load them directly into seagoing vessels in the town's spacious harbor rather than to transport dried fruits, cottons, wools, and leathers to Çeşme, load these bulky goods on to coastal vessels, cross the narrow channel to the port of Chios, and transfer them to seagoing vessels bound for the west. The report İbrahim veled-i Davud and Davud veled-i İbrahim filed confirms that by 1607 Chios had lost its monopoly, at least de facto, on goods exported to the west and that Izmir had replaced it as the dominant port in the region.

Chios's commercial malady did not infect other sectors of its economy. Between 1604 and 1607 duties on mastic, a substance coveted both in the empire and the west, consistently remained above two-million *akçes*, market charges did not decrease, and duties on raw silk even rose marginally (see table 7). Mastic had been and remained the economic mainstay of the island and while adjustments in trading patterns and a transplanted and privileged Muslim population dealt a terrible economic blow to the town of Chios, they had little effect on its countryside and villages. The only restructuring that occurred was in interregional and international trade.

THE ATLANTIC SEABOARD
INVESTS LEVANTINE TRADE

Between 1590 and 1610, then, merchants from Christian Europe chose Izmir from among the cluster of small eastern-Aegean ports to foster as a port of transit for the commodities of western Anatolia. This refocusing of commerce coincided with the intrusion of Atlantic seaboard trading companies into the formerly French- and Venetian-dominated world of Mediterranean trade and, although the veteran trading states suffered gravely from Dutch and English competition, other factors also contributed to the deterioration of their Levantine commercial networks.

For the Venetians, decline was particularly sudden and severe. The seaborne spice trade, demographic changes within the Republic, shortages of shipbuilding materials, rapid fluctuations in real wages within the city of Venice, the loss of the German market during the Thirty Years' War, an intensification of piratic operations in the Mediterranean, and the ruthless attack especially of the English Levant Company upon the Venetian textile trade all contributed to the rapid Dutch and English acquisition of Levantine trade.[39]

Although the French experienced many of these same difficulties, for them the result was less catastrophic. The merchants of Marseilles began auspiciously enough in the middle years of the sixteenth century. During the Veneto-Ottoman war of 1570–73 they lodged themselves in Aleppo and Alexandria. Then, during the French religious wars of 1562–98, their trade suffered a setback.[40] Not only did domestic turmoil divide the French government, distract Paris from commerce, and disrupt communications between the capital and Marseilles, but the port city's merchants split into factions supporting or resisting their staunchly Catholic and pro-Spanish mayor.

More forebodingly, the Ottomans suspected French merchants of nurturing clandestine relations with the Spanish Habsburgs. When in 1590 Sultan Murat III wrote to Marseilles demanding that its subjects pledge allegiance to the Huguenot-turned-Catholic Henry of Navarre, who the year before had been crowned king of France as Henry IV, the inhabitants of the French port replied:

> We understand that you wish us to declare ourselves subjects of the King of Navarre, claiming to be King of France, and you threaten, if we refuse, to ruin our commerce.
>
> We beg you to believe that we are all resolved to live and to die Frenchmen of Marseilles, but never Spaniards, still less Savoyards. We have always been Catholics, and therefore cannot become subjects of Navarre, who is a heretic and a Huguenot.
>
> M. de Brèves is Ambassador, not of France, but merely of the King of Navarre.[41]

The Marseillans composed this letter during a period of eroding relations between themselves and Istanbul. Although the sultan's government supported Henry of Navarre because of his opposition to the Spaniards, not his Huguenot background, the Sublime Porte understood that the bloody French war was as much religious as political and suspected the devout Catholics of Marseilles not only of despising the new king, but also of supporting his Spanish nemesis. At a time when rival companies threatened to topple French commercial hegemony in Ottoman domains, Istanbul's wariness as much as the rift between the French ambassador de Brèves and the merchants of Marseilles or the infamous venality of French consuls hindered French trade and aided the English in obtaining favorable capitulatory terms despite intense French opposition.[42]

A SEA OF PIRATES AND PILLAGERS

Although Dutch and English intruders did not at once eclipse French merchants, who ably competed at least until 1636, the new trading states began to usurp French and Venetian Levantine commerce even before the turn of the century.[43] They burst into the Mediterranean world not as merchants, but as pirates. In spite of favorable terms granted in the capitulations of 1591, English merchants often found it easier, more profitable, and more in accord with their Atlantic training to pillage French, Ottoman, and Venetian shipping than to engage peaceably in commerce.[44]

The Venetians in particular writhed in the tempest induced by warring states, unable to ally themselves fully with anyone for fear of antagonizing others with whom they profitably traded. In the last years of the sixteenth century the city-state through diplomacy pressured the English to cease their depredations, even unrealistically supposing in 1600 that Queen Elizabeth would revoke the Levant Company's charter because of continuous molestation of Venetian shipping. In February of that year the frantic bailo in Istanbul, Capello, expressed to the Doge and Senate that he had "had a most favorable occasion to speak to the English ambassador about the audacity of the English ships which, in the waters and harbors of your Serenity, molest all other shipping, including that of the Republic," and added that the English ambassador had assured him that "when the Queen hears of these complaints, she will revoke the charter of the Levant Company."[45] Not only was the charter not revoked, but pirates became increasingly intrepid with the English, Uskoks, Maltese, Barbaries, Dutch, and Spanish roaming the Adriatic, Aegean, and eastern Mediterranean almost at will, disrupting shipping and turning the seas into a perpetual war zone.[46] The infestation was especially thick around the ports of Alexandretta and Alexandria, with the English ambassador in Istanbul boasting that the ships of his state could "harry the commerce on the coasts and islands of Turkey, and . . . seize the shipping of Syria and Alexandria" at will.[47]

Piracy also disrupted the vital provisioning route between Alexandria and Istanbul. In 1594 an Ottoman fleet of galleons, in an unusual success, rescued a provisioning vessel carrying rice and other goods from Alexandria to Istanbul, which had fallen prey to infidel ships off the coast of Rhodes.[48] The Ottomans, who in 1522 had laid seige to and captured that haunt of crusaders, thereby securing the strategic sea lanes linking Egypt to their capital, seventy years later again lost control of the crucial passage. In 1606 the sultan's government even considered breaking relations with the English because of their maraudings, and did order the removal of the port of Aleppo from Alexandretta to Syrian Tripoli because the former was "an open roadstead, . . . a veritable temptation to pirates."[49] Three years later, after Istanbul accomplished the move, the English, French, and Venetian communities in Aleppo quickly realized the disadvantages of the new arrangement and began issuing noisy complaints against the abuses of customs collectors and other officials in Tripoli.[50] The Ottomans reinstated the port in Alexandretta in 1613.[51]

Izmir, boasting a spacious port within a large and well-protected gulf, was better situated than Alexandretta, Chios, and other eastern Mediterranean ports to repel the raids of corsairs. It also was closer to Leghorn, Venice, and other western Mediterranean ports than Alexandria, Alexandretta, or even Istanbul, and the innumerable islands of the Aegean, within which merchantmen as well as pirates hid or sought ports of safety, guarded its approaches. As the high seas became unsafe and, with the advent of northern European shipping into the Mediterranean, as costs and dangers made long voyages riskier, Venetian commerce contracted and the city-state's vessels rarely hauled freight beyond the Adriatic and Aegean seas. In 1611, only three Venetian ships embarked for Syria, three for Alexandria, six for Istanbul, twelve for Izmir, and fourteen for Crete.[52] The days of venturesome galleys projecting Venetian commercial interests throughout the Mediterranean basin had passed.

NEW TRADING COMPANIES REJECT
OLD TRADING CENTERS

The Dutch and English observed the fiscal, administrative, and social upheaval besetting older Levantine centers of transit and hesitated to fill the partial vacuum left by the Venetian exodus. Particularly in Aleppo, heavy surcharges and disruptions along caravan routes, the semi-autonomous principalities of Canbuladoğlu Ali Paşa (who established himself in northern Syria in the early 1600s) and other rebellious emirs, and the venalities of Ottoman officials within the city wore down French and Venetian merchants and put off new trading states.[53] The result was a sudden downturn in commerce along the Syrian coast in the first decades of the seventeenth century.[54] In 1611, the Venetian ambassador in London reported that an Englishman who had just returned from Aleppo confided that his state voluntarily had abandoned the entrepôt because of the "great price which is necessitated by the cost of transport to Syria partly by sea and partly by land," adding with unintended irony that piracy also was a dissuading factor.[55]

Even without the infamous corruption of Ottoman officials in the established entrepôts of the Ottoman empire and the sporadic delivery of supplies from the east, the Dutch and English would have sought alternatives to the trading routes terminating in Aleppo, Alexandria, and Istanbul. English merchants not only strove to circumvent the empire entirely in their silk trade, abortively exploring the Russian course to Persian silks in the mid-sixteenth century and vainly endeavoring to inaugurate a cape route in the 1620s, but they also searched for new arteries to Persia through the Levant.[56] In 1610 a delegation of English merchants in Istanbul endeavored to open commercial houses in Trabzon and Persia and thus evade Syria.[57] Although they failed and the English did not regularize the Trabzon route until the nineteenth century, the incident reveals an innovative seeking for new commercial outlets within the empire.[58] The Dutch and English wanted them in part because of high and unpredictable surcharges and irregular caravan arrivals in Aleppo. Also, the French and Venetians, who had well-established consulates in Aleppo and well-placed connections with Ottoman officials both there and in Istanbul, long had been commercially dominant along the Syrian littoral, and the Atlantic seaboard states found it difficult to crack their hegemony.

In Aleppo, the Dutch encountered the frustration of trying to break into an established trading center. Upon successfully negotiating capitulations with Istanbul, merchants from the Netherlands still had to contend not only with French and Venetian competitors in Aleppo, but also with Bedik, an Armenian tax collector (*mültezim*). Bedik, who had obtained his office by 1611 and held it sporadically at least until 1627 (when he probably was executed), exercised the authority to collect customs dues on all exports and imports in Aleppo, and symbolized for western merchants entrenched interests in the port.[59] His clashes with foreign merchants were myriad and legendary. In 1611, a representative of the Venetian bailo in Aleppo sold Bedik some goods and precious stones, for which the collector would not fully pay. When the Venetian consul had him dragged before the town's *kadı* to demand that he be thrown into jail, Bedik reportedly huffed in response: "I am the *emin*. No one will imprison me."[60] In 1613, he stood with the Venetian consul in the presence of the *beylerbeyi* of Aleppo, where the fiery collector allegedly directed an abusive tongue-lashing against his opponent.[61] By appealing to authorities in Istanbul, the indignant consul managed not only to pry an apology out of Bedik, but even to secure his removal from office and imprisonment for indebtedness.[62] The Venetian triumph was shortlived, however. Three years later the community's bête noire was back in office, where he was on and off to remain—despite the vociferous protests of Venetian, Frenchman, and Dutchman—for at least another decade. It was this intimidating figure against whom the Dutch, flush with their release from French protection, ran afoul in 1612. He and his agents, wise to the maneuverings and tricks of western merchants, helped thwart the Republic's ambition of building an extensive trading network in Aleppo's hinterland.[63]

INTEGRATION INTO A SUPERIMPOSED
COMMERCIAL NETWORK: THE EXAMPLE OF MANISA

The Dutch and the English built in the environs of Izmir a systematized and far-reaching trading network, which, in Aleppo, had been defeated by the conflicting interests of the Venetians, French, Ottoman officials,and Arab and Armenian merchants. Izmir's commerce benefited from both Chian and Aleppan difficulties and the richness of its own hinterland. Many of Chios's Greeks, Jews, and Venetians drifted over to the mainland port, and, during the second and third decades of the seventeenth century, European consuls resident there followed; European merchants also streamed into the town from Aleppo, Alexandria, and Istanbul as well as from their home countries.[64] These commercial groups fanned out along the agriculturally rich valleys and into towns to which Izmir was the closest and most accessible port. The most important such town was Manisa, which lies in the Gediz river valley a short day's journey from Izmir.

Manisa not only was within reach of the overnight peddler, but also in the sixteenth century it possessed flourishing textile and tanning industries.[65] Mountain ranges below and to the east of the Gediz river sheltered transhumant nomads who provided Manisa with the raw woolen fibers and leathers that fueled its industries. The rich river valley in which the town is nestled yielded grapes, olives, and cottons to Izmir. A traditional training capital for Ottoman princes, Manisa also profited from a royal retinue and exemption from many taxes.

The provisioning network the Ottomans had established in the late 1400s and early 1500s linking the rich region surrounding Manisa to Istanbul was disrupted in the last decades of the sixteenth century. This development did not concern the producers and manufacturers of Manisa's valley, who happily sold their surplus goods to westerners at exorbitant profits. Then, in the early seventeenth century, middlemen and traders from outside the region pushed beyond town markets, outbid native artisans for raw materials, and thereby disrupted supply lines from villages and nomadic groups along the Gediz river valley to Manisa. Shortages were felt not only in Istanbul, but also locally, and the guildsmen of Manisa added their complaints to those of inhabitants of the capital city.

Tanners and other craftsmen at first simply protested against trafficking in raw materials. Villagers traditionally had brought skins to Manisa, where tanners chose the best and paid fixed prices for them; outside traders then could buy from the picked over stock.[66] In 1599, however, a representative of the community of tanners in Manisa traveled to Istanbul to elicit assistance in apprehending a certain Ali who, claiming to be a member of the guild of tanners, diligently scoured the villages around Manisa for high-quality horse, donkey, and mule skins in order to spirit them away to buyers from outside the province before the guildsmen of Manisa even saw them.[67] Ali's poaching depleted local stocks and threatened the quality of and rigid price structure for leathers.

In the following decade, disruptive peddlers, middlemen, and itinerant merchants poached materials vital to industries other than tanning. In 1607, the weavers of Manisa faced competition from "middlemen and traders from the outside, . . . [who] bought the cotton fibre that came to market in Manisa and took it elsewhere;" two years later the cobblers of Manisa turned upon fellow guildsmen, the tanners, whom they accused of selling leathers to foreign merchants at exorbitant prices; and in 1612 morocco leathers vanished from the town's market because of outside demand.[68]

By the 1610s, merchants scurrying through Manisa's rich hinterland had depleted the raw materials of vital manufactures to the point of threatening that town's economic life. While the Jews and Muslims of Manisa's textile industry traditionally had depended upon "fleece produced in that area" in order "to manufacture common broadcloth and blankets," by 1615 speculators hoarded the material in order to "send it to the land of the infidel and . . . harm the tradesmen who cannot find wool to produce textiles" and who consequently abandoned their professions and their domicile.[69] Six years later these middlemen had so disrupted Manisa's textile industry that "few Jews remained" in the town, but had fled to seek opportunities in Izmir.[70]

CONSOLIDATION IN WESTERN ANATOLIA

It is no coincidence that these shortages manifested themselves in the same period that Izmir began to outpace other ports in the region. European traders recently settled in Izmir had begun constructing a network of factors and wholesalers who together with peddlers and middlemen fanned out along the river valleys and plains to the east. The interlopers who trekked across the western-Anatolian landscape enjoyed considerable capital and, combing the region for leathers, cottons, woolens, grains, and fruits, they funneled their purchases westward through Izmir.

While this European-inspired economic system appeared only spottily in the 1620s, two decades later the network was firmly in place. In 1641, Istanbul documents changes in western Anatolia's commerce, for the *kadıs* of Izmir and Manisa and other provincial officials, declaring:

the merchants of Istanbul . . . cannot procure sufficient soap, sultanas, raisins, apricots, wild apricots, figs, dried pears, nuts, shelled nuts, split-eyed beans, olives, grape syrup, jam, sesame seeds, walnuts, almonds, pomegranates (*inar*), olive oil, and other provisions. Although I have not given permission for infidel and non-native traders to buy them, for several years [a number of Jews as well as] . . . Osman and his brother from Izmir, and Hacı Mehmet, Blind Bayram, and İbrahim from Doksanlu, Zeytun, and Eğerca, have received stock from infidels and, traveling from village to village, acquired provisions at a high price. They have brought tools for barrels from Europe and made more than four-thousand large barrels and filled them with goods in the villages and loaded them on [camels] and [cattle]. Merchants from other places [than Istanbul] also are in distress [because of shortages]. The soapmakers cannot make sufficient soap and their soaps are spurious.[71]

Here both Muslim and non-Muslim traders receive capital and equipment from European merchants in order to undercut Ottoman price structures, package provisions and remove them from the empire. The Dutch, English, French, and Venetian directors mobilized both beasts of burden, who trudged down the roads and paths into Izmir, and the expertise of native traders, who congregated in the growing port. This superimposed commercial operation wreaked havoc with both Istanbul's carefully constructed provisioning network and manufactures, which depended upon suddenly scarce supplies.

The European network affected every segment of the western-Anatolian economy. Even the famous soap of Urla suffered from "spurious" manufacture because of western incursions. The soap makers of Urla utilized extensive olive groves for their product, which consumed ten *kantars* of olive oil per fifteen or sixteen *kantars* of soap. As a port town, however, Urla naturally drew sea peddlers to its olive oil and raisins.[72] By 1593 the rising price of olive oil and other goods compelled soap makers not only to produce thirty-five or forty *kantars* of soap from every ten *kantars* of olive oil but also to use impure water and other inferior ingredients.[73] Twenty years later soap houses in Urla and its environs were "broken down and decrepit" and, as European merchants spread out across Izmir's hinterland, the crisis reached Manisa and other soap manufacturing towns in the interior.[74]

AGRICULTURAL TRANSFORMATION

European interest in commodities native to western Anatolia and the ability of western merchants to outbid native consumers

and to transport goods cheaply to the coast, then, created shortages in crucial raw materials. The penetration of western trading
states more indirectly influenced the region's economy and society, dispossessing and transplanting natives, jarring industries,
and altering agricultural structures.

Although cash-crop farming in western Anatolia became
most pronounced in later centuries, even in the early seventeenth
century both European and subject merchants who superimposed their own commercial network upon the official Ottoman
one had specific needs and, as shortages materialized and prices
rose, farmers slowly responded to them. Innovative representatives of the government and ambitious peasants planted cotton
(often for export to Europe) rather than wheat in their fields
and tobacco (principally for domestic consumption) rather than
vegetables in their gardens.

Whereas Anatolians had harvested cotton for centuries and
simply put more land into production as demand increased, tobacco was introduced to the Ottoman empire only in the 1590s
and appeared in Istanbul in 1601.[75] Despite the most ruthless
suppression of its cultivation and use, the substance almost in-
stantaneously became overwhelmingly popular throughout the
empire.[76] The first concerted attempt at the suppression of tobacco came in 1633.[77] But, Istanbul was aware of its widespread
use twenty years earlier, proclaiming in 1613 to the *kadıs* within
the province of Saruhan, including Manisa, that

> wax needed for the imperial larder always has cost 1,400 *akçes* per *kantar*.
> . . . The people of Saruhan however have become accustomed to opening
> tobacco houses and a *kantar* of wax now costs 2,400 *akçes*. This state of
> affairs harms the state and is a bad innovation. . . . You should not let them
> open tobacco houses and you also should not permit tobacco cultivation in
> the gardens within the district.[78]

Decades before the state expressed concern about the effects
of tobacco on the moral fiber of the empire's subjects, Istanbul
was voicing alarm that its cultivation might hinder the sowing
of other crops. In the case of beeswax they misdirected their accusations, for tobacco was less responsible for inflating the price

of beeswax in 1613 than was demand from Christian Europe. Istanbul's objections to tobacco supplanting vegetables and to the proliferation of tobacco houses, however, were well founded. As the seventeenth century progressed, more and more arable land around Manisa was given over to tobacco and cotton, thereby drawing its inhabitants further from subsistence agriculture into a market economy.[79] Meanwhile, in towns and villages throughout western Anatolia, establishments devoted to the imbibing of tobacco joined the coffeehouse, a sixteenth-century addition to the urban Ottoman milieu, and other such institutions of alleged conviviality, idleness, and conspiracy.[80] While this atmosphere of relaxed seediness would beget state obsession with the influence of tobacco on the moral fiber of the empire's subjects, in 1613 Istanbul was more uneasy over tobacco's effect on food production.

• • •

Izmir's hinterland, rich in newly marketable goods, attracted the merchant companies of the Atlantic seaboard. The English sought new markets at the turn of the seventeenth century in part because the collapse of the Antwerp cloth market in 1585 forced them to find other outlets for their textiles.[81] They pursued novel commodities because the Dutch locked them out of the southeast Asian spice trade and threatened also to cut off their recently secured share of Indian pepper.[82] It was this uncertainty in the supplies of luxury goods that prompted English merchants to market cotton textiles from India. Indirectly, it also encouraged the state's domestic textile industry, which, completely dependent upon imported cottons and other industrial crops, spurred vessels of the English Levant Company during the late sixteenth century to scour first Syrian Tripoli and other Levantine ports and subsequently western-Anatolian shores.[83]

Izmir became the principal exchange for this commerce not because of a realignment in caravan routes, but because a largely fortuitous redistribution of regional trade had focused commerce upon the town. An increase in the volume of trade followed this initial concentration as western merchants installed themselves in the port and threw their commercial nets eastward across Anatolia. Had a new transit center for trade between Asia and Europe emerged in Foça, Chios, Izmir or Manisa, Istanbul would have welcomed it. Such was not the case. The concentration of western interests upon native Ottoman materials interfered with internal trade and upset the social, industrial, and agricultural order of Izmir's hinterland. Even after silk reappeared in Aleppo after the Ottoman reconquest of Baghdad in 1638, Izmir continued to grow and, although silk kept flowing across Anatolia, its share of the trade declined and cotton, wool, and other local commodities, which had been the catalyst for Izmir's early development, again became the mainstay of the city's commerce.[84]

4

Non-Muslim Ottomans in a Frontier City

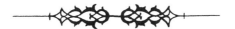

In the first decades of the seventeenth century, Izmir's rapidly expanding commercial infrastructure was spurred by brokers, bankers, translators, tax collectors, administrators, wholesalers, retailers, ship caulkers, bazaar merchants, middlemen, porters, innkeepers, camel-drivers, and international traders. Arabs, Armenians, Greeks, Jews, and Turks, seeking to occupy these positions, inundated the town. Individuals and communities clustered in professions where they had expertise. Thus in the 1620s Armenians, who with their fluency in Persian, Turkish, and European languages and customs already had established an international commercial web, recognized Izmir's potential and created a silk mart in the port; and Jews, who in the sixteenth century had secured communal wealth and political power as Ottoman financial administrators, dominated the position of tax collector in Izmir.[1] Arabs, whose camels in the sixteenth century had hauled salt from the pans of western Anatolia, managed the caravan network thrown eastward by Izmir's entrepreneurs; however, Muslims were not allotted a large part in the port's trade.[2] Whereas longstanding commercial systems and entrenched traders had often resisted and occasionally made capital of European merchants in Aleppo, Bursa, and other silk-oriented entrepôts, trading companies setting up shop on the western-Anatolian frontier constructed their own networks and traded with whom they pleased. Consequently, Ottoman Christians and Jews captured many of the positions as intermediaries and agents for westerners. While the cultural admixture of these linguistic, ethnic, and religious groups eventually shaped a cosmopolitan and commerce-oriented "Levantine" subculture, in the seventeenth century they constituted relatively autonomous communities, of which the liveliest, most contentious, and most explosive was the Jewish.

IZMIR AND THE SIXTEENTH-CENTURY SEPHARDIC
SETTLEMENT IN THE OTTOMAN EMPIRE

During the late fifteenth and early sixteenth centuries Ottoman Jewry had been unstable as an expanding and evolving empire and a fluctuating population composition disrupted the community's administrative, economic, and social structure. After 1453, Mehmet II employed economic incentives and forced migration (*sürgün*) to lure Greeks, Jews, and other commercially sensitive groups to Istanbul. The new capital city's spectacular rebirth assured that they would remain. Jews transplanted from long residences in the dissimilar settings of Rumeli and Anatolia had to intermingle in their new surroundings and readjust their religious and societal regulations. Added to this strain was a massive influx into Istanbul and other Ottoman cities of Jews fleeing from repression in, and after 1492, expulsion from, Iberia. This migration continued through the first half of the sixteenth century and exacerbated intra-communal discord as a vigorous Sephardic civilization slowly assimilated or exiled to the borderlands of the Ottoman empire the native Romaniote Jewry. Relations between the Jewish community and the Sublime Porte also changed during the sixteenth century, in large part because Jewish leadership changed hands several times. First, head rabbis in Istanbul, then, provincial rabbis in Jerusalem, Safed, Cairo, Salonica, and elsewhere, and finally, a secular elite represented the interests of Ottoman Jewry before the sultan's government. Although the fifteenth- and early-sixteenth-century Jewish minority formed an integral part of Ottoman administrative, economic, social, and religious life, its role within the empire was fluid. Within the Jewish community itself, political and economic power was mutable and disputatious, its contours shaped largely by communal relations with the empire of which Ottoman Jewry was a part.

A gradual slowdown in Ottoman expansion and a diminished Jewish migration from the west as the sixteenth century progressed allowed Ottoman Jewry's communal organization to strengthen and its relations with its Muslim overlord to steady. By the end of Süleyman I's reign (1566), the Ashkenazic, Karaite, Romaniote, and Sephardic elements of Ottoman Jewry had resolved most of their differences and integrated themselves into the Ottoman economy and society. The economic and spiritual centers of Ottoman Jewish life were Istanbul, Salonica, and Safed. A powerful, predominantly Spanish, secular elite had overturned Middle Eastern Jewish culture and grasped communal leadership.

The sixteenth-century Sephardic settlers disregarded western Anatolia and the port of Izmir. Mehmet II, in his eagerness to remake Istanbul, had seized most of the peninsula's Jews and forced them to settle in his new capital, and few chose to return to the impoverished province. Consequently, there were few commercial and industrial centers or even Jewish communities to attract immigrant Sephardim and Ashkenazim. Although small Jewish communities thrived in Manisa and Tire, both within peddling distance of Izmir, opportunities in these towns were few and communities modest when compared to the twenty-thousand or so Jews dwelling in Istanbul, or to Salonica where a majority of the inhabitants were Jewish.

While the settlement pattern of sixteenth-century Ottoman Jewry reflected the empire's commercial network, Jewish merchants peddled their wares across western Anatolia. In 1582, Jewish, Christian, and non-Ottoman infidel producers and marketers of wine wandered across the districts of Mytilene, Ayazmend, Edremid, Yeni Foça, and Karaca Foça filling barrels with

grapes. Ten years later Christians and Jews transported casks
through the Dardanelles in order to procure wine in Ayazmend
and elsewhere in the Aegean basin.[10] Jews were active in the
wine trade not only because they were non-Muslims, but also
because Sephardic merchants, most notably Joseph Mendes of
Naxos who under Selim II monopolized wine sales to Poland,
directed this industry.[11]

Another merchant, Jacob ben Judah Ashkenazzi, provides
evidence of a more regularized, if still inchoate, Jewish peddling
network in western Anatolia. This author of a preface to the
"Song of Songs" fled the plague in Safed in 1599 and disembarked on Chios en route to Venice just in time to witness the
abortive Florentine invasion of that island. Unable in the resultant confusion to find a ship to carry him westward, he instead
sailed to Izmir where, he reported:

certain kindhearted people said to me: "Why do you remain here? You
should go to the great city of Manisa where you will find a resting place.
For the ships sailing to Venice are delayed." So I went to Manisa. But
suddenly they wrote to me to return to Izmir, for a ship was sailing for
Venice. Then I returned but could not find the vessel, for they told me it
had already left for Urla. So I went to Urla, but failed to get it. I found,
however, a ship sailing for this city of Salonica.[12]

This passage not only suggests an informal grid of Jewish commerce flung across western Anatolia and the eastern Aegean,
but also fixes Manisa at its hub. Izmir was one of several
ports through which these Jewish merchants rather haphazardly
joined the sea lanes to inland trade.

Although late-sixteenth-century Ottoman survey registers
do not mention Jewish taxpayers in Izmir, a Jewish presence
is indicated by the writings of travelers, such as Sanderson who
journeyed from Damascus to Jerusalem in 1601 with "Jacob ben
al David, habitant in Esmirna;" the existence of a Jewish tombstone dated 1565 in Izmir's graveyard of Bahri Baba; and Jacob
ben Judah Ashkenazzi's fuzzy regional peddling network.[13] The
presence of peddlers and itinerant merchants, however, must
have been an occasional one, for before the establishment of a

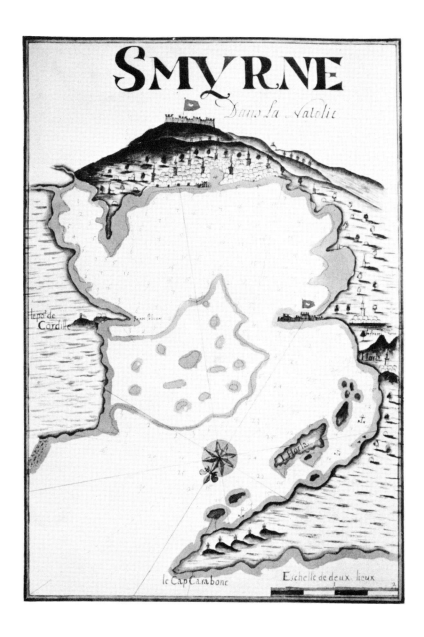

This stylized depiction of the Gulf of Izmir marks the strategically placed fortresses with Ottoman flags and shows the path vessels entering the port had to thread. From Christian Mechlin, *Flambeau de la mer et plan des ports de la Méditeranne* (manuscript). (Courtesy of the James Ford Bell Library, University of Minnesota)

This glorious panorama of Izmir, its port congested with shipping, reveals how important the entrepôt had become by the seventeenth century. The scene represents Izmir as Cornelis de Bruyn saw it before the destructive 1688 earthquake (although his account was not published until two decades later), and is a valuable record of the location of many sites. In it, de Bruyn identifies (1) the castle Kadifekale, (2) the Church of St. Polycarpe, (3) the ruins of the amphitheatre, (4) the kiosk and entertainment house of Hagmet Ağa, (5) the caravansarai for Greek families, (6) the home of the Greek consul, with a flagpole indicating when it was safe for ships to enter the harbor, (7) the residency of the Dutch consul, (8) the residency of the Venetian consul, (9) the house of Kara Mustafa Paşa (grand vezir 1676–83), (10)

the residency of the English consul, (11) the residency of the French consul, (12) the customs house, (13) the bedestan, (14) a fireproof *han* built by Kara Mustafa Paşa in 1677–78 for storing merchandise, (15) the lower castle (Aşağıkale), (16) the inner port (İçliman), (17) the small toll house where ships brought goods from Egypt and elsewhere within the empire, (18) the mountain St. Veneranda, (19) the Armenian and Greek cemetery, (20) the Dutch, English, and French cemeteries, each delineated by a small wall, (21) and the Jewish cemetery. From Cornelis de Bruyn, *Reizen van de Bruyn, dorr de vermaardste deelen van Klein Asia, de Eylandin, Scio, Rhodus, Cyprus, Metelino, Stanchio* . . . (Delft, 1708?), pl. 3. (Courtesy of Special Collections, Regenstein Library, University of Chicago)

An array of foreign vessels, banners flying, rides in Izmir's harbor in this early-eighteenth-century view of the town. Stretching out along the shoreline, Franks Street is a clutter of grand homes and warehouses. From M. Tournefort, *A Voyage into the Levant: Perform'd by Command of the Late French King* (London, 1718), pl. facing p. 374. (Courtesy of Special Collections, Regenstein Library, University of Chicago)

View of Izmir. From Petrus Schenk, *Hecatompolis, sive totius orbis terrarum oppida nobilora centum,* (1702), p. 75. (Courtesy of the Library of Congress)

The buildings seem flimsy and the streets suspiciously broad in this unusual street scene of Izmir. In the background rises a steep hill, crowded
with houses and mosques, and topped by the fortress (Kadifekale). This
woodcut depicts the town that existed before the destructive earthquake of 1688. From Eberhard Werner Happel, *Thesaurus exoticorum
oder eine mit ausländischen raritän und geschichten wohlversehene
schatz-kammer* (Hamburg, 1688), sec. 2, p. 205. (Courtesy of the Library of Congress)

Although the costumes of the stiff figures in the foreground are the artist's subject, the background offers an interesting view of a caravan train descending into the bustling port of Izmir from the north. From Pieter van der Aa, *La Gallerie agreable de monde*, vol. 50 (Leiden, 1729?), pl. 50. (Courtesy of the Library of Congress)

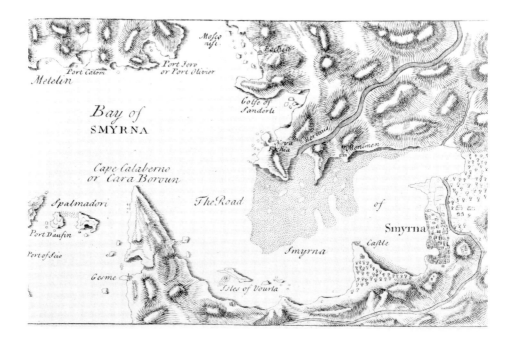

This crude yet clearly drawn *Bay of Smyrna* shows the region's rugged topography and the Gediz River threatening to strangle the port of Izmir with deposits of silt. The slender sea route through the gulf is called "The Road." From M. Tournefort, *A Voyage into the Levant*, pl. facing p. 378. (Courtesy of Special Collections, Regenstein Library, University of Chicago)

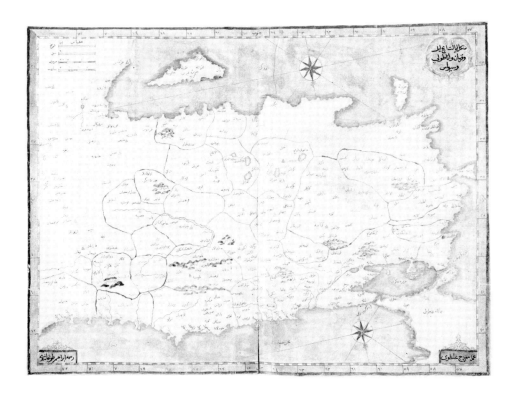

This map taken from an Ottoman world geography, which was written in the mid-seventeenth century, shows Anatolia from the Ottoman perspective with north at the bottom of the map and the *sancak*s of Anadolu outlined. From Kâtip Çelebi, *Cihannüme* (Istanbul, 1732/33). (Courtesy of Special Collections, Regenstein Library, University of Chicago)

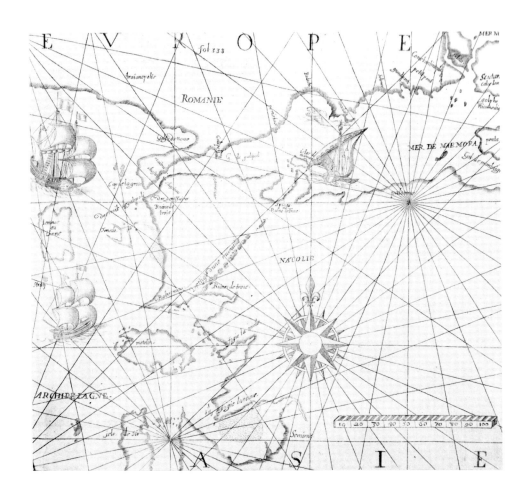

A portolano of northwestern Anatolia. From D. Courmenin, *Voiage de Levant fair par le commandement du Roy en l'année 1621* (Paris, 1632), facing p. 338. (Courtesy of Special Collections, Regenstein Library, University of Chicago)

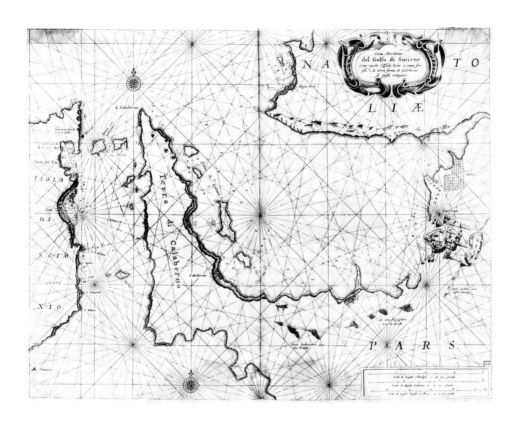

This detailed map of the Gulf of Izmir, published in the mid-seventeenth century, shows the routes into the ports of Izmir, New Foça, and Chios, but does not indicate Çeşme or other sites. From Francesco Maria Levanto, *Prima parte dello specchio del mare* (Genoa, 1664), pl. 22. (Courtesy of the Library of Congress)

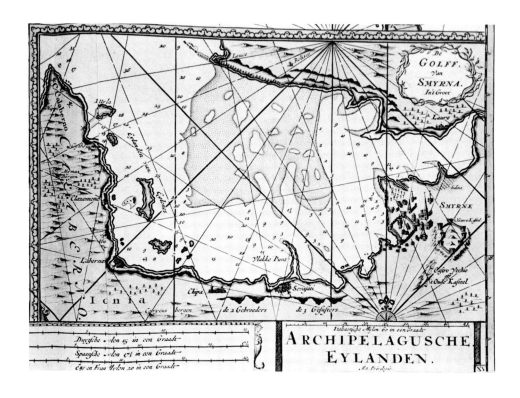

A navigational map showing Izmir and its gulf. The fortress (Kadifekale) on a hill overlooking the port, the old city walls, and the massive sandbar partially blocking the entrance into the gulf are drawn in fine detail. From Nicolas Visscher, *Atlas minor sive geographia compendiosa qua orbis terrarum* (Amsterdam, 1717), pl. 67. (Courtesy of the Library of Congress)

This map of northwestern Anatolia shows the peninsula's fertile coastal plains and rugged interior. Typically, it carries Greek rather than Turkish place names and abounds with geographical errors. From Visscher, *Atlas minor*, pl. 67. (Courtesy of the Library of Congress)

Above, This watercolor of New Foça shows the defenses that made it so valuable as a port of safety. From Mechlin, *Flambeau de la mer*. (Courtesy of the James Ford Bell Library, University of Minnesota)

Top left, New Foça's forbidding fortifications loom menacingly in this scene of the port from the the the sea.

Bottom left, The rock projections that protect New Foça's bay can be seen in this view from the hills behind the city. From de Bruyn, *Reizen*, plates 57 and 58. (Courtesy of Special Collections, Regenstein Library, University of Chicago)

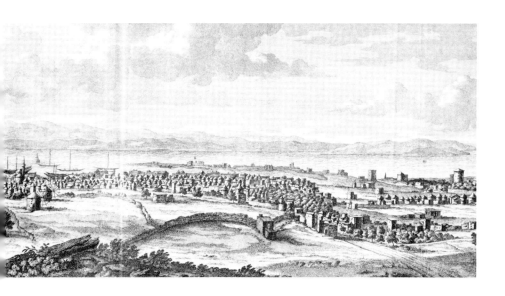

Above, This panorama of the town of Chios depicts the city in its waning days as a seaport. From de Bruyn, *Reizen*, pl. 61. (Courtesy of Special Collections, Regenstein Library, University of Chicago)

Bottom left, The setting of Manisa with mountains towering behind and a river flowing in front contributed to making the city a thriving market center. Wool and hides from the sheep of transhumant nomads were worked into textiles and leathers in Manisa and shipped to Izmir and other western-Anatolian ports. From de Bruyn, *Reizen*, pl. 21. (Courtesy of Special Collections, Regenstein Library, University of Chicago)

MAGNESIA

Titled *A View of Magnesia from Mount Sypili*, this print shows the town of Manisa nestled in the Gediz river valley. From Tournefort, *A Voyage into the Levant*, pl. facing p. 371. (Courtesy of Special Collections, Regenstein Library, University of Chicago)

Each cape and inlet on the east coast of the island of Chios is clearly marked in this navigational guide to the port of Chios. From Visscher, *Atlas minor*, pl. 67. (Courtesy of the Library of Congress)

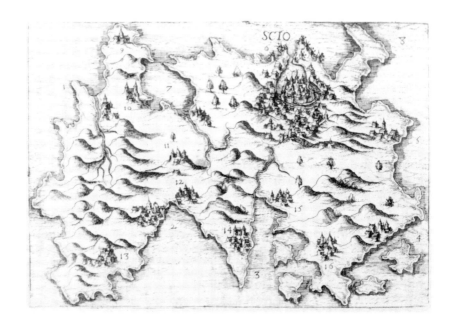

In order to place north at its top, this detailed drawing of the island of Chios must be turned ninety degrees clockwise. The artist, working in the first years of the seventeenth century, sketched in both the town, from which Christians were expelled after the Florentine attack of 1599, and the suburbs, in which they resettled. Points of interest are identified by the artist: (1) Fonte Nao, (2) Valizo, (3) Antornista, (4) Cap des Mastic, (5) S. Mastic, (6) Moulins avent, (7) Port Dauphin, (8) Le Pasazo, (9) Cardanela, (10) Pino, (11) S. Auge, (12) Heluas, (13) S. Helie, (14) S. George, (15) Poligno, (16) Pigri. From Henry de Beauvau, *Relation Iournaliere du voyage du Levant faict et descrit* (Nancy, 1615), p. 28. (Courtesy of Special Collections, Regenstein Library, University of Chicago)

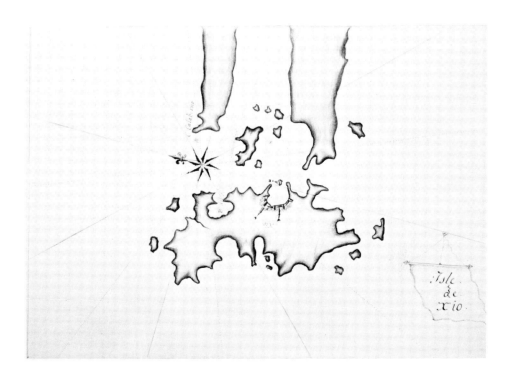

In this drawing of the island of Chios (Sakız), Çeşme, perched on the tip of its peninsula, seems to stretch out and almost touch the port of Chios. From Mechlin, *Flambeau de la mer*. (Courtesy of the James Ford Bell Library, University of Minnesota)

Tax farmers had to report their income. This customs register reveals income at several ports in western Anatolia, including Izmir, in the years 1604–5. From Başbakanlık Arşivi, İbnülemin (Maliye) 640, pp. 1 and 2. Istanbul, Turkey

This copy of a decree to the *kadı* of Izmir describes disputes and conspiracies between the brigand Cennetoğlu, the Dutch consul Nicolini Orlando, and the paşa Hüseyin. From Başbakanlık Arşivi, Maliyeden Müdevver 6004, p. 124. Istanbul, Turkey

In 1650 two men, Henry Hyde and Thomas Bendysh, struggled over the English ambassadorship in both Istanbul and Izmir. The battle ended tragically for Hyde when Bendysh had him shipped back to London, where he was beheaded. From *The Speech and Confession, of Sr. Henry Hide Embassador for the King of Scotland, to the Emperour of Turkie* (London, 1651), frontispiece. (Courtesy of the Lilly Library, Indiana University)

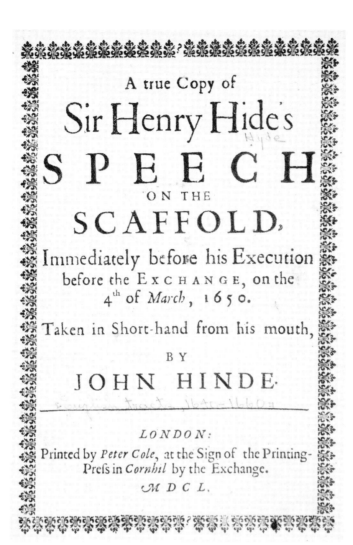

A true Copy of

Sir Henry Hide's
SPEECH
ON THE
SCAFFOLD,

Immediately before his Execution before the E X C H A N G E, on the 4th of *March*, 1650.

Taken in Short-hand from his mouth,

B Y

JOHN HINDE.

LONDON:

Printed by *Peter Cole*, at the Sign of the Printing-Prefs in *Cornhil* by the Exchange.

ᴍ D C L.

The final speeches of the condemned became a popular genre in seventeenth-century England. The mob and the sheriff urged those sentenced to death to prattle on, both as entertainment and for information about other traitors. The gutter press of London produced at least two tracts describing Sir Henry Hyde's speech on the scaffold in 1651. This frontispiece introduces the more antiroyalist, and more detailed, of the two. (Courtesy of Special Collections, Regenstein Library, University of Chicago)

The French consul is provided a chair as he presents his credentials (capitulations and firman) to the *kadı* of Izmir. All figures are clearly identified: (1) the *kadı*, (2) the *kadı*'s adviser, (3) the French consul, (4) the consul's dragomans, (5) the capitulations, (6) the sultan's firman, (7) French merchants, (8) the consul's janissary guards (*yasakçıs*), (9) the *kadı*'s servants presenting coffee, (10) the *kadı*'s servants bringing cologne, (11) miscellaneous servants of the *kadı*, and (12) the consul's promenade. Framed in the background of this stylized scene is a view of Izmir. From Jean Du Mont, *Voyages de Mr. Du Mont, en France, en Italie, en Allemagne, à Malthe, et en Turquie*, vol. 2 (La Haye, 1699). (Courtesy of Princeton University Library)

The *beylerbeyi* of Anadolu, the chief Ottoman military officer of the province in which Izmir was located (although his jurisdiction did not include Izmir itself), sits sternly upon his steed in this woodcut. From Happel, *Thesaurus exoticorum*, sec. 2, p. 16. (Courtesy of the Library of Congress)

An Ottoman official in full regalia poses for this beautiful wood-cut, probably the work of the master Jost Amman, commis-sioned for the volume *Turkische Chronica* . . . (Frankfurt, 1577). (Author's collection)

Murat IV, shown here as a confident and proud ruler, is the best known seventeenth-century Ottoman sultan. His reign (1623–40) spanned the crucial years of Izmir's growth. From Happel, *Thesaurus exoticorum*, sec. 4, following p. 14. (Courtesy of the Library of Congress)

Cadilesquier a Iudge in spiritual and temporal matters.

The *kazasker*s of Rumeli and Anadolu were, after the *şeyhülis-lam*, the most important religious officials in the Ottoman empire. From Nicolas de Nicolay, *The Navigations, Peregrinations and Voyages, Made into Turkie* (London, 1585). (Courtesy of Special Collections, Regenstein Library, University of Chicago)

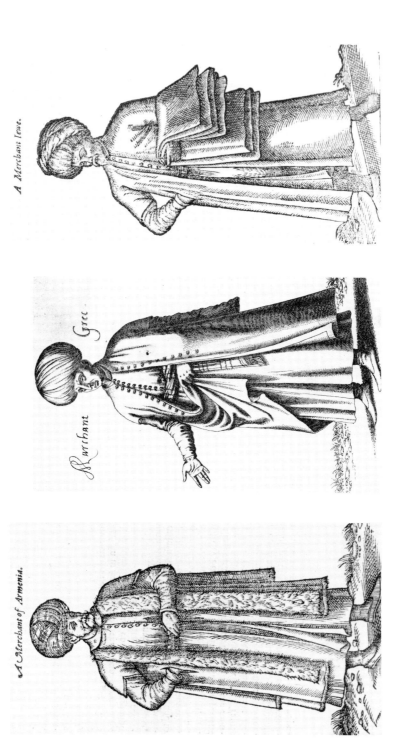

Armenian, Greek, and Jewish merchants were active participants in Izmir's economic life. From de Nicolay, *The Navigations*. (Courtesy of Special Collections, Regenstein Library, University of Chicago). Greek merchant from author's collection.

formal communal organization (*kehillah*) there in 1605, Izmir was unable to support even the requisite ten males of a Jewish community.

JEWISH MIGRATORY PATTERNS
IN THE OTTOMAN EMPIRE

Fifty years after Ashkenazzi's brief and alarming sojourn, a large Jewish community thrived in Izmir. Tavernier in 1631 mentions a community of seven-thousand Jews, and Spon and Wheler in 1675 speak of fifteen thousand. Although the community could not have numbered over two thousand in 1660, more than a natural propensity to hyperbolize inspired these European travelers in their descriptions of this community. To foreign merchants, who depended upon translators and middlemen in their dealings with native traders and Ottoman officials, the Jews of Izmir seemed vigorous, prosperous, and ubiquitous. Western travelers did exaggerate their figures; but in the decades preceding Tavernier's visit, Jewish migrants from Salonica, Manisa, Chios, Istanbul, and elsewhere had established a community that surpassed others in the empire in size, wealth, and creativity.

The first decades of the seventeenth century witnessed a great uprooting and resettlement in western Anatolia. The social unrest that plagued the region and drove many peasants into the cities certainly accounts for some of this turmoil. The *celâli* rebellions were principally a rural phenomenon, however, and thus had relatively little affect on perennial urban dwellers, among whom were Armenians, Greeks, and Jews. The district of Izmir, in any case, was not spared the depredations of brigands, the shortages, and the peasant unrest, which characterized the period. While the dispossessed sought refuge from this onslaught in cities, towns, and castles, Izmir was only one of many safe holds and, although refugees may have been impressed with the opportunities in the port, the rebellions cannot claim primary responsibility for attracting Christians and Jews.

Non-Muslims were, however, attracted by the same structural crisis in international trade that helped transform Izmir into a commercial center. Jews and other religio-ethnic groups lost their positions in established guilds and industries and were compelled to pursue new employment, often in new locations. A crisis in Salonica's textile industry helped feed this internal migration. In the early seventeenth century, not only Salonica, but all textile towns within the empire suffered under the impact of the rising costs of raw wool, the burden of providing the janissary corps with quantities of woolens at ruinous prices, a changing demand for textiles, and the influx of inexpensive fabrics from the west. An economic depression struck Salonica's Jewish population, which had thrived as long as domestic textiles dominated Ottoman sales. Jews whose families had lived in the city for a century and who subsisted on this industry began seeking alternative employment.

Many of them left the city, pushed out by its troubles, and migrated to various cities and towns in Rumeli and western Anatolia. In 1610, Istanbul expressed dismay "that some Jews who manufacture the Janissaries' broadcloth in Salonica have moved to Izmir and Manisa," complaining to the *kadıs* of those two towns that "few people remain in the broadcloth business in Salonica. . . . Broadcloth is in great scarcity. . . . You should send these Jews back to Salonica immediately." Salonica's crisis ousted these Jews, whose ancestors had helped found the city's broadcloth industry. They went to Manisa because not only did it boast an established and sizeable textile industry, but in the sixteenth century had housed the court of an Ottoman prince and consequently enjoyed exemption from many taxes. Others, perhaps more economically adventurous, went to Izmir because the port presented an expanding frontier of opportunity. Istanbul expressed alarm at these moves, wanting to maintain the broadcloth manufacturers (who clothed the empire's army) in Salonica rather than allow the city's Jewish artisans to scatter. Despite the administration's protests, however, few fugitives resumed their fruitless labors in Salonica. Ottoman textile manufacturing centers other than Salonica felt the impact of rising prices, changing demand, and competition from abroad. Safed experienced a parallel growth and decline in its Jewish element and textile industry.[22]

Izmir's commerce also drew families from western Anatolia and the islands of the Aegean. The Jews who had emigrated from Salonica to Manisa in the first decade of the century confronted there debilitating shortages of supplies.[23] Western demand had driven up the price of raw wool and put out of work many Jewish and Muslim textile workers, thereby exacerbating the already chronic lawlessness plaguing the region. By 1621, realizing that Europeans stationed in Izmir took the best fleece and other unfinished goods for themselves, many Jews had abandoned home and employment to work for their wealthy rivals in the booming port town.[24] Forty years later, Izmir supported six times as many Jews as did Manisa (see table 8). In 1661, the vezir İsmail Paşa conducted a survey of the non-Muslim populations of western Anatolia. He found that although the number of Armenian, Greek, and Jewish households in the region had risen since the previous survey from 726 to 945, there had been a decline in the number of non-Muslim inhabitants in Kuşadası, Manisa, and Urla. The population increase occurred exclusively in Izmir.[25] Whereas sixteenth-century Kuşadası had boasted a sizeable Jewish com-

TABLE 8

Non-Muslim Populations of
Major Towns in Western Anatolia in 1661

(*In* nefer*s*/hane*s*)

	Armenians	Greeks	Jews	Total
Kuşadası	–	79	–	79
Izmir	61	301	271	633
Manisa	154	54	41	249
Urla	–	377	–	377
Total	215	811	312	1,338

SOURCE: BBA, MM 14672. In this survey, *nefer* and *hane* are interchangeable. The last two of the seventy-nine "Greek" taxpayers in Kuşadası have Armenian names, Ermeni Hasun and Ermeni Kalıç.

munity, in 1640 only three households remained and by 1660 there were none. A similar decline occurred in the Armenian community of that ancient town. In Urla, an old center of olive cultivation, soap manufacturing, and fish farming, Greeks comprised a majority of the population. In 1660 there were more Greeks here than in Izmir, despite a tripling of the latter port's Greek population over the previous sixty years. Urla's economy apparently remained viable during these difficult years.

The names of families buried in the Church of St. Polycarpe indicate that many of Izmir's Greeks migrated not from mainland towns like Kuşadası, Manisa, and Urla, but from the languishing island of Chios. After the conquest of 1566, the resultant commercial crisis at the port, and the persecutions that followed the Florentine foray of 1599, these Greeks had crossed the narrow channel to the mainland and relocated in Izmir. Chian Jews changed domicile at the same time. The Jews of textile centers such as Manisa, Salonica, and Safed and commercial centers like Aleppo and Chios streamed to Izmir because violent fluctuations in trade patterns at the same time depressed certain areas of the economy and stimulated Izmir's commerce.

While a changing industrial and commercial climate in the empire drew Jewish, Greek, and Armenian migrants to Izmir, light taxes in the new port also attracted them. Jewish communal organizations in seventeenth-century Salonica, Manisa, and Safed endeavored to revive deteriorating industries and strained under the burden of overdeveloped infrastructures and corrupt officials. In order to survive, they imposed crippling dues upon their members, which often merely spurred emigration. Young and thriving communities had no reason to introduce such measures. As Izmir's community grew, its riches enabled it to attract not only Jewish artisans, but also great merchants and rabbis, whom the community took pride in feeding, clothing, and housing.

NON-MUSLIM PROFESSIONS IN IZMIR

Not only Ottoman Jewry, but also the Greeks of Chios and other Aegean islands and the Armenians of Aleppo, Bursa, and Istanbul had compelling economic reasons to leave ancient domiciles and resettle in Izmir. An Ottoman census undertaken in 1640–41, which the government thought necessary because of rapid changes in the population composition of western Anatolia, discloses the employment structures of these communities. The document describes itself as "a registration of the *cizye* of non-Muslims in the district of Izmir on account of various dispersals in Anatolia" and, rather than listing all dwellers, is limited to those newly settled. In it, are listed 47 *cizye*-paying Armenians, 265 Greeks, and 92 Jews. In 1640, those Armenians, Greeks, and Jews who had arrived in the previous twenty or thirty years outnumbered by four to one the entire non-Muslim population of the town in 1575.

Although this register does not faithfully record the livelihood of each listed individual, enough are included to elicit some sense of how the communities supported themselves. Among the Armenian immigrants were three weavers of cheap cotton goods, three merchants, one bathhouse attendant, one jeweler, one perfumer or spice dealer, one priest, two tailors, two chinaware dealers, and two importers. In the Greek community were six tavern keepers, nine tailors, one sesame sweets seller, two caulkers of ships, three priests, one oarsman, one fisherman, one dealer in straw, two makers/sellers of homespun wool, one person who lays mats, and one innkeeper. Among the Jews, the scribe recorded only the professions of three rabbis, one jeweler, and one so-called priest (certainly an error for rabbi). This small sampling suggests that the Armenians and Greeks were well represented in the small shops and businesses of the city— the former specializing in luxury goods from the east (perfumes, jewels, and chinaware) and the latter in more mundane items such as straw, lime, and homespun woolens. While the Armenians dominated international trade as merchants and importers, the Greeks played a crucial role in the service industries—as innkeepers and tavern owners—and in employment dealing with the sea. Even the presence of four rabbis in this in-pouring of persons denotes a rich and diverse economy, for scholars flocked to thriving communities that could support their esoteric studies and economically nonproductive students. The census implies rapid integration of non-Muslim migrants into the city's expanding economy.

Within economic life, Jews figured prominently in the most visible professions—those of tax collectors, middlemen, moneylenders, and translators—and thus appeared ubiquitous to foreigners, who relied upon indigens in order to transact their commercial dealings. In their formative years, Levant trading companies in Izmir not only employed such men as factors and translators, but even appointed "strangers" to the exacting position of consul. Nicolini Orlando, the first Dutch consul in the city, was no Dutchman at all, but a "Levantine."   Although no Jew in Izmir rose to a position to rival Orlando's, Jews often acted as dragomans and agents for company factors and consuls.

Non-Muslim natives aspired to the position of dragoman in particular because, even in the first decades of formal Ottoman relations with Atlantic seaboard trading states, this office afforded its holder privileges that an Ottoman subject as a rule could not attain. A Jew named Aaron Levi in 1621 received a letter of privilege appointing him second dragoman to the Venetian consul in Izmir, allowing him to receive pay from the Venetians, and granting him exemption from extraordinary levies.   Ottoman subjects coveted especially this last privilege during a time when the government more and more resorted to extraordinary levies in order to replenish a depleted treasury.   In addition, the position granted the holder certain legal rights: most notably it specified the transfer of lawsuits involving the dragoman from Izmir to Istanbul. While this move did not free him from all corruptions and artifices, it did alter lines of authority and remove him from those particular intrigues and briberies that typified legal proceedings in Izmir.

JEWS AS COLLECTORS OF CUSTOMS

All the important trading companies, not only in Izmir but throughout the Levant, appointed Jews to positions of responsibility in administering their own communities and commerce and in their dealings with Ottoman officialdom. At first glance, this state of affairs seems odd. Neither Londoner nor Parisian had seen a Jew since the fourteenth century, and the Venetians recently had waged a bitter campaign against Jewish commercial interests in the Levant, which cooled off only with the death of Joseph Mendes in 1579. While Amsterdam welcomed some Spanish settlers in the sixteenth century, Levantine Jewry associated more closely with the English, French, and Venetians than the Dutch. Merchants from these states, despite domestic enmity, were willing to cultivate business dealings with Levantine Jewry because of the commercial nature of their mission in the eastern Mediterranean; in addition, while the Jewish community had found one niche in the Ottoman economy in textiles, it found a second as tax farmers and collectors of customs. In Izmir during the early seventeenth century, Jews monopolized positions as government officials, particularly as customs officials, at a time when the city was growing rapidly (see table 9). Western merchants endeavored to secure the good will of customs collectors at least as guarantors of fair dealings, and at times as conspirators in circumventing tariffs and other dues.

The collectors knew how to exploit their powerful posts. Venetians and other Europeans frequently petitioned Istanbul about officials' transgressions, such as impounding of broadcloth and other textiles, inflated estimates of the value of cotton, conspirings with messengers from the Sublime Porte, and refusal to accept suspected currencies. Although the Jewish collectors in these petitions appear to be venal and ruthless rogues searching methodically for new means to increase their income, the reality was considerably more complex and not to be judged in terms of individual or communal traits. Western merchants and customs officials, who dealt with each other almost daily, struggled

most bitterly over percentages of assessed duties. Whereas the
customs officials purchased their positions from the government
and sought to turn a profit, the Venetians and other westerners
strove to reduce their dues, frequently resorting to bribery and

TABLE 9

Jewish Customs Collectors in Izmir, 1604–30

Description	Title	Dates
İbrahim veled-i Davud Davud veled-i İbrahim	tax farmers in Izmir Chios, etc.	3 May 1604– 3 May 1607
Haham al-Kaz Haham Ali Baba	customs collectors in Izmir and Chios	23 Nov. 1605
İbrahim	tax farmer	21 Nov. 1607
İbrahim	customs collector in Izmir	19 Feb. 1616
İbrahim al-Kaz	customs collector in Izmir	8 April 1617
al-Kaz	customs collector in Chios	24 July– Aug. 1617
Jewish	customs collector in Izmir	29 Dec. 1617
İbrahim al-Kaz	customs collector	29 Nov.– 8 Dec. 1618
İbrahim al-Kaz	customs collector	29 Nov.– 8 Dec. 1618
Jewish; served for several years	customs collector in Izmir	24 Nov. 1623
Jewish	tax farmer	25 Oct. 1623
Jewish; served for several years	customs collector in Izmir	25 Oct. 1623
Jewish	customs collector in Izmir	23 Dec. 1623
Jews named Betrozi and Macar	customs collectors in Izmir	29 Oct. 1630

SOURCE: The sources in order of mention are BBA, İE (Maliye) 640; ED
13/1, p. 38; ED 13/1, p. 57, no. 2; ED 13/1, p. 140; ED 13/1, p. 151; ED
13/1, p. 181, no. 3; ED 13/1, p. 185, no. 3; ED 13/1, p. 186, no. 3; ED
13/1, p. 189, no. 1; MM 6004, p. 30, no. 3; MM 6004, p. 47, no. 2; MM
6004, p. 50; MM 6004, p. 53; MD 85, no. 329.

smuggling. By the 1620s European merchants had acquired most of the properties along the shoreline in Izmir. While merchants, travelers, and Orientalists later would depict this strip of land as an island of western culture in an Islamic sea, its homes and warehouses also had direct access to the water, making it an ideal location for smuggling. Merchants sometimes protected their establishments from Ottoman inspectors by arguing that to them, as in Islam, the home was a sacred place and thus inviolable. In 1644, François Dupuy, who for seven years shared the consulship with his brother, Jean, and in 1651 became the sole occupant of the post, even formalized this arrangement in his letter of appointment, which declared that "no one from the Ottoman administration, police superintendents, or others shall enter his house."

Customs officials not only had to contend with this development, but also deal with the vagaries of an inflated and easily counterfeited currency. Because of monetary and other irregularities, they justly were suspicious of the prices for cotton that Venetian factors purchased in the countryside of western Anatolia. The two groups battled over assessment, with Venetians arguing that customs fees should be paid according to declared purchase price and the governmental agents insisting upon collection according to current rates in Izmir. Such disputes arose not out of duplicity, but merely reflected differing perspectives; however, they increased friction between the protagonists. Under such circumstances, it is not surprising that European consuls and merchants sought out Jewish translators and factors who, apart from other duties, might influence their powerful coreligionists.

Customs officials and translators did not dominate the economy of Izmir's Jewish community. Although their influence was considerable and communal vigor owed much to their success (and subsequent communal decay followed their failure to retain control of these critical posts), the bulk of the community concerned itself with other businesses characteristic of a commercial port—as brokers, money-lenders, factors, and wholesalers—and in the guilds of the city and community. Exchanges of money and goods naturally initiated disputes between Jews and foreigners. In 1609–10, two Venetian merchants proceeded in the Ottoman law courts against a Jew named Solomon who allegedly owed them 1,600 *akçes*; forty years later a French merchant foolishly enlisted a certain Joseph to carry seventeen clocks from Izmir to Istanbul for a Frenchman in the capital city; and several years after that a Haim Muvari complained that a French merchant in Istanbul was indebted to him. Although western merchants in each case spoke disparagingly of Jewish brokers and money-lenders, it is a mistake to conclude habitual suspicions based in an unrelenting and deep-rooted hatred. Europeans depended upon and usually trusted their Jewish money merchants. In May 1661, the French consul, lashing out at a chief broker who blocked his nation from employing a Jew named Abraham Solomon as its messenger and broker, wrote that Solomon completely satisfied him and his merchants, and insisted upon retaining his services. This testimony probably represented the rule rather than the exception in commercial dealings between the peoples.

IZMIR AND SABBATARIANISM

Izmir certainly was the most vital and cosmopolitan center of Levantine culture in the early seventeenth century and it is not coincidental that as social and economic distress agitated the world around it these prosperous surroundings bore an explosive messianic movement. While in 1666 the ideas and personality of the false Messiah, Sabbatai Zvi, were to infect every Jewish community (and many Christian and Muslim ones as well) in Europe and the Middle East, Zvi's father, Mordecai, had come to Izmir from Greece sometime after 1614 as part of the wave of Jewish migrants from Salonica, Manisa, Urla, and elsewhere. The Zvi family were typical immigrants to this expanding urban milieu. Mordecai struggled at the fringes of communal life as an egg-dealer before penetrating its more secure and profitable economic hub as a rather wealthy broker and agent for some English merchants. Together with his sons, he held this position for much of Sabbatai's youth. Exposure to new ideas followed Mordecai's change of domicile and profession. Not only did he and his young sons confront a culturally diverse Jewish community, but in the city's bustling markets they mingled with Armenians, Greeks, Turks, and Franks. The family secured employment with English merchants during the 1630s and 40s and was exposed not only to the cultural swirl and profligacy of Franks Street, but also to the ideological and religious disputes of the English civil war. English merchants could not escape these issues and, along with practical fears regarding the safety of family, friends, and estates in England, they initiated lively debates concerning grace, the Old Testament (for which they had rabbinic authorities at hand), and the bases of authority in England and the world. Zvi and his coreligionists imbued the English (as well as the continental and Muslim) mystical and millenarian notions of the period and mixed them with their own rabbinism and kabbalistic lore to help create the persuasive, disruptive, and at times violent Sabbatarianism.

● ● ●

The Armenian, Greek, and Jewish presence in Izmir during the years of Sabbatai Zvi's youth was a recent and volatile phenomenon. A mass of displaced individuals searching for new careers lived in remarkably close relations with representatives of the emerging nation-states of western Europe, and were bombarded with new ideas and cultures. Izmir in the mid-seventeenth century was a city of temptation for these migrants. It represented something confusing, something frightening, something enticing, something revolutionary, and it gave individuals and communities the opportunity to develop new political vocabularies and worldviews. Izmir, enjoying a singular position in the Ottoman economy, lying on the edge of one empire and attracting the merchant-adventurers of another, exploded upon the international scene during the early years of Zvi's youth.

The Sabbatian crisis may have exploded out of Izmir, but it had the least impact there. The prosperity and administrative dominance of Jews in early-seventeenth-century Izmir was unique in the Ottoman empire. While the rest of the empire's Jews, faced with the erosion of their economic positions, embraced Sabbatai's eschatology wholeheartedly and almost universally, Jewish leaders in Izmir, prospering mightily, voiced serious doubts. Seventeenth-century Ottoman Jewry was in a slow descent from the economic pinnacle of the sixteenth century. A Balkan-Greek ascendancy in trade with the west and a Jewish withdrawal from worldly affairs in the aftermath of the mid-century Sabbatian debacle may have been elements in this decline.   More important, however, the bulk of Jewish merchants and industrialists remained closely linked to the Ottoman administration in a relationship that had been productive in the late fifteenth and early sixteenth centuries, but that by the seventeenth century was becoming secondary to a vigorous western trade empire. This decreasingly productive Judeo-Ottoman union is apparent even in early-seventeenth-century Izmir, where Jews dominated the administration of customs revenue. The Jews already had found their niche in Ottoman administration and were unable, or saw no necessity, to adjust to the economic frontier induced by western European expansion. Just as the seventeenth-century success of the city of Izmir can be ascribed to this transformation in Levantine trade, so can the Jewish presence and prosperity. In both cases also, the changing patterns of trade had deleterious effect in other parts of the empire, and ultimately upon the Jews of Izmir as well.

5

The Venetians in Izmir, 1604–1624

The policies of European trading companies were instrumental in encouraging Izmir's commercial advancement and cultural diversification. Merchants representing both established Mediterranean states and the new companies from the Atlantic coast crowded into Franks Street in the early seventeenth century. Their attitudes, abilities, and particularly their leaders and governing structures molded the companies' relations with officials in both Izmir and Istanbul, and in large part defined their roles in the new commercial network being carved out of Izmir's hinterland.

Conventional attitudes toward commerce in the Mediterranean did not circumscribe or obstruct the Atlantic seaboard states, whose representatives initiated and exploited the realignment taking place in the region's market. Levantine ways of thinking however did affect the French and Venetians, who had invested much in traditional trading networks and relied upon longstanding relations with the Sublime Porte. Appeals to the Ottoman central government, which had been effective in the past, no longer always worked. The economic transformation of the Ottoman empire had loosened administrative ties between agricultural regions and Istanbul and created other authorities to whom a foreign state or merchant could address grievances, thus enabling natural economic centers, such as Izmir, to develop without the constraints of a highly cen-

tralized administration.[1] Innovations in the structures of the
new companies enabled them to exploit this change in the empire's administration better than their French and Venetian
rivals.[2] In addition the Ottomans were more receptive to the
Dutch and English states because they were not Catholic and
so not encumbered with a tradition of ideological strife with
Islam.[3]

A comparison between the conservative Venetian consular
system and the innovative English one reveals some of the
advantages enjoyed by the Atlantic seaboard over established
Mediterranean trading states. The Venetians operated within
well-defined lines of authority. The Department of Commerce in
Venice appointed consuls from the ranks of the nobility; they
served for three-year terms and answered directly to the bailo.
The system, centralized and mired in bureaucratic and diplomatic tradition, provided neither incentive, time, nor money
for a Venetian consul to explore innovations in trade. In the
English case, however, the Levant Company appointed its own
consuls, who were not directly responsible to the ambassador
in Istanbul or the government in England, but who, together
with the merchants under their jurisdiction, were free to assess their own surcharges and deal with local authorities and
special dues (*avanias*) as they saw fit.[4] Although this structure often generated acrimonious disputes among Levant Company directors in London, the ambassador in Istanbul, consuls
in the provinces, and merchants everywhere, it also guaranteed flexibility in the face of transfiguring Ottoman patterns
of power and ensured that competent and creative men who
had earned the respect of the community of traders over whom
they presided usually served in positions of authority within
the company. Thus, the English system was tailor-made for
the unstable environment of western Anatolia in which lines
of authority were not rigidly fixed, social disorder was constant, and opportunities to manipulate the provisioning network
abounded.

MANIPULATION OF CHAOS

Significant variances distinguished the two new trading companies. While the Dutch and English communities in many ways resembled each other, the English consul had an advantage over his rival. The Englishman's basic salary was fixed; the Dutch official's pay depended upon special duties on goods imported by Dutch traders, which naturally led to friction between consul and merchant. In spite of this disadvantage, the Dutch community skillfully utilized the partial breakdown of central authority in order to enhance its own position in Izmir. In September 1625 Istanbul wrote to the *kadı* of Izmir that

> the ambassador of the Netherlands has petitioned that Cennetoğlu recently came to Izmir and the consul of the Netherlands, Nicolini Orlando, and the Dutch merchants of Izmir had to send a letter and tribute to him so that the brigands of Cennetoğlu would not do them harm. Hüseyin, who recently became the *beylerbeyi* of [Anadolu?] and who is charged with conquering Cennetoğlu, used this excuse to harm the consul and merchants of the Netherlands, claiming that "you sent a letter and tribute to Cennetoğlu. . . ." I command that . . . henceforth Hüseyin should not harm them with this excuse.[5]

Cennetoğlu, operating in the aftermath of the *celâli* rebellions, inhabited that profitable, dangerous, and shadowy area between soldiering and outlawry. He was a cavalryman stationed in western Anatolia who capitalized on widespread bitterness and rebelliousness against the Ottoman government by establishing an unauthorized and independent military presence in the western-Anatolian provinces of Aydın and Saruhan. In 1624, leading perhaps 2,500 men, he defeated an Ottoman military force. In the following year, Istanbul appointed Hüseyin Paşa to suppress Cennetoğlu and the Ottoman commander routed him near Manisa, probably in August 1625. By October of the same year, Cennetoğlu was dead.[6] Istanbul issued the above decree in the midst of this turmoil, after Cennetoğlu's defeat, but perhaps before Hüseyin Paşa was certain that the brigand would not arise again.

The Dutch community in Izmir thrived in the uncertainties that brigands such as Kalenderoğlu, Cennetoğlu, and İlyas Paşa helped spawn in the first decades of the seventeenth century. The Levantine consul, Nicolini Orlando, was the first man to serve in Izmir as consul to the Netherlands.[7] The directors of the nascent Dutch Levant Company, realizing that they possessed no men knowledgeable enough to compete with the established consuls of rival states, employed members of the cosmopolitan communities of resident Armenians, Greeks, and Jews. In the present case, the Dutch policy proved effective as their representative astutely manipulated the multiple sources of authority in Izmir. The tribute that the consul paid to Cennetoğlu was a form of protection money, for the outlaw roamed those very regions of western Anatolia where the westerners had established their provisioning network.[8] Whereas a Venetian consul probably would have directed his plea against Cennetoğlu to Istanbul, Orlando preferred to drive a wedge between Ottoman central and provincial officials. He requested the Dutch ambassador in Istanbul to complain to the Sublime Porte not against the depredations of the soldier-turned-brigand, with whom the consul and merchants had fostered an expedient relationship, but against the oppressions of the government's own military appointee Hüseyin Paşa.

Orlando's accommodation with Cennetoğlu freed Dutch merchants and their representatives, if fleetingly, not only from the ever-present menace of raiders and pillagers, but also from the restrictions and tolls the Ottoman state imposed, thereby foreshadowing the rise of provincial notables who later were to strip Istanbul of much of its authority in local politics and commerce.[9] Despite the willingness of the Dutch and many native inhabitants of the region to support him, Cennetoğlu failed in his perhaps premature bid for power. It is not surprising that Hüseyin Paşa, whose victory earned him the governorship of Anadolu in May 1626 and command of a massive army rushing against the Safavids at Baghdad, should urge punishment of Dutch as well as Ottoman subjects who aided and abetted Cennetoğlu.[10] Orlando's initiative and his understanding of local conditions, however, frustrated Hüseyin's request and the Dutch community of Izmir was able to take advantage of the chaos Cennetoğlu had generated, and evade the consequences of its actions once order was restored.

Neither the Venetian nor French consuls had the ability, the authority, or even a sufficient stake in the fate of their communities in Izmir to do likewise. The Venetian consul would have had to "go through channels," seeking permission from his bailo to conclude a pact with the brigand, and it is doubtful that the cautious Venetian representative in Istanbul would have jeopardized Venetian influence there by allowing him to do so. The French, notorious for their administrative ineptitude, were also burdened with the exceptionally hotheaded and greedy Jean Dupuy as consul in residence in Izmir during this period.[11]

COURT VERSUS COUNTRY AND THE CONSULAGE

Merchants from the Netherlands, England, France, and Venice feared that rivals might secure an edge in commerce. The Venetians, confronting their own commercial demise, became intensely vigilant against the partialities and perceived venalities of port officials, the avarice of Armenian and Jewish middlemen and brokers, the favoritism and exorbitant exactions of guards and porters on Izmir's wharf, and the maneuverings of competitors in Istanbul and Izmir. They particularly opposed the English Levant Company's establishment of a trading community in Izmir and feared England's opportunistic incursions into commercial spheres which, according to both tradition and capitulation, had belonged to the Venetians.

In 1619, the two trading powers clashed over cargo charges. In order to provide consuls and ambassadors with salaries and administrative monies, a mother state or company typically imposed surcharges—referred to as "rights of consulage" (*konsolos*—or *konsolosluk—hakkı*) or less frequently "customs dues" (*kotimo*)—on all goods in which the merchants of the community traded. The consul generally collected a 2 or 3 percent duty on all imported and exported merchandise and divided it among company officials according to prearrangement. The company treasurer then would "remit any surplus to Constantinople . . . and the treasurer there sent it home."[12] At times, however, rivalries, petty jealousies, and simple greed forced directors to divide the spoils more formally. For much of the early seventeenth century, the French in particular assessed two distinct 2 or 3 percent charges: one for the expenses and debts of the ambassador and the other for those of the consuls. Although the percentages of customs collected and the apportionments between ruler, company, ambassador, and consul varied according to state and period, these dues were vitally important to all company officials and triggered bitter quarrels between governments, companies, ambassadors, consuls, and merchants. In the 1630s during "the affair of the Strangers Consulage" England's Charles I, desperate for funds, spent long years bickering with the directors of the English Levant Company and their dependents in the Ottoman empire over income from surcharges on foreign merchandise transported in English bottoms.[13] In 1636 the English consul in Izmir, upholding an "order from the company . . . to withstand all" assaults from the king upon the consulage (and naturally reluctant to relinquish these monies) and resorting to Turkish courts in his opposition to royal supporters, drove the royalist ambassador to dispatch his dragoman to Izmir. Only then, "the Consull gave waie."[14] In the following decades, English merchants of Izmir were caught up in a whirl of ambassadors, consuls, royalists, and parliamentarians bickering over, among other things, debts and consulage.[15]

The French even more than the English stumbled over the issue of consulage. French consuls faced a dilemma. While they received from Marseilles no salaries or regular payments for emergencies and bought their posts in the expectation of reaping riches from the consulage, they could neither force French merchants to contribute funds nor negotiate a harmonious division of revenue with the French ambassador, who was equally desperate for funds.[16] These dues were less important to the English and the Venetian consuls, both of whom received fixed salaries, but they also needed them to administer their communities, to pay emergency levies, and to support their embassies in Istanbul. The surcharges constituted the financial underpinning of foreign commerce and diplomacy in the Levant. In 1619, when the Venetian consul lashed out against the English for infringing upon his rights of consulage, he defended the very life blood of Venetian trade in Ottoman domains.

Consulage imposed on the goods of Venetian merchants passing through Izmir traditionally had been the bailo's and consul's. Although this arrangement seems sensible and proper, rival traders struggled to circumvent the extra expense. For example, in 1605, 1616, and 1622, Ottoman subjects loaded their goods bound for Venice onto vessels anchored in Lemnos, Patmos, and other places that Venice could not police.[17] Such incidents, in which individuals and groups of merchants searched for means to reduce the expense of transport, reveal a constant pressure upon the bases of Venetian ascendancy in the Aegean.

English incursions into that sea in the early decades of the century simply accelerated an already present trend. When in 1609 the Venetian Senate strove to block foreign shipping with tolls and navigation laws it succeeded only in turning the trade to other Italian ports, especially Leghorn and Genoa.[18] By the second decade of the century it was common for English ships to sail directly into the harbor of the formerly great trading state to do their business.[19] Tremors from this audacity vibrated across the Levant, giving the English leverage in Izmir and elsewhere. As early as 1608, the English consul in Aleppo tried to seize consulage from merchandise shipped aboard a vessel recently arrived from Venice.[20] A decade later, the Venetian consul in Izmir, working through his bailo, elicited from the Sublime Porte the pronouncement to the *kadı* of Izmir that

the Venetian merchants in the city of Venice send their goods to their compatriots in Izmir upon English ships and pay the freight accordingly. After paying their customs dues, they have always given the consulage and other surcharges to the consul of Venice. Now, however, when the Venetian consul sought his dues from the English ship, the *Eagle*, which recently arrived in Izmir from Venice, the English consul and other persons interfered and acted contrary to the command that was issued to the Venetian consul. . . .

I order that . . . you should have these dues given to the consul of Venice and let no one interfere.[21]

In the second decade of the century, Venetian merchants often transported their merchandise on English bottoms and Ottoman customs officials routinely awarded to the Venetians the right of consulage and the bailo's customs on these goods. In 1619, however, the English wrested this precious income from Venetian hands. The English enterprise coincided with the transfer of their consulate from Chios to Izmir, which occurred at some time between 1610 and 1620 as a result of the sudden increase in Izmir's commerce and its concomitant reduction on Chios.[22] In Izmir, the English escaped from the ancient and ritualized Latin commercial network, allowing their merchants to test their competitiveness within the Levantine market.[23]

In this affair of the right of consulage, the English proved devastatingly effective. Collection of consulage depended upon Jewish customs authorities and other officials in Izmir, and the English utilized dragomans and brokers such as Mordecai Zvi in aggressive and innovative schemes against Venetian interests. In the question of consulage, the English in Izmir outmaneuvered the Venetians who consequently turned to Istanbul to rectify what they considered an injustice.

At the Divan, the bailo argued that these dues traditionally had gone to the Venetian consul and should so continue, whereas the English ambassador contended that the surcharges should go to the English consul because the merchandise had been shipped on an English vessel. The English had a strong argument; a passage in their capitulations of 1601 stated explicitly that all merchandise brought to the empire under English banner was liable to English surcharges.[24] Despite this, the Ottoman government in this decree ruled in favor of the Venetians on the grounds that the Venetian state always had received such dues on its traders' merchandise.

In the past, provincial officials, bound to the central government and unconcerned with infidel squabblings, would have complied with Istanbul's ruling. In 1619 they did not. Port officials in Izmir willfully disregarded their government's injunction and continued to award consulage on Venetian merchandise to the English consul. In 1620 the tension between court and country emerged unequivocally when Istanbul protested rather querulously that "the Sublime Porte has repeatedly said that no matter what ship Venetian goods travel on, the consulage should go promptly to the Venetian consul. But the English consul, contrary to habit and custom, persists in not returning it."[25] Although the bailo had exploited his state's vast experience in Ottoman intriguing in order to sway authorities in Istanbul, the machinations of English merchants and Ottoman customs officials in Izmir frustrated the city-state's designs.

More than the full weight of a vigorous trading state lay behind the English consuls and ambassador. The Venetians also had to contend with an Ottoman sympathy to the English as fellow protagonists against the Habsburgs and as suppliers of high-quality tin, steel, guns, and gunpowder. The Venetians found themselves in the almost hopeless position of being virtually dependent on the goodwill of the Ottomans to defend their trading rights against this natural ally.

The Venetians explored other avenues in protecting their rights of consulage, seeking to forbid compatriot merchants from shipping merchandise on English ships. If Venetian vessels had been active in the Aegean, such a boycott may have worked. But few such vessels dropped anchor in Izmir, and the policy soon proved untenable. With purchases awaiting sanctioned cargo space rotting on the port's wharf, Venetian merchants often lost patience and hired space on English ships.[26] In 1628, the bailo wrote to the doge and Senate that although Venetian merchants in Izmir promised not to pay dues to the English, it was doubtful that "they will do so, as I fancy the English are determined on this advantage. . . . I fancy they are not only lading the English [vessel] already hired but hiring others from the Greeks."[27] Venetian traders simply could not afford to entrust their goods to ships that were unreliable, slow, costly, and easily and frequently plundered. In order to ward off ruin,

they resorted to whatever other ship was available and English
captains capitalized upon the city-state's misfortune.

The English community of Izmir was not content to expand
its trade legally only. In 1619, Venetian merchants shipped two
large lengths of broadcloth aboard the *Eagle*. When the vessel touched port in Izmir, English merchants confiscated the
fabric, even though Venetians had documents proving their
ownership.[28] Such pilfering violated local traditions, capitulations, and certainly agreement between the English ship's captain and the Venetian merchants transporting goods on his
vessel, and demanded collusion from either Ottoman customs
officials or someone on the docks—perhaps janissary guards
(*yasakçıs*). Whoever actually conspired in the seizure of fabric, this clash between English and Venetian subjects substanti-
ates a growing Venetian isolation from provincial officials and
locals.

FAVORITISM ON THE WHARF

Deteriorating relations between the Venetians and the janissaries
who protected merchants and their goods in Izmir more starkly
reveal an eroding Venetian influence in Izmir vis-à-vis other
western trading states. Customarily, a trader who had goods
on the dock paid a gratuity to janissaries assigned to guard
them. In the first decade of the seventeenth century, however,
disputes over payment erupted between Venetians and janissary
guards. Janissaries appear to have initiated the quarrel, complaining in 1605 that the captains of Venetian ships anchoring
in Izmir no longer presented to them a gift of broadcloth.[29] The
Venetian community in Izmir responded several months later to
this charge, insisting that the janissaries who protected their
merchandise and consul were unreliable.[30] In spite of a capitulatory clause allowing consuls to select their own guards, the
janissary captain sensed Venetian weakness and sought to usurp
this privilege, perhaps in order to reap some of the benefits that
accrued to those assigned to foreign service.[31] The dispute also
had its personal side, for the captain of the janissaries had been

engaged for some time in litigation against the Venetians over a debt.[32]

The Venetians at least emerged victorious in their struggle with the captain of the janissaries. When in 1607 the local Ottoman commander suddenly dispatched one of the Venetians' loyal guards, İbrahim, to the Persian front, the bailo managed to have the order countermanded in Istanbul. By 1608 İbrahim again was in Venetian service.[33] The incident not only displays Venetian influence in the capital city, but also indicates that in the early seventeenth century the sultan could not rely even upon his slave army. Both İbrahim and the janissary captain had resided in Izmir long enough to develop the local networks of support and regional loyalties characteristic of that period and province.

Although the Venetian consul won the skirmish of 1608, the prestige of his compatriots gradually slipped as encounters along the pier continued. Whereas in 1605 janissaries guarded goods for a small gratuity, in 1613 and again in 1620 they demanded in compensation for their service thirty *guruş* per Venetian vessel.[34] Two years later the guards regularly received five *guruş* from every ship entering the harbor of Izmir. They coveted even more, with the bailo contending in Istanbul that "contrary to law janissary guards seek not only enough cloth to tailor suits for five members of their corps, but also fifteen *guruş*."[35]

Added to the Venetian grievance against excessive janissary demands was the humiliation that the guards did not request as much recompense from other foreign merchants. In 1622 and again in the following year the bailo, citing the services of janissaries in earlier times and denouncing the growing favoritism of the guards toward rival traders, objected that

the captains of Venetian ships anchoring at the port of Izmir customarily have given a little money and broadcloth to the janissary guards . . . by their own inclination. Now they day-by-day seek more money and other extras. . . . Recently, they demanded from Venetian captains more than the five-hundred *akçe*s, which the French and English captains pay. . . . The janissaries are not satisfied with the five-hundred *akçe*s, but seek ten or fifteen *guruş* from every [Venetian] ship.[36]

The janissaries at first had served gratis with their recompense only gradually evolving into wages. While the guards desired higher wages from all the foreign communities, they witnessed Venetian failures against the English and other foreigners and focused their demands against the weakened city-state.

Venetian difficulties did not end with the janissaries. The porters (*hamals*) "who lift and carry the packages of Venetian merchants" also clamored for higher wages in the early 1620s.[37] In 1620 not only did the porters demand as much as three times their customary pay, but they also formed an alliance in order to stop Venetians from hiring other more accommodating (or more desperate) carriers. In other words, they initiated a work stoppage and resisted strikebreakers. The porters, emulating the protests of the more privileged janissaries, understood that they could paralyze Venetian trade and realized that with the janissaries also agitating against the consul and with Venetian influence over the *kadı* and port officials at a nadir, the foreigners could do little to quash their labor movement other than protest feebly to Istanbul.

The turmoil on Izmir's pier was one facet of the social strife gripping the western-Anatolian peninsula; the demands of workers also manifested an Ottoman monetary crisis in the early seventeenth century. The value of silver in relation to gold had declined steadily since about 1580. At the same time, the government repeatedly had debased its silver *akçe* in order to pay the burgeoning janissary corps and other dependents of the state.[38] With Ottoman infantrymen rebelling against their own sultan or his advisers because of corrupt coinage and delayed payments, how much more likely that they also should rise up against suspect and insufficient remuneration from infidels? Nor were the port workers satisfied with higher wages. The janissaries knew that textile prices would tend to remain stable or even increase during a period of steep inflation, particularly in Izmir's rapidly expanding market, and they insisted upon broadcloths and clothing as a hedge against rising prices.

FAVORITISM IN THE HINTERLAND

The deterioration of Venice's position vis-à-vis other western traders in Izmir extended far beyond the wharf. In the procurement of goods in the city proper and in its hinterland also, Venetian merchants encountered growing resistance from local inhabitants and fierce competition from Dutch, English, and French merchants. Even as social unrest engulfed western Anatolia in the first decade of the century, inhabitants of the valleys radiating from Izmir obstructed Venetian middlemen gathering commodities in the port's environs. In 1605 the bailo informed authorities in Istanbul that two Greek brothers named Konstantine and Jean Kiya, who represented Venetian merchants in Izmir, could not trade in peace in the environs of Izmir, Tire, Manisa, and several other districts.[39] Local officials incessantly hindered their commerce with litigations, disputes, and false witnesses.

The Venetians themselves had to contend with indigens as they pushed out into Izmir's hinterland. One night in the summer of 1609, while Jacmo Musaveti slept in the Franks quarter of the town of Tire, several *zimmi*s allegedly crept into his room and stole 300,000 *akçe*s worth of cash and merchandise.[40] Three years later, some natives insisted that two Venetian merchants who had ridden out from Izmir in the direction of Lemrodlu, a village near Manisa, had swooped down upon a woman named Ayşe and murdered her.[41] Even Nicolini Orlando, who some years later assumed the Dutch consulship in Izmir, acquired his cunning and familiarity with local conditions by itinerant peddling through the western-Anatolian provinces of Aydın, Saruhan, and Menteşe in the 1610s. Between 1613 and 1617 he acted as creditor to various resentful *sipahi*s, janissaries, *zimmi*s, and Jews scattered across the region.[42]

Despite such harassments and obstructions, the Venetians persevered in their struggle to establish a commercial network in western Anatolia. They did not, however, do so by negotiating with those local officials and outlaws who frustrated their agents. Rather, through their bailo they channeled petition after petition to the Sublime Porte. In 1609, the consul obtained an

imperial rescript authorizing Venetian representatives to travel
and trade in peace in accordance with their capitulations and,
more creatively and venturously, convinced Istanbul to allow
a Venetian merchant to wander across the districts of Aydın
and Saruhan in disguise in order to conceal his identity from
"brigands and thieves."[43] The intrepid trader, who was an agent
procuring cotton, oil, and other goods for several compatriots,
chose curious garb. He and his men "mounted horses, carried
weapons, and dressed like janissaries, wearing the white tur-
ban." Whereas a more conciliatory policy similar to Orlando's
(who must have learned from his experiences during the 1610s)
may have pacified the undisciplined soldiers roaming roughshod
across western Anatolia, this indignity against janissary prerogatives merely helped to fuel provincial discontent against the
Venetians. By 1612, a coalition of assistant *kadıs*, policemen,
janissaries, and cavalrymen forced "traders from Venice to buy
cotton from them at high prices, to transport their purchases
on animals provided by them, and to pay exorbitant prices for
the animals."[44] Venetian merchants persisted in seeking safety
in janissary attire and the military class continued to view the
pretensions of the infidel as a travesty of its own privileges. Although the Dutch experience with Cennetoğlu in 1625 demonstrates that other foreigners faced similar difficulties, the Venetians, wedded to their outdated perception of a centralized Ottoman state, singularly could not adapt to and exploit these and
other developments in regional trading patterns. Their ineffec-
tiveness is most visible in their attempts to market cotton.

THE COTTON PREDICAMENT

The Italians, especially the Genoese and Venetians, had long
dominated the western-Anatolian export of cotton.[45] In the
first decade of the seventeenth century, Dutch and Englishmen
cracked their monopoly and participated ever more actively in
the cotton trade. The English in particular became great buyers
of the crop because of the development, principally in Lancaster,
of a fustian-producing industry. By 1621, merchant vessels from

the Levant imported through the port of London over 43,000 pounds of cotton per year.[46] The competition from the Netherlands and England not only propelled foreign merchants deep into Izmir's hinterlands in search of cotton, but also encouraged customs officials in Izmir to solicit more revenue from the crop. They exerted pressure particularly upon the weakened Venetians.

In 1606 Venetian merchants accused two Jewish customs officials who inspected cotton in Izmir of imposing surcharges of more than the 5 percent agreed to in their capitulations.[47] Although Istanbul condemned the exactions, two years later the Ottoman inspectors grumbled that "the cotton the [Venetians] buy with cash in the countryside and villages should be assessed according to the market price in Izmir" for they could not verify purchase prices and suspected Venetians of doctoring the receipts in order to reduce customs payments.[48] Since cotton prices were higher in Izmir than elsewhere in western Anatolia—which is why foreigners ventured beyond that frontier city in the first place—merchants resented these assessments.

Fifteen years later, the controversy still raged. In 1623 the bailo denounced customs officials in Izmir and Foça for charging dues on Venetian cotton according to its market value in these ports rather than its purchase price.[49] The Venetian official further condemned them for demanding broadcloth, sugar, and bottles in order to compensate their own "vexations and servants" and for requiring payments of 9 percent in duty rather than the customary 5 percent.[50] The collectors, no less than the guards and porters on Izmir's pier, recognized Venetian weakness in the 1620s and the advantages of payments in goods rather than cash during that inflationary period.

By the 1620s, then, fierce competition from the Dutch, English, and French had eroded Venetian influence in Izmir considerably. As early as 1618, some *sipahis* and janissaries illegally prohibited Venetians from purchasing cotton, cotton thread, and honey, and four years later Ottoman subjects in the environs of Izmir not only hindered the city-state's merchants from buying cotton, cotton thread, wax, buffalo hide, and morocco leather for cash, but allowed the Dutch, English, and French to purchase such commodities freely.[51] In the following year some cavalry-men and janissaries extorted monies from the Venetians with the excuse that "permission has been given to the French and other trading communities to buy cotton and cotton thread whereas none was given to the Venetians."[52] Even though these Ottoman officials correctly granted the French special privileges in their purchases of cotton because permission to buy cotton was given in their capitulations of 1604, Venetian agents in Istanbul succeeded in attaining an imperial decree against such preferential treatment.[53]

FAVORITISM AMONG BROKERS AND PEDDLERS

Ottoman officials and members of the military class were not alone in exploiting Venetian difficulties. The city-state also clamored against native brokers and peddlers whom it accused of reneging on promises to exchange cotton for other commodities. In early 1610 a Venetian merchant loaned four Jewish merchants—Abraham Kohen, Nazri Kalvano, Mosi son of al-Kaz, and Isaac Kohen—some merchandise and money with the stipulation that they would repay it in kind several months later when the cotton crop was harvested. The foreigner accused the Ottoman subjects of never honoring this pledge.[54] Ten years later the Venetian consul in Izmir, Angelo Marni, gave ninety-five pieces of broadcloth to Jacob Levi, Michael Kohen, and Mosi Suryan in exchange for cotton. Marni later claimed that his business associates delivered only a portion of the cotton.[55] In this instance, the litigants disputed the quantity of cotton at issue, for it was impossible to predict prices of goods in Izmir's volatile market, and when the value of cotton suddenly soared because of competition from other foreigners, speculators and hoarders hesitated to honor standing contracts with Venetian merchants.

A long and acrimonious dispute between several Venetian merchants and a Greek named Dmitri veled-i Mihal displays how evolving conditions in western Anatolia undermined the system of barter through which Venetians habitually conducted their business. In 1622 Dmitri received from a Venetian merchant twenty lengths of broadcloth ostensibly worth 248,000 *akçes*, in exchange for which he agreed to deliver a specified quantity of cotton four months later. The Greek subsequently delivered 260 *kantar*s of cotton worth 1,000 *akçes* per *kantar* and maintained that with this consignment the deal was closed. The Venetians disagreed, arguing in bitter litigation that Dmitri had contracted to repay according to exchange rates current when he received the broadcloth and that he still owed 26.5 *kantar*s. Three years passed, a combination of inflation and demand pushed the price of cotton to 4,000 *akçes* per *kantar*, and Dmitri returned to the law courts, now contending that he had delivered 260 *kantar*s of cotton to the Venetian at 4,000 *akçes* per *kantar* and was "seeking accordingly 4,000 *akçes* from each *kantar*, or I will take back my cotton."[56] While the protagonists perhaps never resolved their differences, their simmering disputation displays the complexity and fragility of the barter system and the ease with which misunderstandings and outright frauds occurred under it. The unexpected and precipitous rise in the value of cotton over the three-year period between 1622 and 1625 reflects an increasingly zealous competition, perhaps brought on by the sudden demand for cotton fiber in England and elsewhere along the Atlantic seaboard. The resultant rise in the worth of cotton had caught these merchants, relying on speculative barter in their transactions, utterly off guard and the chronic shortages in specie, which bound Venetian merchants to such barterings throughout the Mediterranean world, left them exposed in Izmir both to the maneuverings of Ottoman middlemen and to the greater resources of foreign rivals who possessed hard metals.[57]

Venetian and other European merchants in Izmir depended on native middlemen, without whom they could not comb the port's hinterland effectively. Strikes on Izmir's docks and spats with local Ottoman officialdom, however, tempted native merchants to desert their enfeebled Venetian partners. For example, in 1612 a certain Hacı Arslan b. Hacı Torbalı, whom a Venetian merchant in Saruhan had entrusted with sixteen sacks of cotton to deliver to compatriots in Izmir, bolted from Venetian service.[58] In the 1610s and early 1620s Venetian influence with suppliers and transporters of goods in Izmir's hinterland plummeted.

FAVORITISM AMONG OTTOMAN OFFICIALS

The Venetians settled into a siege against customs officials in Izmir and other western-Anatolian ports. According to the bailo these officials did not limit themselves to small overcharges, but borrowed large sums from Venetian ship captains and traders, confiscated entire cargoes because of alleged but unproven smugglings, doubled and redoubled customs charges, refused to accept payment in many coinages, extorted loans from merchants, and arbitrarily compelled Venetian captains to disburden their ships for inspections. While opportunity for these abuses derived from the monetary and social crises shaking both the Ottoman and Venetian empires in these years, it was the Venetian inability to adjust to the changing situation that spurred these irregularities on and concentrated them against that trading state.

Rather than confront the customs officials directly, Venetians in Izmir typically asked their bailo in Istanbul to protest abuses and Ottoman authorities often supported their representative's forwarded petitions. In 1605, the Sublime Porte ordered the Vezir Mehmet Paşa, who was battling brigands in the province of Anatolia, and the *kadı* of Izmir to move against janissary guards, police captains, customs officials, and others who disrupted Venetian trade; eighteen years later Istanbul demanded that messengers, collectors, and others cease their interference in Venetian commerce in broadcloth, silk, and cotton.[59] The Ottomans routinely complied with the bailo's desires not only because of capitulations or friendship, but also because they believed Venetian trade "a cause for the cheapness and abundance of such materials in the Ottoman domains."[60] Allowing this commerce to die, the government feared, would threaten the well-being of the empire's subjects.

The lending of money provoked particular tension between Venetians and port officials in Izmir. Customs collectors reg-

ularly borrowed from foreign traders, often contracting to repay their debts in duty remissions. This arrangement suited
both parties. It gave Ottoman collectors ready cash and European traders leverage with those very persons who regulated the
movement of commodities through the port and who could either
extinguish or ignore and even abet a vigorous and expanding
commerce in contraband goods. In the early seventeenth century, however, Ottoman officials began to renege on promises
to repay loans from Venetian merchants. After the Venetian
community in Izmir had lent customs collectors a quantity of
*akçe*s, the officials in 1606 refused to acknowledge the debt.[61] In
the same year, a certain Jean Dofetsu Janbadas in payment for
a loan claimed 100,000 *akçe*s worth of broadcloth and carpets
from two Jewish customs collectors in Izmir and Chios named
Haham al-Kaz and Haham Ali Baba.[62] Many similar incidents
occurred in the 1610s and 1620s and, although it is unclear why
these loans were granted, whether the practice was standard and
typically uneventful, or whether and how much interest accrued
from them, it is unlikely that an individual merchant would lend
or even release custody of 100,000 *akçe*s worth of goods unless
either the risks were low and the expected returns high, or, far
more likely, the loans were merely cleverly disguised bribes con-
cocted to fleece the central government of revenues. Despite the
conspiratorial implications of these loans and the certain knowledge that advance payment for a commodity (*selem*)—under
which category these dealings certainly fell—was contrary to
Islamic law, the Venetians in the 1610s and 1620s repeatedly
presented their petitions in Istanbul and made public their discontent. The Sublime Porte in turn condemned not only the
customs collectors, but also the loaning of money in this way,
calling it a bad innovation (*bid'at*) and ordering it stopped.

Venetian repudiation of local interests in this instance proved
almost fatal to the city-state's comfortable presence in Izmir.
The homes of western merchants along the port's shore not
only were pleasant, but also eased commerce in contraband.
Many houses had entrances facing the sea through which the
residents not only initiated pleasure outings, but also smuggled

goods onto and from small boats. Local Ottoman administrators, responding to bribes, loans, and favors, usually ignored these blatant illegalities. In 1612, however, officials, angry at Venetian attempts to circumvent their authority, marched from house to house along the seashore, ousting their Venetian occupants and demolishing the dwellings.[63] The locals thus assertively took their revenge against the ancient maritime state, which, through communications with and appeals to Istanbul, threatened their lucrative accommodations with the burgeoning foreign communities in Izmir.

The Sublime Porte's concerns, while initially with the legal niceties of Islamic and secular law, soon became more concrete, for the conspiracies and chicaneries in Izmir entangled the Ottoman provisioning network. In 1616, the *kadı* of Izmir received an order that

> the Venetian consul and merchants trading in Izmir gave a quantity of *akçes* to a Jewish customs collector named İbrahim as a loan. İbrahim in return gave the merchants a promissory note. When the Venetians wanted to claim their dues, [İbrahim] plotted with an imperial agent who came to collect fruit for My larder, claiming that "excuses for the fruit are being made." He took an account of the *akçes*, which were being produced from the customs, and prevented the reckoning of the debts of the traders.[64]

The Venetians called this excuse, by which the customs collector reneged upon his promise of repayment, a plot; and the incident indeed possesses an element of prevarication. Nevertheless, monies collected from customs were critical to the provisioning of Istanbul and the central government would have condemned any official who disrupted its network in order to pay off personal debts. İbrahim's balancing act between Istanbul and Venice might have produced great wealth, but he also courted disaster; when the Venetian consul reported his proceedings in Istanbul, he and his cohorts reacted with anger and fear.

Such litigations between Venetian merchants and local collectors occurred often enough to suppose a widespread discontent, and even contempt toward imperial authority. Officials felt increasingly confident that Venetian petitions against them could be frustrated, not only because during that anarchic period provincial authorities feared imperial agents less, but also because of increasing tension between the Ottomans and Venetians over the island of Crete. Although the Muslim power did not attack that Venetian-held island until 1643, Istanbul long had coveted Crete as the door to the Aegean and resented it as a refuge for Christian privateers. Knowing well the diplomatic strains between the two empires, officials in Izmir disdainfully abused the Venetian community and its consul, who continued futilely to denounce them in Istanbul. In 1617, the consul delivered a particularly bitter diatribe against the embezzlements of a Jewish collector, İbrahim al-Kaz, charging not only that this official treated Venetian merchants in Izmir with contempt and delighted in fabricating new ways to swindle them, but that he even had purloined one-hundred *guruş* from the consul himself.[65]

DODGERS AND IMBIBERS

One of the most frequent Venetian accusations against customs collectors concerned smuggling. While the legal punishment for smuggling was a fine, which doubled the duty of 5 percent on cargo, in 1609 officials began confiscating entire cargoes from Venetian ships caught circumventing the tariff.[66] The consul, frustrated in his efforts to overcome locally this flagrant breach of treaty and custom, appealed to Istanbul.

Although the consul had a good legal case against the collectors, local officials had to contend with escalating smuggling in and around the port of Izmir. In concert with imperial agents, they sought to control it by systematically inspecting the cargo of ships in the harbor. Deteriorating Veneto-Ottoman relations in the 1620s tempted customs inspectors to concentrate their exertions against subjects of this maritime state. In 1622 and again in the following year port officials threatened to empty fully laden and ready-to-sail Venetian vessels, even though "two trustworthy assistants to the collector and the *kadı*" already had inspected their cargoes.[67] With Venetian captains insisting that collectors merely wanted to extort additional monies from them,

Istanbul ordered the *kadıs* of Izmir, Chios, Ayasoluğ, Balat, and the two Foças to prevent this unworthy behavior.

Venetian merchants also accused port officials of other extortions. While a vessel engaging in intra-empire commerce paid duty only at its first anchorage, customs collectors in Izmir at times compelled captains of ships that already had stopped at another Ottoman port, or that had returned to Izmir without leaving the empire, to pay tariffs again. In 1623, officials maintained that a Venetian captain, who claimed to have docked at Izmir, weighed anchor, sailed to Istanbul, and then returned, in fact had embarked for Venice.[68] On his reappearance, they demanded not only cargo duties, but also payments to janissary guards, porters, and other servants on the dock.

In other instances, functionaries reassessed and even seized cargo salvaged from wrecked Venetian vessels. Although a clause in each capitulation exempted ships' owners from such confiscations, local officials disputed the privilege. When in March 1607 a ship plying the sea lane from Venice to Izmir ran aground off Chios, the Venetian consul in Izmir accused collectors of customs and inheritances and the captain of the janissaries of "taking unjustly from [salvaged] goods, merchandise, artillery and weaponry."[69] When another Venetian ship foundered off the island of Mytilene three years later, a second vessel ferried much of its cargo and artillery to Izmir.[70] Upon arrival, local officials insisted on customs dues, even though the Venetians had documents proving previous payment.

Collectors in Izmir confiscated merchandise from wrecked ships because they suspected Venetians of passing off contraband goods as the accoutrements of sunken vessels, and because they supposed that foreign merchants used title deeds from lost cargo in order to avoid customs payments on their own merchandise. Their insistence upon collecting taxes on wine is more difficult to explain. In the early seventeenth century, with riotous janissaries often plundering, allegedly drunkenly, through the streets of Istanbul, officials in the Sublime Porte fretted about drinking and drunkenness. On 2 May 1601, the authorities prohibited wine in Istanbul and, despite the infamous Christian devotion to the substance, included non-Muslims and foreign merchants in the ban. The bailo expressed to his superiors the resultant panic that gripped the Frank community, writing: "[I have] obtained an order which covers this Embassy and the houses of the Venetian merchants [excepting them from the prohibition]. But the danger is that when the wine I have is finished it will be impossible to get more."[71] When two months later, on 12 July, some drunken janissaries "rushed with drawn scimitars into the bazzar [*sic*] where the richest merchandise is kept [and] terrified everyone and caused a panic," the grand vezir ordered all casks of wine in the city staved in, houses in which it was found confiscated, and their owners sent to prison.[72]

When similar riotous behavior invaded Izmir and other locales, however, the prohibitions of the capital were not repeated. The government was eager to suppress the sale and consumption of wine in Istanbul, but its attitude toward Izmir reflected a different code for non-Muslims. In 1607, when customs officials in Izmir imposed a duty not only on wines imported by Venetian merchants, but even on wines produced in their own cellars, the government forbade the collectors from taxing the drink and ordered them not to interfere in any way with the foreigners' purchase and production of wine for personal consumption.[73] The empire's traditions and capitulatory understandings allowed native non-Muslims and foreigners to import alcohol duty free, and to produce and imbibe wine as long as they did so inconspicuously. Although the frolicking and carefree foreigner of Franks Street and the sometimes zealous and easily offended native Muslim did not always perceive "conspicuous consumption" in the same light, in outlying communities Istanbul protected the very "loose" behavior by foreigners, which it found unacceptable in the capital city.

VENAL AND RAPACIOUS: A MATTER OF PERSPECTIVE

Officialdom in Izmir appeared corrupt to Venetian merchants not only because of differing cultural milieus, but more concretely because of merchant manipulations of the Ottoman monetary crisis. European merchants, experienced in the clipping and forging of coinage, exploited devaluations, debasements, and other governmental exigencies in order to cheat Ottoman officials.[74] Imbalances in the monetary system became particularly pronounced in 1618 when Osman II acceded to the throne and issued an *osmanî* proclaimed to be worth ten *akçes*. It was not. The *osmanî* quickly became a notoriously overvalued currency and officials in Izmir and elsewhere hated accepting payment in it rather than in the more reliable gold *altın* and silver *guruş*. In 1623, customs collectors in Izmir argued that

Venetian merchants in Izmir traditionally have given . . . 540 *akçes* in customs for every bale of *cayli*[?], violet and other colored broadcloth and 360 *akçes* for every bale of Erekmiya[?] broadcloth. But the Jewish collectors in Izmir say "we are not satisfied with this old rule and we do not want one *osmanî* for every ten *akçes*. We want *altıns* and *guruş* or we will take it in materials."[75]

From the Venetian perspective, this refusal to accept *osmanîs* seemed arbitrary and even avaricious; however, Ottoman officials believed that they merely were responding to existing conditions. The conundrum of converting frequently debased and unreliable currency eventually brought the customs officials to demand payment in goods rather than cash.[76]

The Venetians often condemned officials who strove to legitimize their novel claims with imperial firmans. Although Istanbul routinely denied having issued such decrees and censured the demands as bad innovations, the Sublime Porte was contending with novel phenomena and consequently probably did issue contradictory statements on these matters. Commercial activities in Izmir were expanding and diversifying rapidly and the authorities in Istanbul could not have known intimately the conditions under which officials and merchants there operated. Furthermore, Istanbul could not even rely upon intelligence from its own agents because many of them no longer were salaried appointees of the state. In their search for hard currency, the Ottomans expanded their system of tax farming and by the first decade of the seventeenth century they chronically auctioned off, usually for a three-year period, the right to collect customs.[77] Consequently, the collectors about whom the Venetians complained were not merely salaried servants of the state. They also had a personal stake in generating as much revenue as possible in the shortest time, although their ability to do so quickly deteriorated because the same exigencies of state that extended the system of tax farming also demolished Ottoman finances. Thus, in spite of an increase in the flow of goods through the port, customs collectors in Izmir saw an inflationary spiral erode their incomes. It was this bifurcation between expectations and actualities that drove officials to redefine the rules of collection. The Venetians, because of structural inflexibilities, disintegrating relations with the Ottomans, and pressure from Dutch, English, and French merchants, were particularly vulnerable to these innovations, and the behavior of customs officials tempted others—the *yasakçi*s and porters, the janissaries and cavalrymen, the middlemen, peddlers, retailers, and brokers—also to coerce merchants from Italian city-states.

The Venetians of Izmir, in long-standing custom, relied upon their capitulations to escape this explosive arena and upon their bailo to fight in their behalf through the tangled intrigues of Istanbul. In both 1605 and 1609 the Venetian consul endeavored to transfer all lawsuits between Venetian and native merchants from Izmir to the capital city.[78] One and a half decades later the bailo, remarking upon the intolerable commercial atmosphere in Izmir, bitterly asserted that

some people have been blaspheming and slandering the consul and merchants of Venice [in Izmir] for personal gain, saying "you spirit away our slaves and revile our daughters and women and blaspheme us and do not repay our loans. . . ." They are bringing false witnesses against us [to support these claims]. Because of these obstacles, the consul and merchants cannot trade through [Izmir's hinterland] and they will be forced to abandon commerce. This will bring loss to the treasury.[79]

While all traders periodically condemned Muslim false witnesses and native accusations against them of sexual and spiritual harassments, this threat to abandon all trade in Izmir was not idle. The winter of 1622–23 brought crisis to the port's Venetian community as it almost monthly petitioned vainly to Istanbul to rein in the hosts arrayed against it.[80]

• • •

Neither Istanbul nor Venice fully understood that the abuses and entanglements plaguing the Venetians in Izmir were in part a product of fragmenting authority within the Ottoman state and in part a symptom of a wider malaise that had stricken the Venetian maritime empire. Although Venetian trade had been in a downward spiral since 1602, the city-state's commercial network crashed in the early 1620s.[81] These hard times were reflected in Izmir—in the encroachments of the English on Venetian privileges, in the intensification of janissary and porter demands, in the futile Venetian struggles against the innovations of Ottoman customs agents, and in the erosion of the Venetian marketing web in the villages and towns lying to the east of the port. The Venetian community of Izmir, if left to its own devices, might have thrived in the port's chaotic and burgeoning trade. It did not, however, because its representatives remained wedded to an anachronistic diplomacy in which consuls, wrongly assuming that Ottoman provincial authorities conformed promptly to Istanbul's will, funneled complaints and demands through the capital city. As the English usurpation of Venetian consulage and the Dutch manipulation of multiplying authorities in western Anatolia prove, Venetian strategies no longer worked in the eastern Aegean. The changing world of its provinces also misled the Sublime Porte into genuinely fearing the loss of Venetian trade and thus responding favorably if ineffectually to the bailo's demands. The Ottoman government seems not to have realized that the city-state's trade through Izmir already was negligible and that Dutch, English, and French commerce would more than compensate for its demise.

6

The Crisis in French Trade, 1635–1650

The Venetians never adequately reformed their outdated commercial and diplomatic structure or adjusted to the changing circumstances in Izmir that crippled their presence in the growing port. Although the French merchant community in Izmir also faltered in those years, its difficulties eventually vanished because they were not fundamentally structural. Rather, temporary administrative and political disarray in France and Marseilles spilled over into the Levant and manifested itself in petty squabbles between French representatives and merchants. The two communities' relations with officials in Istanbul and Izmir reflect these contrasting troubles. Whereas the Venetian consul antagonized a whole range of powerful interest groups in Izmir by issuing petitions against customs dues, harassments, and the impingements of other foreigners upon Venetian rights, the consul and merchants of France concerned themselves more with domestic squabblings between ambassador and consul, consul and merchant, and merchant and merchant.

These disputes derived from French mismanagement of Levantine commerce during the first decades of the seventeenth century. After a protracted struggle, Henry IV had come to the French throne in 1589, on the verge of bankruptcy. Consequently, rather than paying the French ambassador in Istanbul a salary, he authorized his representative there to pocket a 2 percent surcharge on French goods passing through Ottoman ports. Although the French abolished this assessment in 1619, the ambassador then in residence, Philippe de Harley, Comte de Césy, ignored the decree from Louis XIII's court and in 1627, in order to finance mammoth debts, he even raised it to 3 percent. This payment was in addition to the 2 or 3 percent consulage imposed upon French merchants to cover local expenses. These internal levies undermined the most-favored-nation status, which, despite Dutch and English opposition, Ambassador de Brèves had secured for the French in 1604. The state's Levantine trade suffered accordingly.[1] The ambassador's grasping policies also generated resentment among French merchants and consuls in the Levant.

Bad as French ambassadors were in this period, French consuls were often worse. They were neither chosen by their fellow merchants nor appointed by French officials in Marseilles. Instead, the French government farmed out these offices to the highest, but rarely best qualified, bidders.[2] As a result, merchant representatives tended to be inept and corrupt, and their posts often became nepotistic, as in Izmir where between 1626 and 1685 first Jean Dupuy, then his brother Franois, followed by their nephew Honore Dupuy, and his nephew du Roure all served as French consul.[3] French merchants, furious over their fumblings and rapacity, lashed out at such consuls and ambassadors with the result that in the first half of the seventeenth century internecine quarreling engulfed the French community in the Levant.

QUARRELS AND COLLUSION IN IZMIR

Jean Dupuy, in his long tenure (1626–51) as French consul in Izmir, fought, often heatedly and openly, with his merchants and his ambassador. France's capitulations long had granted the French Levantine community the right to adjudicate such confrontations autonomously.[4] Dupuy possessed a letter of appointment from the Ottoman government, which not only acknowledged his right to "decide insurrections and lawsuits between his traders" without interference from local officials, but even provided that "when blood is shed between [Frenchmen], they shall be punished according to the consul's customs," and that "if anyone is rebellious, the consul may send him to France."[5] Despite this statement of communal self-sufficiency, neither Dupuy nor his antagonists hesitated to drag each other before Ottoman tribunals. The most common clashes occurred between Dupuy and the merchants whom he ostensibly led. To take one instance: in 1636 the consul accused a French merchant of assaulting his person and instigating various "seditions" against the French community of Izmir.[6] When the French ambassador in Istanbul presented Dupuy's position before the Divan, he argued, in accordance with the capitulations, that "ambassadors and consuls should be allowed to do as is necessary according to their customs." This assertion was irrefutable and the grand vezir readily accepted it. The difficulty was that in a fractious and self-directing city like Izmir such regulations depended upon a disciplined corps of merchants, a uniform legal system, and respected leaders. The French community boasted none of these ingredients and when the irresponsible individual who struck Dupuy fled to Ottoman provincial notables, they protected him and frustrated the consul's desire for retribution. Because Dupuy enjoyed no jurisdiction over these Ottoman officials, his only recourse was to those authorities—first, no doubt, the *kadı* in Izmir and ultimately the Sublime Porte—who might pry the fugitive from them.

Exactly what had angered the merchant to such an extent that he physically abused his consul remains a mystery, although money probably was its root cause. French merchants resented yielding to the ambassador or consul a percentage of the value of their goods, particularly when such payments soared above their Dutch, English, and Venetian competitors, and Dupuy, stretching to the utmost his authority in order to reap the harvest of his tax farm, imposed various innovative and disabling duties upon his charges. In 1649, he demanded from French merchants who provisioned their ships in the port of Izmir a due called the *baylaç hakkı*, probably a 2 percent "right of the ambassador."[7] In order to collect it, Dupuy required that a vessel's provisions pass either through his home on Franks Street into boats tied at his pier, or under the supervision of his representative. These impositions upon provisions meant for personal consumption infuriated French captains and merchants. They faced no such exactions from other consuls or the Ottoman government. To circumvent their consul's greedy order, they smuggled supplies "to the edge of the sea" with the assistance of "hirelings" (*âcirs*), loaded these goods onto ships' boats or small Ottoman coastal vessels (*kayıks*), and transferred them surreptitiously onto their ships lurking in the harbor. Dupuy's avaricious policy thus pushed his compatriots into a conspiring opposition. The utilization of Ottoman hirelings and their boats exposed the conceit of communal loyalty and autonomy and necessitated the consul's recourse to local Ottoman officials. When Dupuy proved unable to defeat the combination arrayed against him in Izmir, he petitioned Istanbul for assistance. Even this maneuver, however, was unavailing. Local officials ignored the resultant imperial decree and four years later, in 1653, the consul's brother still confronted the same unified opposition.[8]

The smuggling affair was not an isolated instance of intracommunal strife. To the annoyance of other merchants, Dupuy in 1648 insisted that as French consul he should have precedence over them in loading the valuable valencia acorns onto his ship.[9] In the same year the consul complained of a conspiracy between the French merchant community and Ottoman customs collectors of Izmir aimed at depriving him of his "rights of consulage."[10] Three years later, the dispute was still unresolved.[11]

This concern with consulage is reminiscent of Venetian difficulties. The city-state twenty years earlier had resisted both the English seizure of funds and the hostilities of Ottoman officials in Izmir. The striking contrast between the two instances, however, is that French merchants attempted to evade payments to their own officials, not to competitors. Perhaps Dupuy needed the funding in order to cover administrative expenses and the occasional extortions of Ottoman local and naval officials. If so, rather than assume Dupuy's confrontational posture, which polarized the French community, introduced Ottoman laws and persons into its management, and weakened it in its rivalries with other foreign merchants, a more astute and sensitive consul would have consulted, and if necessary hammered out differences with, his compatriots in order to maintain the communal autonomy his predecessors had won and to present a united front in Izmir's fiercely competitive market.

AMBASSADOR AND PORTE VERSUS CONSUL AND PORT

Despite his interminable litigations in Izmir, Dupuy effectively defended the French community against the French ambassador in Istanbul, who endured perennial cash shortages and who periodically alienated his compatriots in the Levant with arbitrary surcharges. In 1626 the ambassador de Césy dispatched a pursuivant, armed with letters and decrees from both French and Ottoman officials, to seize money from the merchants of Izmir. As the ambassador's servant traveled away from Istanbul, however, the power of the central authority weakened and his pile of papers became almost valueless. In Izmir Dupuy and his "friends" easily frustrated the scheme.[12]

Ottoman officials in both Istanbul and Izmir regularly arbitrated such feuds between representatives of the French state. In 1638, the French ambassador in Istanbul clashed with Dupuy and the French community in Izmir over interest payments on a loan.[13] The French ambassador received little salary during those years and depended largely on the uncertain generosity of his compatriot consuls and communities. Consuls, anxious not to apportion their returns, were particularly resentful of ambassadorial interference and resisted Istanbul's efforts to impose surcharges on commerce and collect exorbitant interest on debts. Even after de Césy had rallied his supporters in the capital city, marched before the Divan with the ambassadors of Venice and the Netherlands, and demanded that the French community in Izmir repay him a twenty-thousand *guruş* debt cleverly con-

cocted out of an emergency 3 percent imposition on exported
and imported goods, Dupuy was able to rebuff him, asserting
with candor on behalf of the Frenchmen of the port that "we
are not tied to it."

Even the Sublime Porte's blunt demand that the consul and
merchants of Izmir hand over the money to the ambassador's
deputy did not sway the dauntless consul. Rather than comply,
several months later, in July 1638, he presented a counter-plea
in Istanbul.[14] Dupuy insisted that, in accordance with the capitulations the Ottoman government had granted the French state,
he must supervise those aspects of the affairs of the French merchants in Izmir dealing with the laws and customs of the Ottoman realm. This task cost money, and in order to undertake
it, Dupuy audaciously announced that the merchants of Izmir
must pay him a small tax. It was the rights to this money, the
consul contended, that the French ambassador, with Ottoman
assistance, was striving to usurp. Such meddlings, Dupuy im-
plied, hurt the community's ability to function in Izmir and thus
constituted an injustice.

It is ironic that a man involved in similar undertakings
should condemn his ambassador's cupidity. Yet, it was a case
of two unscrupulous men exploiting their two power bases—de
Césy's in Istanbul and Dupuy's in Izmir—for personal gain. Nor
did their rivalry die in 1638; it continued to simmer. When a
year and a half later de Césy arbitrarily rewarded a loyal servant with goods from French vessels anchored in Izmir's harbor, the French community, presumably led and abetted by the
consul, adamantly refused to relinquish the commodities.[15] As
in earlier incidents, the Ottoman position in this dispute was
uncertain. Istanbul vacillated between the two French parties
and, while it is possible that the Sublime Porte was too dis-
tracted by the siege of Baghdad and other urgent business to
take seriously such a peripheral and petty dispute, it is more
likely that Dupuy and his compatriots (who united in opposition to this outside menace) influenced and bribed local officials who then ignored and undermined their masters' demands.

INTERFERENCE FROM PARIS

At times it was French rulers in Paris who drew the Ottomans into these bickerings. Particularly under the mismanagements of ambassadors de Césy and Henri de Gournay, Comte de Marcheville, who resided in Istanbul between 1619 and 1640, French debts in the Levant swelled.[16] In the early 1630s, Marseilles began dabbling in Levantine finances because of this debt crisis. With the king's blessings, the mayor and merchants in that port city sought to liquidate their debts by imposing duties on commodities passing through Levantine ports. It was not the resident ambassadors and consuls who administered this levy, however. In order to raise money quickly, the French government auctioned off such posts and a member of the merchant community in Izmir, a certain Bagasar, farmed the surcharge. By 1636 he had collected several thousand *guruş*.[17]

While the conditions of Bagasar's appointment are obscure the harvest from his tax farm was rich, and the French ambassador coveted a piece of it. When he dispatched a dependent named D'Aramon to wrest some money from the merchant, however, the agent discovered that Bagasar and several other French entrepreneurs in Izmir were sinking the windfall capital into their own businesses. Although such diversion of tax monies was illegal, the enterprising traders sidestepped prosecution by remaining outside French territory and linking up with French ports through loyal agents. Obviously, in order to apprehend these expatriates who were constructing a kind of reverse Mediterranean "trading diaspora" and who relied upon local Ottoman military and civil officials for protection, the French ambassador had little choice but to enlist Ottoman aid.[18]

In 1652–53 Paris interfered more directly in Levantine affairs by requesting the sultan's government to extract 2,545 *guruş* from the French community in Izmir to help settle their debts. The French ambassador Jean de la Haye presented the royal letters from Paris at the Divan and then, with weighty backing from two powerful states, sent his dragoman to seize the money. Although Dupuy finally had departed his post the year before and so could not personally check the ambassador's maneuver, the French community in Izmir, under Dupuy's brother François, continued to resist compliance.[19]

Because of inept leadership and undisciplined traders, Ottoman subjects, officials and laws became decisive factors in these controversies between French consuls and merchants, consuls and ambassadors, and merchants and French domestic authorities. Wayward and libertine young Frenchmen, tasting the novelties of a new culture in a melting pot environment, sought and found refuge with Ottoman officials and subjects in Izmir. While this behavior constituted a provocative bridge over a deep religious divide, it also damaged French trade because the fraternizing and conspiring of French merchants and officials with Ottomans externalized administrative and legal affairs and set Frenchmen against each other. Despite the resultant financial losses, disarray among French officials together with Izmir's virtual administrative independence from Istanbul ensured that neither the French ambassador nor even the Ottoman and French central authorities could prevent the self-destructive conduct.

While the fluidity of Ottoman administration bore the potential for innovative and profitable commerce, it also tempted individuals within the foreign communities to venture beyond the limits of state or company policy. In the cases of the Dutch and the English, little damage was done because consuls were appointed, salaried, and given room for maneuvering. The bounty of these policies manifests itself in Dutch handling of the brigand Cennetoğlu and his conqueror Hüseyin Paşa and in English triumphs against the Venetians. The loyalties of Venetian officials and merchants also negated many of the uncertainties of western-Anatolian commerce, although the decentralizing tendencies of the Ottoman state in this period permitted trading rivals to trample across many Venetian prerogatives. French difficulties, however, derived from their internecine feuds and their willingness to bolt to Ottoman authorities in order to gain advantage over compatriots. The French policy of farming out consular positions and disallowing French communities in Levantine ports from assessing their own surcharges also spawned disloyalty. Among all European trading states, only the French routinely resorted to Ottoman authorities in order to resolve intracommunal spats.[20] It was a practice that guaranteed perpetual and self-destructive recrimination and gravely handicapped the French in their battle against vigorous Dutch and English encroachments.

CLASHES BETWEEN CULTURES

The freewheeling lifestyle of French factors in Izmir also triggered numerous collisions with Ottoman subjects. In such cross-cultural confrontations, the foreigners effectively utilized their extraterritorial privileges. A clause in the French capitulations allowed for the transfer of lawsuits between Frenchmen and natives from provincial ports to Istanbul, and the French community in Izmir habitually shielded itself behind this right when confronting powerful local officials or when it was dissatisfied with proceedings in the *kadı*'s court.[21]

Legal disputes between Frenchmen and Ottomans almost always concerned inheritance and the transfer of funds or property and often involved Jews because of their exposed positions as tax farmers and collectors. In 1635, when the Jewish customs collector İbrahim al-Kaz died, a fierce legal battle commenced between his sons, Menachim and Mosi, and the French consul Dupuy.[22] Eighteen years earlier İbrahim had feuded bitterly with the Venetian consul over an unsettled loan.[23] He similarly estranged Dupuy by borrowing 2,500 reals from him and died still owing 2,000. While İbrahim's sons acknowledged the debt and reimbursed a portion of it, they maintained that the last 1,264 was fully mortgaged ("pledged in pawn") in real estate.

The disputants first hastened into court in Izmir, where the *kadı* endorsed Dupuy's plea and ordered İbrahim's sons to fulfill their father's pledge. When they still procrastinated and refused to raise funds by selling their real estate, Dupuy exercised his privileges as consul and dragged them in front of the Divan in Istanbul. There he convinced the grand vezir that he needed the money immediately because of his imminent departure for France.

Dupuy did not leave his post in 1635, however. He remained in Izmir for sixteen years and his lawsuit against the Jewish inhabitants may very well have been his ploy to acquire the insolvent brothers' buildings. Five years before the litigation, he bought an inn (*menzil*) from a certain Umur Ağa (although Umur's widow in 1650 denied the sale) and it seems that one of the consul's many enterprises in the booming port town was the accumulation of real estate.[24] Dupuy also projected his financial dealings beyond the port of Izmir. Around 1644, he demanded that officials in Kuşadası seize 450 reals from the heirs of a Greek *zimmi* who had moved there from Chios.[25]

Dupuy was not the only Frenchman who clashed with native inhabitants, and *zimmi*s were not their only adversaries. Several years after İbrahim's death, the French merchant Bogasan lent 350 *guruş* worth of merchandise to a Muslim merchant, Hacı Mehmet, and his son, Mustafa.[26] When in 1644 Hacı Mehmet secretly fled Izmir, his son refused to accept responsibility for the debt and drove Bogasan to bring action against him in Izmir and Istanbul.

The French did not always initiate these litigations. French as well as Ottoman subjects fled from their debts in Izmir and, despite a capitulatory clause forbidding the practice, frustrated creditors sometimes tried to punish the French consul for his merchants' malfeasances. In 1639, two such French factors hastily abandoned the port, leaving behind various creditors.[27] The merchants' troubles had begun not because of suspect dealings, but because of an unlucky encounter with Algerian and Tunisian corsairs, who were prowling along the Anatolian coasts of the Aegean. The French ambassador knew of the presence of these pirates, feared them, and in December 1638 petitioned Istanbul to protect his community from them.[28] The Sublime Porte could do little to discipline its fractious dependents, however, and two months later the corsairs struck. Contrary winter winds had forced both a fully laden French vessel and some Barbary ships to ride out a storm in the port of Foça at the mouth of the Gulf of Izmir. When the winds subsided, and as the captain of the castle of Foça (whose guns perhaps could have foiled the decamp) quietly looked on, the corsairs cut the French boat's mooring line, took it in tow, and headed out to sea.[29] Aboard this ship were the persons and merchandise of the two French merchants who, after escaping from or being released by their captors, proved unable either to rescue their goods or appease their creditors (apparently Hacı Ali, Hacı Çelebi, and Hacı Mustafa).[30] They disappeared from Izmir later that year.

After unavailingly demanding recompense from Dupuy, the angry and influential Muslim lenders vengefully sought to punish him for his merchants' misconduct. They first secured the French consul's detention in prison, and when after three days the *kadı* ordered him released, they appealed directly to Istanbul for redress. This maneuver proved a mistake, for the transfer of the case to the capital deprived the Muslim claimants of their power base in Izmir and left them at the mercy of the French representative in Istanbul, who was well acquainted with the city's political ins and outs. When Dupuy asked him to quash the creditors' case, the French ambassador issued a petition to the Divan explaining that the plaintiffs possessed neither the backing of the *kadı* in Izmir, nor documents proving that the consul had accepted bond for his merchant's debts (according to French capitulations no one could hold a member of the community responsible for another's debts). The Ottoman authorities agreed that the accusers should stop harassing the consul and his community of merchants.

In these lawsuits between native and foreign merchants Ottoman authority appears fragmented and unpredictable. When the verdict of a lower court was satisfactory, the victor sought to realize his gains and keep the central government at bay. When dissatisfied with the decision of provincial authorities, a disputant simply turned to Istanbul. Merchants also had to contend with local notables, brigands, and corsairs whose powers were uncertain and whose actions were fickle. Thus, the prosperity of a Frenchman in Izmir depended as much upon his legal deviousness and political influence and initiative as upon his commercial acumen. Dupuy may have been an astute trader, but his wealth and power derived also from his skill in outmaneuvering his rivals in Izmir's legal and political jungle.

PROVISIONING ISTANBUL AND THE FRENCH

Although French and Ottoman subjects occasionally were at odds, foreigners depended upon local Ottoman officials to travel, to secure adequate provisions, and simply to survive day to day. In their wanderings through the Ottoman countryside, particularly across hazardous terrain, they regularly obtained imperial passes eliciting protection from army and naval officers, captains of castles, *kadıs*, customs collectors, and guards. In 1636 such a decree, permitting a representative of the French ambassador, his men, his goods, and his livestock to move freely between the ports of Izmir, Chios, and Kuşadası, ordered officials to assist him in buying provisions as needed and at the going rate.[31]

The French also needed local officials to help provision their seaborne journeys. A ship did not dare set sail without adequate food and water, the lack of which threatened sailors with starvation or dehydration. Although Istanbul acknowledged this requirement and agreed to furnish French ships with necessary provisions at current market prices, shortages in Izmir and its hinterland, diversions to Istanbul, and suspicions that merchants smuggled foodstuffs sometimes frustrated French procurements and upset scheduled sailings. In 1648, the Vezir Süleyman Paşa, in Izmir "for some important matters," strictly regulated French purchases, allowing merchants and ships to buy only enough provisions and necessities "for [their] needs."[32] Two years later a messenger from Istanbul, ordered to procure foodstuffs for the capital, grew frustrated over the scarcity and expense of commodities in Izmir, condemned foreigners for creating shortages, and harshly limited the quantity of goods permitted to the French consul and merchants residing in the port.[33] When the French protested these cruelties, the Sublime Porte ordered its agent to ease his rationings. The French however were not presented with a carte blanche; Istanbul warned the foreigners not to sell food to the Venetian enemy (*harbi*).[34]

The Sublime Porte fired off more directives to Izmir in 1651 and 1652.[35] In the latter year, an Ottoman official, Hüseyin, became so incensed over French purchases that he refused to allow subjects of France to load their ships at all and, when the consul protested, he threw the French dragoman into prison, releasing him only upon payment of a large bail. Istanbul condemned Hüseyin's strong-arm tactics, ordering him to release the dragoman, return the bail bond, and provide the Frenchmen with provisions.

Istanbul, however, generally moved reluctantly against these abuses because of the conflict in the Aegean, and the capital itself was contending with desperate food shortages, rioting, a weak sultanate, and factional rule. Since 1644 a Veneto-Ottoman war had raged, or at times sputtered, over the island of Crete. In this confrontation, Venice several times deployed its relatively strong navy at the Dardanelles straits in order to cut off Istanbul's access to the Aegean.[36] Although unable to sustain such a blockade for long, the Venetians sporadically severed the vital supply route. This closure meant not only that Crete became inaccessible to Ottoman supply vessels, but that provisions coming via the Aegean Sea could not reach Istanbul. Istanbul's massive and influential populace grew hungry and restless. Responding to the clamor, in 1648 and 1650 the Sublime Porte dispatched important officials to Izmir on urgent supply missions. In panicked and zealous pursuit of fruits and grains, these agents prohibited the French and other traders from securing valuable stocks. Furthermore, the Ottomans knew that since Crete sprawled across the sea route linking the Aegean Sea with the west, French, English, and Dutch ships could easily slip provisions to the embattled Venetians in Candia, no doubt at grossly inflated prices. Although Istanbul did not want to antagonize its French allies unnecessarily, Ottoman authorities needed to frustrate this smuggling operation, which threatened their besiegement of Candia. Thus, they carefully limited foodstuffs sold to the French and other foreigners. The Ottomans remained in this crisis situation at least until 1656 when Mehmet Köprülü came to power.

CAPRICIOUS AUTHORITIES

Brigandage in western Anatolia and tensions between rival trading states illuminate the regional crisis in Ottoman authority and resultant dangers and opportunities. In October 1650, the French ambassador complained that an Anatolian rebel active in the area had murdered a French merchant resident in Izmir.[37] Two and a half years later, the consul himself became a prey. A representative of a governor's assistant, a local sergeant at arms, and their band of brigands drew their swords and fell upon the French consul, François du Roure, and several accompanying merchants who were on excursion to Karataş, a suburb of Izmir.[38] They wounded du Roure, and stole some diamond-studded and inlaid ivory as well as money. Even at Izmir's very portal, Istanbul was unable to suppress the violence of Ottoman officials gone astray.

Rivalries among and between foreign states aggravated these perils. Early in 1650, competition between the hotly contentious English and French communities in Izmir boiled over when a certain Acılır, in the service of the English ambassador in Istanbul, Sir Thomas Bendysh, and several companions "swept down, halberds in hand, upon the house of the French consul," Jean Dupuy, forcing him to abandon his home and seek refuge, probably on a ship riding in the harbor.[39] The same ruffians allegedly also attacked and crippled a French vessel (perhaps the one sheltering the consul). The Ottoman government subsequently appointed a guard in order to protect the Frenchman.

This mid-century rivalry between the English and the French was not simply commercial. It reflected the complex and devious course of political and diplomatic affairs in England and France. The beheading of Charles I in 1649 and the consequent domestic uncertainties confused and made wary representatives of the English Levant Company. It is even unclear whether the

English ambassador in 1650, Bendysh, was a royalist or a par-
liamentarian, although it seems likely that he was fundamentally an opportunist who navigated the narrow course between
causes.[40] Whatever Bendysh's politics, Sir Henry Hyde's arrival
in Istanbul in 1650 threatened his authority. Hyde claimed to
be an extraordinary ambassador of Charles Stuart and enjoyed
the support of the French. Hyde's pretensions, at a time when
no one, including the perspicacious Venetians, knew what would
happen in England and how the English Company would fare
in that state's volatile politics, precipitated complicated maneuverings in the Ottoman capital and Bendysh's eventual triumph.
The resident ambassador masterfully exploited the blurring lines
of Ottoman and English authority in Istanbul and Izmir. In May
1650, he orchestrated Hyde's kidnapping in Istanbul and shipped
him to Izmir from whence, despite the endeavors of the French
ambassador to have him returned to Istanbul, he was dragged
off to England along with three other royalists where in the
following year he was tried and beheaded.[41]

This affair kindled the smoldering rivalries between the foreign communities of Izmir. Bendysh wrote of the charges, coun-
tercharges, and muddled inter- and intra-company belligerency
in which local Ottoman officials fully participated:

all the chief officers of the Janissaries were engaged against us; . . . the
French and [Hyde's] English party persuading them that Sr. Henry was not
gone but concealed among the English; hereupon the Agha of the Janissaries
seizing on two of Our Nation, . . . imprisoned them in his house. . . . Nor were
Our adversaries contented herewith, but sent thither a very strict command
for the seizing on the English Consul and Nation and delivering them into
the hands of the French, but they being timely advertised thereof by me,
got into an English ship in port, their standing upon their guard, till they
had seized on some sure considerable persons of the French Nation, as that
they were content to make an exchange, and set our men free.[42]

This passage exposes the freedoms, bafflements, rivalries, manipulations, and dangers of life in the new port city.

Laid over this bewildering swirl was an ever-present fear of
the Barbary corsairs, who at any time might descend upon the
city. In April 1636 Barnard, the English consul in Izmir, ad-

dressed a letter to his ambassador in which he related an incident, which began because the English ship *Concord* entered the Gulf of Izmir flying its colors while North African vessels looked on.[43] A corsair of Algiers became incensed at this apparent provocation and shot one of the *Concord*'s crewmen. When the consul protested this treatment to the *kadı*, the Ottoman official brusquely exclaimed that "these were unruly fellows not subject to his domain." In retribution, and also probably in fear, the consul, without allowing it to unload, dispatched the *Concord* directly to Istanbul. Half a league from Izmir, the vessel again unfurled its flag and fired a gun, an action that enraged the corsairs anew and inflamed the inhabitants of Izmir, so that "this beastly people were on a sudden all man uproar, and tumult upon the pretense of religion, raging that the Gawies [infidels] should dare to wear their Cross aloft in the port of the Grand Signeur." Barnard wrote that this fury continued for three or four days and that all of the consuls finally went together to the *kadı* and threatened to quit the city if their capitulations were not honored and their rights protected. The *kadı*, together with the principal men of the city, then "caused the Corsairs to be quiet and appeased the fury of the people."[44] This passage demonstrates not only the cultural chasm between foreigners and the native population in Izmir, but also the intense antipathy the corsairs provoked among western merchants dwelling in the city. Nor was this an isolated incident. The foreign community reacted in much the same way to the arrival of the Ottoman admiral (*kapudan paşa*) and his fleet. In 1631, the English consul in Izmir sent to Istanbul a detailed description of the tyrannies the admiral had perpetrated against foreigners in the port.[45]

Unfurling of flags and attacks by corsairs and Ottoman naval officials throughout the seventeenth century heightened tension in Izmir. In 1662 the French complained that brigands in the city prevented them from flying their flag in the Gulf, in 1663 janissaries from the *kapudan paşa*'s fleet indiscriminately attacked all of the consulates in Izmir, and in 1690 a brawl broke out between Algerian corsairs and French sailors.[46] When in this last incident a Frenchman killed one of the corsairs, the Algerians threatened a bloodbath against all western traders. Although such threats brought the Dutch, English, French, and Venetians together in a show of unity, such accord was rare. In commercial matters especially, ruthlessness was the rule.

FRANKS STREET

European merchants, who helped make the city of Izmir and carved out a commercial network in its hinterland, also turned the port into a cultural outpost of the Christian west. In the first decades of the seventeenth century, the site expanded physically and demographically as well as commercially. By the 1620s Christian homes, shops, and taverns snaked along the town's sea front, the physical symbol of an increasingly aloof enclave of Christian culture in an Islamic state.[47] The haughtiness of Franks Street's inhabitants was not only cultural. They also showed little interest in contributing to the physical beauty and protection of the city. Izmir's notables, fearing that the town's riches would attract Christian pirates and Muslim brigands, in 1607 decided to repair the inadequate fortifications and decrepit castle walls at their own expense.[48] When they solicited Venetian merchants for funds to help in the renovations, however, the Italians argued that their capitulations forbade contributing.[49] The Venetians also viewed the demand as extortion and, haunted by memories of their precarious condition on Chios, feared any action that might identify them with subject peoples and thereby undermine their privileges in Izmir.

While unwilling to contribute to the infrastructure or defense of the town, the foreigners of Franks Street built secure homes and warehouses for themselves. They also set out to construct churches in order to make their lives more homelike and further isolate them from their surroundings. The Islamic stricture against construction of new churches and synagogues, the fact that Izmir was predominantly Turkish, and the need for separate establishments for Catholics, Anglicans, Calvinists, Capuchins, and Jesuits complicated this endeavor. Yet Izmir had been the site of one of the seven Churches of the Apostles and as an important Byzantine city boasted numerous ruined churches, several of which Istanbul approved for renovation in the early seventeenth century.[50] Having obtained the *kadı* of Izmir's confirmation that a church had previously stood on a certain site and an assurance of protection against rioting Muslims, the Venetians began reconstructing one of these churches (perhaps the Church of St. George) in 1612.[51]

The Ottomans carefully established the location and size of a structure before consenting to the reconstruction of ancient churches. Even after the physical devastation of the earthquake of 1688, Christians could not rebuild without the authorization of Ottoman architects. In the case of the Church of St. Polycarpe, administered by the French consul, inhabited by the Capuchins, and leveled by an earthquake, the architects issued a permit specifying exactly how the church was to be rebuilt.[52] It was to be thirty-three cubits in length, nineteen in width, and thirteen in height. It was to have thirteen windows with thirteen glass plates, three guest rooms upstairs, and ten pillars and four doors on the ground floor.

Despite the government's caution, Turkish inhabitants of the town resented these Franks who undertook a "Christian renewal" program, insultingly sang psalms within earshot of Muslim worshipers, and snubbed the municipality. As early as 1605, the Venetians there objected against interference in their religious rituals.[53] The year before construction of the Church of St. George commenced, inhabitants of the town harassed worshipers in the "church of the Frank," and even after its renovation in 1618, the Latins continued to demand protection against local subjects.[54] Five years later, in 1623, a flurry of Christian complaints against the intrusion of townsmen into their place of worship induced Istanbul to condemn the Turkish mob, albeit ineffectively.[55]

These incidents provide a hint of the societal tensions accompanying Izmir's commercial and demographic growth, which continued apace. Although the great earthquake of 1688 initially discouraged the city's entrepreneurship, merchants soon realized that they could rebuild the devastated site in a style amenable to their foreign traditions and preferred tastes. In 1700 Izmir boasted two Greek, one Armenian, and three "Latin" churches and there remained no doubt that western culture had inundated this Islamic-Ottoman town. As the traveler Tournefort observed in 1700:

the Turks are seldom seen in the *Franks* Street, which is the whole Length of the City. When we are in this Street, we seem to be in *Christendom*; they speak nothing but Italian, French, English or Dutch there. Every body takes off his Hat, when he pays his respects to another. There one sees Capuchins, Jesuits, Recolets. The Speech of *Provence* shines there above all others, because there are more from *Provence* than any other parts. They sing publickly in the Churches; they sing Psalms, preach, and perform Divine Service there without any trouble; but then they have not sufficient Regard to the *Mahometans*, for the Taverns are open all Hours, Day and Night.[56]

Tournefort, arriving in Izmir during a tour of the east, felt almost that he had entered a European city. In a rare display of Frankish sympathy with Islamic culture, he even questions the impunity with which confident Christian merchants flaunted their misbeliefs and caroused drunkenly. If western merchants, over the fierce objections of natives, had intended in the early seventeenth century to turn this new commercial center into an outpost of western culture, by the turn of the eighteenth century they had succeeded.

7

A Colonial Port City

One of the Ottoman dynasty's primary concerns, in accordance with the religion upon which its legitimacy rested, was with the physical well-being of its inhabitants. This preoccupation meant that the crux of Ottoman economic policy was not, and could not have been, mercantile.[1] The authorities never grew preoccupied with imports and exports or in balances of trade as barometers of wealth; rather, the Ottomans sought to ensure adequate and dependable provisions for the various peoples within their domains. The populace of Istanbul itself was particularly well-placed. It shared the capital of this highly centralized state with a large bureaucracy to whom it could voice demands and dis-contents; thus, the people of this city enjoyed a special influence and the Sublime Porte sought to placate them by presenting to them the surpluses of the Black and Aegean sea coasts.[2] These regions served as Istanbul's hinterlands. Needs and desires from within the empire dictated the economic policies by which Istanbul administered the fertile coastal areas accessible to and controlled by it. International trade remained ancillary.

As long as they were able to do so, the Ottomans maintained these domestic priorities. For a period during the late sixteenth and seventeenth centuries, Istanbul with rare exception excluded foreign merchants from the Black Sea.[3] In the Aegean, which was open to the Mediterranean, sprinkled with innumerable islands, and thus difficult to police, the Ottomans sought merely to limit international commerce to commodities deemed nonessential or already abundant. Prohibited items varied according to place, time, and circumstance. Although smuggling was chronic, the Sublime Porte for much of the sixteenth century was able to restrain it and to transform the Aegean into an Ottoman lake responsive to Istanbul's requirements.

The sixteenth-century demography and geography of the western-Anatolian littoral physically conditioned Ottoman economic policy. No single port dominated trade. Rather, small active trading towns dotted the coast. The presence in western Anatolia of a number of river valleys feeding into a series of natural bays facilitated this preponderance of regional entrepôts; and the authorities strove to maintain the tapestry of unassuming settlements because the produce of western Anatolia consisted of valuable yet difficult-to-transport grains, fruits, and fibers. The decentralized network of ports provided quick access to the sea, thereby reducing greatly the cost of—and in fact making practicable—transport to Istanbul. To funnel such goods through a single terminal would have entailed long overland hauls as well as a regional concentration of population, which might compete with the capital city for locally grown foodstuffs and consequently defeat the network's chief purpose. Thus, both geographically and demographically the western-Anatolian coastline of the sixteenth century reflected Ottoman economic policies.

In the first decades of the seventeenth century, this system changed suddenly and dramatically as, within thirty years, the port of Izmir came to dominate the region commercially, economically, demographically, and even socially. This transformation can be quantified in various ways. In 1580 the settlement's population was about two thousand; by 1650 it had risen to thirty or forty thousand. In 1600 no European consuls were resident in Izmir; by 1620 the Dutch, English, French, and Venetians all had consular representation there. In 1580 the town was fundamentally Turkish; thirty years later large Armenian, Greek, and Jewish communities lived there. In 1604 the government collected almost twice as much customs from the town of Çeşme as from Izmir; by 1608, while there was no appreciable increase in the *total* customs revenue that western Anatolia generated, the distribution had been virtually reversed—Istanbul in the latter year collected far more in customs from Izmir than from˙any other port on the littoral. In the first years of the seventeenth century, then, the scattered commerce of western Anatolia, both domestic and international, collapsed onto Izmir.

Istanbul would have been happy, indeed it endeavored, to maintain its decentralized distributing web. The network's consolidation in Izmir, which began commercially but which also had far-reaching economic, social, and demographic ramifications, occurred principally because of the confluence of a regional crisis in western Anatolia (which created *conditions* that accommodated change) with a revolution in international commerce (which constituted the principal *impetus* for change). The latter phenomenon had taken a hundred years to transpire. It was born in the Portuguese discovery of an all-water route to Asia and grew to maturity in the relative success of the Dutch in severing the ancient spice road through the Middle East. Thus, when new and resurging commercial states—the Dutch, the English, and the French—attacked the Levantine market at the end of the sixteenth century, they found no exotica to exchange for their specie and cloths. Silks they did find; but merchants and companies (Armenian and Jew, Venetian and French) of long experience dominated the terminals of the caravan routes in Aleppo, Alexandria, and elsewhere; and the Atlantic seaboard companies not only found it difficult to crack their hegemony, but also found discouraging the voluminous tolls and regulations under which especially Aleppan merchants labored. It was in their search for alternatives to spices, to established emporiums, and to the well-traveled caravan roads from Persia that Izmir emerged as a trading center of international import.

Coincidentally, at the very moment new Levantine companies searched for new markets, new supplies, and new hubs for commerce, Istanbul momentarily lost its grasp over its western-Anatolian provinces. Musket-toting brigands terrorized town and country, with the more powerful establishing effective, if ephemeral, principalities. These *celâlı* rebels helped loosen Istanbul's hold over both the provisioning network and local officials. Customs collectors, janissaries, and other representatives of the Ottoman state became more willing to strike deals on their own initiatives, thereby undercutting (or at least redefining) the state's authority and depriving it of desperately needed revenues and foods. Consequently, the innovative and vigorous northern trading companies, looking for new commercial outlets and searching for ports in which their representatives could trade unencumbered with archaic mechanisms and a highly centralized authority, found both in Izmir and its hinterland. Within decades after the Dutch and English Levant companies were established, they had discovered this port's potential and were engaged in lively commerce there in cottons, wools, dried fruit, and other commodities of local provenance. By the mid-1620s, Armenian traders had perceived that a European-inspired commercial infrastructure in Izmir opened for them also an alternative to the Aleppan and Bursan caravan roads, which were smothered in tolls and regulations and which, in the case of Aleppo's approaches, Ottoman-Safavid conflict periodically obstructed. For these reasons, despite the lengthier overland trek through Persia and across the Anatolian plateau, silk quickly joined other commodities channeled through Izmir. This fabric so quickly and thoroughly dominated trade there that by 1630, which is approximately when western sources—principally travelers' accounts, and consular letters and reports—join Ottoman ones in our reconstruction of Izmir's history, observers assumed that disruptions in other silk routes wholly determined Izmir's commercial emergence. This explanation for Izmir's ascent, proclaimed in the correspondence of consuls and merchants and disproven in Ottoman sources, has held sway almost to the present day.

Whatever economic and social permutations Izmir and western Anatolia underwent in successive centuries, however great the rise in the volume of trade during the Age of Enlightenment, however profoundly Europeans influenced western-Anatolian society during the Age of Imperialism, the transformation that

determined the region as their arena and Izmir as their hub occurred when the settlement developed from a regional port into
an international entrepôt at the beginning of the seventeenth
century. More can be asserted. Although the ethnicity of its directors varied and its direction fluctuated in the eighteenth and
nineteenth centuries, the outlines of a western-inspired, and initially at least western-controlled, commercial network emerged
quickly after 1600 and, with it, the demographic, economic, and
social alterations associated with such penetration.[4]

The demographic changes were the most pronounced. Izmir
in 1580 was over eighty percent Turkish. While a small Greek
community lived in the town, there were neither Armenians
nor Jews. Small groups of these religious minorities lived scattered about the region, in Kuşadası, Manisa, Aydın, Chios,
and Çeşme; but Izmir itself had not drawn these commercially
sensitive groups. By 1630, circumstances had changed dramatically. Greeks from Chios, Urla, and elsewhere had joined their
brethren in Izmir. Jews from throughout western Anatolia, and
from more distant centers such as Salonica and Istanbul, had
migrated there and formed a community of some two-thousand
souls. A smaller, yet influential, assemblage of Armenians, some
from Aleppo and Persia, also had settled in the new city.

The motives for this sudden and rather massive dislocation
were many. The Armenians came principally because of the silk
trade; they quickly and effectively linked the port to an already
extensive trading diaspora that stretched from China to Amsterdam and beyond. The Jewish migratory wave, while somewhat
more complicated in origin, was also encouraged by the magnetic
pull of the growing commercial center. Most of these Jews had
migrated to the Ottoman empire from Iberia and Italy in the
previous century and had found employment in major commercial and industrial towns such as Aleppo, Istanbul, and, most
notably, the textile producing site of Salonica. By 1580, Salonica and other textile towns faced crises of supply, demand,
and competition from western manufactured cloths, and many
Jews who had found an economic niche in this industry searched
for new employment; some found it in Izmir. By 1620, most cus-

toms officials and tax farmers in the port were Jewish. By 1640, Jews also served as translators, factors, leather tanners, and jewelers. Although the third non-Muslim group in Izmir, the Greeks, already in the sixteenth century boasted a small settlement, an influx of perhaps four-thousand coreligionists in the early seventeenth century revitalized the ancient community.

Between 1580 and 1640 the non-Muslim settlement in Izmir increased tenfold and more, thereby producing a multi-ethnic, multi-religious, and multi-linguistic metropole. By the latter date, the port was well on its way to becoming the cosmopolitan cultural center with which the eighteenth- and nineteenth-century world associated it. The activities of European merchants were instrumental in this creation, just as they later were to be in other nonwestern or "colonial" port cities. In Calcutta, Manila, Batavia, and Singapore the European search for markets and marketable products drew those individuals—whether Indian, Chinese, Arab, Armenian, Jewish, or Greek—best able to serve, inform, and survive in a world of middlemen. In Izmir also Europeans attracted such people; and here as elsewhere their western associates benefited and eventually protected them.

Such social consequences of Izmir's ascent emerge more vividly through an examination of the movements of specific communities to the port. In sixteenth-century Manisa, one of the guilds associated with textile manufacturing enjoyed the privilege of purchasing the fleece that peasants and nomads brought to the town market. This symbiosis continued until, in the first decades of the seventeenth century, a shortage materialized, not because nomadic sheepherders had drifted elsewhere, or because sheep were dying, or because of a dispute between supplier and manufacturer, but because outside merchants had begun going directly to producers and giving more for fleece than the guilds of Manisa would, and perhaps could, pay. This disruption proved ruinous for native industry and both Jewish and Muslim textile workers threatened to abandon Manisa in search of more reliable and remunerative employment elsewhere.

Under different circumstances, perhaps such textile workers would have weathered this storm of innovations; perhaps, having few alternatives, they would have adapted to, even emulated, their new competitors.[5] Perhaps the Muslim workers eventually did some such thing. For the Jews, however, there was an option of lesser resistance and potentially great reward. This alternative was to join with those who were innovating, to integrate themselves into the western-inspired trading network radiating out of Izmir. For these intruders who possessed the opportunity, the capital, and the commercial acumen to penetrate the villages surrounding Manisa and purchase raw materials at their source were factors—sometimes Armenian or Jewish, sometimes (surprisingly) Venetian or French—of European merchants resident in the port city.

So, by 1625 or 1630 the demands of western merchants for goods and manpower and their ability to finance their operations already had brought severe dislocations to Izmir and its expanding hinterland. Their influence was demographic; Izmir within decades changed from town to city, from relative homogeneity to economic, ethnic, and religious diversity, from provincial to cosmopolitan, and from one among many in western Anatolia to one without peer. It also was economic; western Anatolia evolved from regional conduit to international supplier, from having a reasonably autonomous economy to partial integration into a larger economic system. Finally, the region became exposed to newly introduced crops, which in the long run would transform western-Anatolian agriculture.[6] Even in the seventeenth century, however, there is evidence that peasants responded to the demand for certain raw materials marketable or manufacturable in northwestern Europe.

There were of course sophisticated markets in western Anatolia before the seventeenth century. After the turn of the century, however, the demands and offerings of European merchants stationed in Izmir greatly accelerated and centralized economic diversification. Venetian involvement in the cotton trade documents this evolution. Although the city-state quickly succumbed to vigorous Dutch, English, and French competition, Venetian trade exhibited the characteristics of the typical superimposed network and bitter complaints to the Ottomans against the trading practices of the waning power's rivals facilitate reconstruction of the commercial web being spun across Izmir's hinterland. European merchants did not await cotton in Izmir, but sought it where it was produced. The considerable price, differential between the port, a market town becoming city, and regions of production made this movement to the interior profitable. By 1650, these activities had helped introduce new crops (such as tobacco) and seriously threatened production of others (such as sesame). Perhaps most indicative of the sweeping change underway was that by the 1620s speculation on cotton futures, of accepting goods or borrowing money against crops not yet in the soil, was common.

The Ottoman government understood that their western-Anatolian provisioning system was being undermined. It knew well that Istanbul was not as well supplied as previously, in part because Izmir was growing uncontrollably. Merchants of the capital city complained that they could not locate and buy essential provisions because "infidel" and non-native traders stealthily wandered about from village to village and bought commodities at "high prices"—high, of course, only to those accustomed to a regulated economy in thrall to Istanbul. To the European interloper, the merchandise seemed cheap.

During the first half of the seventeenth century, a sort of centrifugal evolution in Ottoman lines of authority destabilized western Anatolia's relations with Istanbul; it helped disrupt supplies, unleash brigands, and push people into new employment and domiciles. Izmir was formed in the midst of this upheaval, as European companies and merchants in search of goods and markets centered at the port a commercial network, which immediately began influencing the commercial, demographic, economic, industrial, and social make-up of the region. The town quickly became a cosmopolitan city acting like a magnet upon commercially sensitive communities and establishing itself as a rival to Istanbul for the people and products of its expanding hinterland. Seventeenth-century Izmir strikingly resembles Braudel's vision of the early-modern European city. He writes of "autonomous worlds" of "unparalleled freedom" that had "outwitted the territorial state" and pursued "an economic policy of their own." He proclaims that they ruled "their fields autocratically, regarding them as positive colonial worlds before there were such things," and asserts that they were "capable of breaking down obstacles and creating or recreating protective privileges."[7] The new city of Izmir conformed to this path first trodden by the European city; other nonwestern ports were to follow. By the nineteenth century a lattice of colonial port cities acting as conduits for wide hinterlands and following in broad outline the network constructed in seventeenth-century western Anatolia had been created. In many other ports, however, political upheavals followed this initial commercial transformation as Dutch, French, English, German, Italian, Portuguese, and Spanish colonials replaced commercial administrations with political ones. The surprising resiliency of the Ottomans, who clung to their political integrity into the twentieth century, preserved western Anatolia from a similar fate. Although the region fell increasingly under western economic influence, although the capitulations loomed ever more prominent in Ottoman administration, although Izmir became the chaotic outlet to a gushing river of trade, the changes of the eighteenth and nineteenth century were a matter of degree rather than kind. They arose naturally from the network created in the seventeenth century.

APPENDIX 1

The Registers of Foreigners

The great trading states of early-modern Europe—Venice, England, France, and the Netherlands—and their powerful and structurally fascinating Levantine companies and commercial colonies have received much attention from historians. The directors of these trading networks and the ambassadors, consuls, merchants, and factors who represented them produced masses of account books and correspondence, which scholars such as Masson, Steensgaard, Tenenti, and Wood have exploited in order to assess relative strengths, to compare structures, or simply to write narrative histories of one or another trading state.[1] In such works, historians also have utilized the recollections of European visitors to Levantine ports, a rich addition to often dry official papers. Such reminiscences have provided insights into the daily lives of western merchants (whom the travelers themselves often were) in the Levantine world.

While of much value, such histories share a rather obvious, but largely ignored, shortcoming. The merchant adventurers who populate these studies traded and dealt with the Ottomans. Although in the sixteenth and seventeenth centuries their fortunes depended heavily upon the policies and attitudes of this empire and its subjects, Ottomans have remained virtually voiceless. Admittedly, the administrative nature of Ottoman sources rule out a lively anecdotal narrative. Nevertheless, such

147

material exists and historiography has failed to incorporate it into its analyses. Consequently, however penetratingly scholars have interpreted western records, their results have been lamentably one-sided.

This intrinsic bias is particularly distressing because Ottoman sources, especially the registers of foreigners (*ecnebi defterleri*), are so revealing.[2] The registers consist of more than a hundred volumes of varying length, covering the period 1567 to 1922 and devoted to everyone from Americans to Venetians; in all, thirty-two states. And within these are individual registers concerning appointments (*nişans*), capitulations (*ahdnames*), and rescripts (*ahkâm*). The first of these classifications simply records Ottoman consent to various appointments of ambassadors, consuls, translators, and other "protected" individuals. This series helps ascertain the names and dates of appointments; and through it one can undertake quantitative studies of the numbers and ethno-religious make-up of Ottoman subjects taken under capitulatory umbrellas at different times and locations.

The second series records and confirms commercial understandings between the Ottoman state and other governments. While copies of these capitulations have been exhaustively (and misleadingly) exploited as the exclusive expression of the Ottoman role in Levantine commerce, interspersed with the capitulatory texts are decrees regarding their implementation. These rescripts make the registers of foreigners invaluable. When a foreign merchant, a consul, or an ambassador resident in the empire held a grievance against an Ottoman subject, a competing national, or even a compatriot, he could petition the Ottoman government through his ambassador, who presented the complaint to the Divan. Istanbul then forwarded firmans summarizing the problem and instructing the appropriate provincial officials— janissary captains, *kadıs*, beys, and *beylerbeyis*—to follow a prescribed action. Scribes copied these decrees into registers, and in this form they remain extant.

The topics of these documents are almost always commerce related. Through them emerge the policies of various states active in Levantine trade, the structures of companies representing them, and their day-to-day dealings with the Ottoman state and society. Both the Venetian bailo and the French ambassador, for example, regularly forwarded to the Sublime Porte their consuls' complaints against Ottoman customs officials in the empire's principal port cities. Both often claimed the protection of the Ottoman state when they collected grapes in order to produce wine. Both also petitioned against Barbary and other corsairs. Beyond these and other commonalities, however, lies the striking contrast that Venetians regularly petitioned against *rival* company officials, and Frenchmen against *French* company officials.

Venetian petitions echo the doge and Senate's realization that new states were carving out commercial networks in regions and among commodities that traditionally had been theirs. These infringements occurred both on sea—in the Dutch and English seizure of the carrying trade—and on land—in Atlantic seaboard penetration into cotton and wool producing areas along the Syrian, Balkan, and Anatolian littorals. When in the early seventeenth century these invaders broke the long Italian hegemony over such activities, the Venetians appealed to the central Ottoman government (an old trading partner) to protect their interests. Although the Venetians ultimately lost their campaign, the registers disclose how they employed their entrenched diplomatic corps to draft Ottoman aid and how this strategy failed in the face of superior company structures and growing opportunities for the new states to operate through Ottoman subjects who purposely misinterpreted, circumvented, or simply ignored orders emanating from the Sublime Porte.

Whereas the Venetians lashed out at rival trading states, the French utilized their right of petition to devour themselves. In the French registers, one encounters ambassadors undermining compatriot consuls, consuls demanding the capture of renegade French merchants, and merchants taking recourse to the rival Ottoman religio-legal system against their own superiors. Dozens of decrees addressed to Ottoman officials in the major Ottoman trading centers consider controversies between Frenchmen intent upon assisting the commerce not of the merchants of Marseilles or the French state, but only of themselves. The French merchant's ability to circumvent the authority of his directors and government—as well as his willingness to do so— derived from a commercial structure characterized in part by a consular system in which consulships were farmed out. While this structure tended toward anarchy, its laxity alone does not explain the opportunities that the Levantine environment provided for private initiative. Under what conditions could a merchant in Aleppo flout his consul's authority? Upon whose authority could he do so? How might a consul respond to such transgressions? What do these clashes reveal of the transparency of international trade? Its fluidity? Its scope? Its liabilities in the Ottoman milieu? The registers of foreigners not only help us recreate Ottoman administration of western commerce, but also guide us in framing and grappling with such questions.

The registers also aid us in specific issues of Levantine commercial history. Any complaint that western ambassadors, consuls, or merchants wanted to air before the Ottomans found its way into this source. Four categories of particular interest are piracy on the Mediterranean Sea, the activities of priests in the Ottoman empire, the internal system of revenue collection by which companies supported their overseas bureaucracies, and the physical presence of traders in the empire.

Piracy was unceasing in the seventeenth-century Mediterranean. Every trading state claimed in their capitulations Ottoman protection against corsairs, seizure of goods, and enslavement. Accordingly, pirates could not legally take refuge or sell contraband, captured vessels, or slaves in Ottoman ports; but they often did so. Maltese, Spanish, Uskok, Barbary, English, and others roamed and plundered quite freely. The clamor against such outrages was frequent and heated. The Venetian and Dubrovnikan registers in particular bristle with complaints against the Uskoks, a small and elusive band of brigands who operated off the Dalmatian coast and harassed Adriatic shipping and the city and surroundings of Dubrovnik.[3] Pertinent decrees elucidate where the Uskoks struck, which populations they affected, and, most interestingly, the diplomatic and military wranglings undertaken between Dubrovnikans, Ottomans, and Venetians over responsibility for their attacks and appropriate responses. The Venetians several times protested to the Sublime Porte that, despite Dubrovnikan accusations to the contrary, Venice was not in league with the Uskoks and, in fact, would welcome an Ottoman alliance in order to annihilate this persistent menace to shipping. At other times, the Dubrovnikans complained against Uskok raiders who, allegedly with Venetian collusion, burned their ships, leveled their orchards, and murdered or enslaved their populations. The two city-states promoted their interests in Istanbul not only in regard to the Uskoks. The struggle for commercial dominance in Ottoman Europe also is played out in the registers, as when ambassadors from Dubrovnik accused the Venetians of interfering in their lucrative salt monopoly.

Virtually every type of corsair swaggers through the pages of these registers. When pirates disrupted Venetian sea roads in the early seventeenth century, the bailo argued that the Ottomans did not properly police their coastal waters. Most often condemned were freebooters, who resembled the Uskoks but who operated off the coasts of southern Greece and the islands of the Aegean. These outlaws built small coastal vessels, darted en masse against larger ships, and towed them to the protection of the guns of Ottoman fortresses dotting the coasts and islands. The Venetian navy could not act unilaterally against such pirates, who sheltered in fortified bays and gulfs. The bailo was reduced to pleading with the Ottomans not only to punish these brigands and burn their boats, but also to discipline janissary captains who obligingly offered the marauders refuge under the cannon of fortresses and permitted the sale of contraband in nearby markets. The bailo also argued that these black market goods deflated the value of Venetian cargoes, at times so much that merchants on vessels that did escape the pirates' net found themselves unloading merchandise at ruinously low prices.

Ambassadors brought priests as well as pirates to the attention of Ottoman officials, not to destroy but to protect. Pirates meandered across the seas in search of plunder; priests wandered across the empire in pilgrimage and in order to maintain contacts with Christian dwellers in this Islamic state. During the seventeenth century, the French in particular sought to expand Catholic jurisdiction over holy sites in Jerusalem and its surroundings. They directed their endeavors not so much against Muslims as against their Greek Orthodox rivals. The registers often refer to travel and church renovation permits, and to intrigues and squabbles between monks and priests over shrines and churches in Jerusalem, Bethlehem, and elsewhere. The French supervised Capuchin and Jesuit priests not only in Palestine: wherever French merchants operated, men of the frock followed. Through the registers, one sees priests fanning out along merchant networks in the Balkans and Anatolia as well as in Arab lands.

In the nineteenth century, Austro-Hungarian and French protection of Catholic, and Russian protection of the Greek Orthodox became a fiery issue as the Great Powers used the excuse of protecting minorities to squeeze the declining Ottoman empire. Two centuries earlier, however, Dubrovnik more than France projected itself as protector of Catholics. Perhaps because of the city-state's unique status as a vassal, Dubrovnikan priests freely wandered from town to town in Ottoman Europe and preached to Latin worshipers. The registers help trace their movements, detail the conditions under which they operated, and reveal Ottoman attitudes toward them.

While certain European states and companies accepted their obligation to support and propagate Christianity, they also sustained the diplomatic and bureaucratic structures that supported their commerce. In order to compete in the empire, ambassadors consulted regularly with the Divan and other authorities in Istanbul, and consuls and merchants mingled with local officials and notables in the provinces. While the registers prove that a trading community could, and often did, circumvent the wishes of one or another Ottoman authority, they also vividly demonstrate that in order to flourish in the Ottoman milieu, merchants needed the acquiescence, even the support, of some segment of the Ottoman bureaucracy. This dependency, often overlooked, is most apparent in the question of consulage.

Company officials and diplomatic corps exacted this 1 or 2 percent surcharge upon compatriot merchants. The consulage on all goods carried under a certain flag usually belonged to representatives of that banner. Thus, duties on Spanish, Flemish, Portuguese, Sicilian, sometimes even Venetian goods shipped on English vessels went to English officials. The surcharge on such commodities was called the "strangers consulage," over which king and company or ambassador and consul sometimes fought. Their wranglings have been described often.[4]

Never discussed or even mentioned, however, is that without the consent of Istanbul and/or Ottoman customs officials, no one could collect anything. Even after such acquiescence, the empire still decided into whose hands the revenue actually fell. Foreign merchants were as reluctant to deliver these surcharges to their own directors as they were to pay customs to the Ottomans. As the registers make apparent, they endeavored to circumvent the consulage. French officials in particular could not rely on their merchants. They received consulage only when Ottoman officials collected it for them. Venetian officials, meanwhile, sometimes lost the cooperation of provincial authorities, as customs collectors gave consulage collected from Venetian merchants to their Dutch or English competitors.

While Venice's great rivals on the sea were Atlantic seaboard states, on the overland route between Venice and Istanbul they battled Armenians, Dubrovnikans, Greeks and Jews, who argued that the system of consulage applied only to commodities carried on vessels with hoisted flags and refused to pay this surcharge on goods caravaned across the Balkans. Here also, the Venetians depended upon the goodwill of Istanbul and its ability to control the extremities of its empire in order to collect these dues.

The registers suggest affirmative answers to important questions regarding all foreign traders. In regard to the Venetians, were the attitude and authority of the Ottoman bureaucracy critical to the city-state's loss of trade? Was Venetian decline linked to the contemporaneous transformation of Ottoman administration and society? Was the relationship between central and provincial Ottoman officials often acrimonious and did innovative foreign states and companies astutely play them off against each other while the Venetians continued an increasingly sterile dependence upon central Ottoman authorities?[5]

Finally, these registers, through the eyes of outsiders, put the European enclave colonies on display. They illustrate where merchants were active, what materials they specialized in, how and where they rented or bought storehouses and living quarters. They identify the taxes they paid and demonstrate how the Ottomans made them pay them. As foreigners, merchants were not liable to the head tax (*cizye*). Since their residency often was long and since they tended to fraternize with Ottoman Christians and Jews, however, local officials sometimes perceived them as subjects and sought to register them as such. To Ottoman tax farmers, this endeavor was a logical extension of their system of administration and taxation. To foreign merchants, it constituted an intolerable harassment.

Although the registers offer an occasional glimpse into diplomatic and political relations between the Ottomans and western Europe, their principal importance lies in the commercial sphere. They effectively sweep away the perception of the vast empire to the east as static and impenetrable and indicate the Ottomans' critical influence in eastern Mediterranean trade. Companies, ambassadors, consuls, merchants, and factors did contend daily with Ottoman officials and subjects; their ability to adapt to a vigorous and evolving economy and society, to appeal to an appropriate authority, and to grasp an emerging opportunity delineated and in large measure defined the destiny of their commerce in the Levant.

APPENDIX 2

Revenue from the Kaza of Izmir, 1575–1576

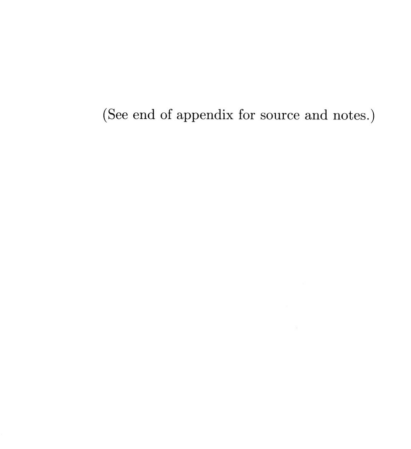

(See end of appendix for source and notes.)

Village	Çift		Nim Çift		Bennak	
	Taxpayers	Akçe	Taxpayers	Akçe	Taxpayers	Akçe
1 Izmir	–	–	–	–	–	–
2 Gümüldere	2	66	30	495	8	96
3 Mesaveli	2	66	28	462	22	264
4 Urba	3	99	37	592	65	780
5 Timurcilu	6	198	34	561	13	156
6 Denizliburnu	7	264	39	646	11	132
7 Malkoç	–	–	3	82.5	3	36
8 Omuzlu	3	99	24	396	54	648
9 Tahtalu-i Kebir	1	33	24	396	96	1,152
10 Tahtalu-i Sağır	–	–	–	–	53	636
11 Akçık Kebir	3	99	13	221	15	180
12 Akçık Sağır	–	–	4	66	7	84
13 Palamud	–	–	2	33	–	–
14 Geldinmen	2	66	34	561	39	468
15 Seki	4	132	75	1,237.5	18	216
16 Buladı	5	165	28	459	24	288
17 Gökbeyan	–	–	25	412.5	34	408
18 Sa'ilkassa	5	165	16	265	13	156
19 Eşen	8	264	70	1,155	41	492
20 Oğlanas	3	99	6	99	4	48
21 Mande	6	198	27	445	131	1,772
22 Burunak	–	–	3	49.5	90	1,080
23 Bayraklu	–	–	15	255	27	324
24 Hamıdlu	1	33	22	396	11	132
25 Haciler	–	–	20	330	8	96
26 Goğulca	1	33	1	16.5	9	108
27 Özeroğlu	8	264	45	742	23	276
28 Kıyaş	1	33	16	264	29	348
29 Karacadağ	–	–	52	858	9	108
30 Kesri	4	132	45	742.5	17	204
31 Suluağaç	3	99	15	247	21	252
32 Camlu	2	66	84	1,386	167	1,524
33 Gökyaka	6	198	29	478	35	420
34 Reb'kordan	–	–	5	82	46	552
35 Kazanacak	–	–	3	49.5	20	240
36 Ilıca	2	66	5	82.5	34	406
37 Dere	–	–	–	–	33	296
38 Haşirler	–	–	1	16.5	16	192
39 Deryanda	39[a]	194	–	–	18	216
40 Unnamed	16[a]	96	–	–	3	36
41 Aymerdoğan	–	–	21	346	14	168
42 Boynuzseker	1	33	4	66	50	600
43 Balıhun	–	–	22	363	77	724
44 Çağış	8	264	18	297	2	24
Total	152	3,524	945	15,651.5	1,410	16,338
Percentage	3		21		31	

	Mücerred		Total		Wheat		Barley	
Village	Taxpayers	Akçe	Taxpayers	Revenue	Bushels	Akçe	Bushels	Akçe
1	–	–	658	31,040	35	3,920	50	3,200
2	24	144	64	32,000	50	5,600	150	9,600
3	31	181	86/83[b]	29,418	15	1,680	35	2,240
4	78	468	181/182	27,687	35	3,960	60	3,840
5	23	128	77/76	25,000	18	2,016	45	2,880
6	78	468	139/135	17,650	3	336	6	384
7	2	12	9/8	7,816	5	560	11	704
8	103	618	182/184	11,650	18	2,016	25	1,600
9	115	690	233/236	15,530	15	1,680	30	1,920
10	50	300	104/103	20,302	40	4,480	60	3,840
11	27	162	62/58	8,252	15	1,680	20	1,280
12	1	6	12	2,000	3	336	7	448
13	–	–	2	6,000	15	1,600	30	1,920
14	37	222	123/112	17,999	30	3,360	75	4,800
15	45	270	161/142	17,200	25	2,800	37	2,361
16	40	240	104/97	14,500	8	896	37	1,792
17	55	330	112/114	7,875	7	784	15	960
18	18	108	52	9,700	25	2,800	35	2,240
19	72	432	195/191	50,250	5	560	7	448
20	6	36	19	13,416	45	5,040	8	512
21	244	1,664	413/408	23,495	50	5,600	32	2,068
22	113	678	214/206	17,466	17	1,904	32	2,048
23	64	768	115/106	9,110	10	1,120	7	448
24	30	180	69/64	8,151	11	1,232	20	1,280
25	21	126	51/49	7,682	8	896	17	1,088
26	7	42	19/18	2,886	2	224	5	320
27	60	360	143/136	31,750	50	5,600	60	3,940
28	20	120	64/66	27,500	55	6,160	110	7,040
29	36	216	99/97	33,570	85	9,520	150	6,400
30	34	204	105/100	11,000	18	2,016	20	1,280
31	46	276	97/85	12,000	17	1,904	28	1,792
32	130	780	351/383	38,712	45	5,040	75	4,800
33	45	270	115	11,030	15	1,680	24	1,536
34	59	354	110	6,780	11	1,232	15	960
35	29	147	51/52	3,572	12	1,344	12	768
36	62	372	104/103	7,000	12	1,344	15	960
37	42	252	76/75	2,228	3	336	6	384
38	24	144	41	8,000	15	1,680	30	1,920
39	21	210	92/78	22,000	55	6,160	100	6,400
40	7	42	26	1,431	30	3,360	60	3,624
41	24	144	60/59	36,000	60	6,720	130	7,320
42	47	262	98/102	31,000	61	6,632	131	8,384
43	75	450	212/174	30,937	55	6,162	125	8,000
44	4	24	32	9,100	20	2,240	35	2,240
Total	2,049	12,900	5332/5213	757,685	1,129	126,210	1,982	121,969
Percentage	45							

Village	Legumes	Cotton	Garden Vegetables	Culinary Vegetables	Dried Fruits	Olives	Figs and Other Fruits
1	2,000	800	50	3,000	9,605	1,500	1,500
2	2,500	1,000	900	25	1,580	1,700	700
3	480	200	10	40	13,433	147	150
4	1,200	300	50	100	11,670	300	50
5	2,013	500	80	560	850	10,000	150
6	400	300	15	$-^d$	4,600	3,443	–
7	500	50	15	10	412	799	200
8	290	256^c	99^c	254	2,255	310	50
9	150	55	70	25	5,000	50	71
10	341	152	15	40	5,500	300	200
11	101	–	–	–	–	1,200	500
12	260	50	10	$-^d$	386	100	20
13	200	50	207	15	–	–	–
14	836	115	27	25	225	3,200	2,000
15	480	329	50	30	1,200	2,500	500
16	285	50	25	–	1,500	2,500	250
17	250	55	20	15	225	1,500	350
18	217	50	25	–	664	1,862	653
19	1,000	300	186	470	$37,000^d$	30	–
20	1,075	–	–	$-^d$	–	10	–
21	315	36	50	55	6,398	1,120	50
22	356	20	15	13	4,348	150	50
23	129	33	215	25	4,093	25	20
24	120	40^c	15^c	10	2,219	600	524
25	100	11^c	4^c	41	2,981	219	58
26	60	18^c	7^c	27	985	118	25
27	1,215	183^c	67^c	175	9,000	3,000	1,000
28	2,480	172	14	50	2,900	150	100
29	1,600	150	55	150	5,000	500	250
30	1,009	650	17	217	1,000	100	150
31	490	650	15	23	4,204	100	200
32	2,212	304	300	323	3,173	5,550	2,000
33	510	200	25	50	1,865	360	57
34	517	25	17	35	1,512	60	115
35	250	32	15	25	150	15	20
36	800	25	28	15	1,500	26	15
37	300	13	36	25	$-^d$	50	40
38	550	25	15	150	200	200	–
39	1,825	66	90	56	1,846	411^c	116^c
40	580	173	116	–	301	55^d	55^d
41	325	450	120	32	12,000	470	500
42	783	170	66	152	10,000	608^c	172^c
43	1,400	620	55	220	5,000	866^c	244^c
44	425	325	25	35	600	150	100
Total	32,929	9,003	3,236	6,513	177,380	46,354	13,205

Village	Citrus Fruits	Mohair	Hemp	Clover	Bee-hives	Mulberry Leaves	Acorns	Sheep	Fisheries	Turnips, Radishes
1	257	200	–	392	300	150	–	–	–	–
2	7[d]	96	550	–	510	–	17	1,500	–	–
3	25	50	–	–	33	–	–	100	–	–
4	25	–	–	–	200	–	–	650	230	–
5	–	–	–	–	50	–	–	450	–	150
6	10	40	–	–	200	19	–	60	–	–
7	20	20	15	–	20	45	–	30	360	–
8	15	55[c]	–	–	167	–	–	200	–	–
9	25	25	–	–	92	–	–	100	–	–
10	55	–	–	–	155	–	–	150	–	–
11	10	–	–	–	10	25	10	60	–	–
12	6	–	–	–	5	10	10	10	–	–
13	15	30	–	–	–	–	–	25	–	–
14	50	20	–	–	15	–	–	228	–	–
15	60	40	–	–	600	–	–	150	–	–
16	–	15	20	–	30	–	–	150	–	–
17	–	21	–	–	37	–	–	31	–	–
18	–	37	–	–	22	–	–	25	–	–
19	–	70	–	–	172	–	–	144	–	–
20	15	50	–	–	30	–	–	100	–	–
21	25	25	–	–	139	–	–	220	–	–
22	50	–	15	–	200	–	–	55	–	–
23	–	–	–	–	15	–	–	24	–	–
24	25	–	–	–	25	–	–	45	–	–
25	25	–	–	–	20	–	–	15	–	–
26	15	–	–	–	25	–	–	11	–	–
27	20	–	15	–	–	–	151	25	–	–
28	15	50	58	–	104	–	–	221	–	–
29	–	–	–	–	1,200	–	–	380	–	–
30	–	–	257	–	500	–	–	866	–	–
31	–	–	–	–	15	–	–	25	–	–
32	–	125	–	–	476	–	50	105	–	–
33	–	15	–	–	20	20	–	150	–	–
34	–	–	–	–	50	–	–	125	–	–
35	–	–	–	–	10	–	–	45	–	–
36	–	–	–	–	13	–	–	220	–	–
37	–	–	–	–	7	–	–	15	–	–
38	–	–	–	–	12	–	–	200	–	–
39	–	15	–	–	–	–	–	25	10	–
40	–	–	–	–	189[d]	–	–	55	–	–
41	–	235	273	–	250	–	–	–	–	–
42	–	150	30	–	–	–	–	50	–	–
43	–	114	–	–	1,260	–	–	600	–	–
44	50	–	50	–	251	–	–	350	–	–
Total	820	1,498	1,283	392	7,429	269	238	7,990	600	150

Village	Sumac Leaves	Imperial Olives[e]	Pears	Chest-nuts	Legal Decisions[f]	Registrations[g]	Fines and Other Dues[h]	Marriage Tax[j]
1	–	–	–	–	1,000	2,133	131	–
2	–	–	–	–	1,397	2,500	1,718	–
3	–	–	–	–	500	2,540	297	120
4	–	–	–	–	200	1,000	236	150
5	100	–	–	–	900	1,012	127	180
6	–	500	–	–	2,294	1,000	1,318	200
7	60	–	–	–	2,000	1,500	172	60
8	–	–	–	–	1,500	500	57	120
9	–	–	–	–	839	1,000	1,410[d]	120
10	–	–	–	–	1,445	1,500	558	120
11	30	–	–	–	1,259	500	90	180
12	–	–	–	–	30	40	36	30
13	–	–	–	–	100	80	35	30
14	–	–	–	–	525	500	352	120
15	–	–	–	–	2,000	1,500	211	120
16	–	–	–	–	1,500	3,500	262	120
17	–	–	45	–	615	1,200	128	60
18	–	–	–	–	44[c]	56[c]	91	120
19	–	–	–	–	657	1,000	197	300
20	–	–	–	–	2,200	150	157	60
21	–	–	–	–	250	750	215	200
22	–	–	–	–	150	171	393	60
23	–	–	–	–	266	720	420	60
24	–	–	–	–	95	105	165	90
25	–	–	–	–	375	500	419	120
26	–	–	–	–	200	240	302	60
27	250	–	–	–	2,500	2,000	159	120
28	–	–	–	–	800	700	1,591	60
29	440	–	–	–	300	2,165	1,908	150
30	–	–	–	–	150	1,000	256	210
31	–	–	–	115	500	250	315	60
32	150	–	–	–	3,500	3,000	718	450
33	50	–	500	–	250	251	878	60
34	–	–	–	–	100	115	334	60
35	–	–	–	–	100	150	120	30
36	–	–	–	–	150	111	250/680[i]	60
37	–	–	–	–	55	25	[ ]/474[d,i]	30
38	–	–	–	–	585	1,200	400/514[i]	30
39	–	–	–	–	–	–	1,057	270
40	–	–	–	–	1,224	1,000	53	120
41	–	–	–	–	730	1,600	80	182
42	–	–	–	–	100	100	82	210
43	100	–	–	–	1,000	2,300	221	285
44	–	–	–	–	350	907	94	350
Total	1,180	500	545	115	34,735	42,571	19,681	5,537

Village	*Deştvane*	Mills		Ruined Mills	Olive Mills		Wind Mills		Flour Mills	
		No.	*Akçe*	Mills	No.	*Akçe*	No.	*Akçe*	No.	*Akçe*
1	–	–	–	4	–	–	–	–	–	–
2	–	–	–	–	3	36	–	–	–	–
3	840	–	–	–	–	–	–	–	–	–
4	295	4	120	–	–	–	–	–	–	–
5	320	–	–	–	5	60	6	144	–	–
6	500	–	–	–	15	180	10	250	–	–
7	50	–	–	–	12	36	2	48	–	–
8	150	–	–	–	–	–	–	–	–	–
9	550	4	150	–	–	–	–	–	–	–
10	200	–	–	–	–	–	–	–	–	–
11	260	10	150	–	2	24	1	24	–	–
12	5	–	–	–	–	–	–	–	–	–
13	10	–	–	–	–	–	–	–	–	–
14	200	–	–	–	1	12	3	73	–	–
15	200	–	–	–	12	144	–	–	2	60
16	350	–	–	–	8	108	–	–	–	–
17	350	–	–	–	2	24	–	–	–	–
18	100	–	–	–	–	–	–	–	–	–
19	3,900	$11/9^k$	$330/540^k$	–	–	–	–	–	–	–
20	100	7	420	–	–	–	–	–	–	–
21	1,000	14	420	–	–	–	–	–	–	–
22	151	–	–	–	–	–	–	–	–	–
23	150	–	–	–	–	–	–	–	–	–
24	300	–	–	–	–	–	–	–	–	–
25	200	–	–	–	–	–	–	–	–	–
26	50	–	–	–	–	–	–	–	–	–
27	500	3	90	–	4	48	–	–	–	–
28	300	2	90	–	–	–	–	–	–	–
29	300	$16/10^k$	$960/300^k$	–	–	–	–	–	–	–
30	300	3	90	–	–	–	–	–	–	–
31	100	2	60	1	–	–	–	–	–	–
32	1,800	–	–	–	6	72	–	–	–	–
33	250	3	180	–	–	–	–	–	–	–
34	60	7	210	–	–	–	–	–	–	–
35	25	–	–	–	–	–	–	–	–	–
36	150	–	–	–	–	–	–	–	–	–
37	100	–	–	–	–	–	–	–	–	–
38	100	–	–	–	–	–	–	–	–	–
39	300	$14/1^k$	$840/30^k$	–	–	–	–	–	–	–
40	500	$10/3^k$	$600/90^k$	–	–	–	–	–	–	–
41	100	–	–	–	–	–	–	–	–	–
42	600	–	–	–	5	50	–	–	–	–
43	400	–	–	–	–	–	–	–	–	–
44	215	–	–	–	–	–	–	–	–	–
Total	16,331	133	5,670	5	75	794	22	539	2	60

SOURCE

BA, TT 537, pp. 8–86. All revenue is in *akçes*. These tables are discussed more fully in Daniel Goffman, "Izmir as a Commercial Center: The Impact of Western Trade on an Ottoman Port (1570–1650)" (Ph.D. diss., University of Chicago, 1985), pp. 40–69.

NOTES

[a] Not included in totals because of special status as *kürekçi* (cultivators of rice).

[b] The first of the figures refers to the number of *nefer*s or taxpayers whom the scribe cited for the village, the second refers to the number of *çift* and *nim-çift* holders, *bennak*s, and *mücerred*s whom I noted for the village.

[c] In isolated cases, the surveyor lumped together crops that normally were separated. For instance, in the village of Omuzlu, cotton and garden vegetables were combined. In such cases, I have tabulated the percentages of the two revenue-producing items in the villages in which they were cited separately and used those figures to estimate the revenue produced by each of the two crops.

[d] I am unsure of the amounts of these crops. Where estimates are present, I arrived at them by adding up the total of all other revenue in the village and subtracting it from the stated total.

[e] There apparently was an olive grove in the public domain (*hassa*) in the village of Denizliburnu.

[f] In the survey, this heading is *resm-i zemin ve hakk-il-kara*. It refers to two separate taxes. The first also was called the *dönüm resmi*. It was a land tax assessed on agricultural lands cultivated in addition to those categorized under the *çift* and *nim-çift*. The *hakk-il-karar* usually is identical to the *tapu resmi*, but since the *resm-i tapu-i zemin* also is listed in this survey (see note g), perhaps it refers to the income the authorities derived from the registration of the lands of the *resm-i zemin*.

[g] This is the *resm-i tapu-i zemin ve zemin-i hane*, or the tax on the registration of lands and buildings. They were dues paid for certification of possession.

[h] The listing of "fines and others dues" lumped together various items that varied from village to village. The most common were *cürm-i cinâyet, badihava, yava, kaçgun, resm-i duhan, resm-i kışlak,* and *resm-i otlak-i yürükan-i kışlakçıyan.* The first four refer to fines in payment for various unlawful acts. The *cürm-i cinâyet* were payments for crimes, including murder, of a serious nature; the *badihava* paid for lesser infringements; the *yava* was a dues paid to *sipahis* for stray or runaway animals; and the *kaçgun* or *resm-i kaçgun* refers to the fine taken when animals were allowed to wander untethered over village pasturage or farmland. *Kaçgun* probably was directed specifically toward the nomadic element. The term also may refer to money earned from such animals whose owners never claimed them. The last three terms refer to dues taken in return for grazing rights. The *resm-i duhan* was a tax that temporary settlers—nomads or wandering peasant youth—paid when they grazed an area. These people were known as *hariç-raiyyet.* The *resm-i kışlak* was collected from the villagers for the right to use land that produced winter fodder and water. This due also was known as *kışlakiye.* Finally, the *resm-i otlak-i yürükan-i kışlakçıyan* was paid by Turkoman nomads availing themselves of grazing lands in valleys during the winter months. All of these dues were combined in the *tahrir* register and no pattern linking their assessments to the size or prosperity of the villages is immediately discernible. On these terms, see Barkan, *XV. ve XVI. asırlarda Osmanlı imparatorluğunda ziraî ekonominin;* İnalcık, "Osmanlılar'da raiyyet rüsûmu," esp. p. 595; and İnalcık, ed. *Hicrî 835 tarihli,* p. xxxciv.

[i] In these cases, the *cürm-i cinâyet* has been given a separate category. The first figure is the cited revenue for all fines other than this (see note h) and the second is the *cürm-i cinâyet* doubled because it is in these cases called *nısf-i* (or one-half) *cürm-i cinâyet.*

[j] The *resm-i arusane* was paid for a marriage certificate.

[k] These give two categories of *asiyab* without stating why they were separated.

NOTES

CHAPTER ONE

1. *Civilization and Capitalism, 15th–18th Century*, trans. Siân Reynolds (New York: William Collins, 1984), vol. 3: *The Perspective of the World*, pp. 469–71.
2. Elizabeth A. Zachariadou, *Trade and Crusade: Venetian Crete and the Emirates of Menteshe and Aydın (1300–1415)* (Venice: Library of the Hellenic Institute of Byzantine and Post-Byzantine Studies, 1983), pp. 125–31. See also Speros Vryonis, Jr., *The Decline of Medieval Hellenism in Asia Minor and the Process of Islamization from the Eleventh through the Fifteenth Century* (Berkeley and Los Angeles: University of California Press, 1971); Paul Lemerle, *L'Emirat d'Aydın, Byzance, et l'Occident: Recherche sur 'La Geste d'Umur Pacha'* (Paris: Presses Universitaires de France, 1957); Helene Ahrweiler, "L'histoire et la géographie de la région de Smyrne entre les deux occupations Turques," *Traveaux et mémoires* 1 (1965): 1–204; and Himmet Akın, *Aydın oğulları tarihi hakkında bir araştırma* (Ankara: Ankara Üniversitesi, 1946).
3. See Edward D. Sokol, *Tamerlane* (Lawrence, Kansas: Coronado Press, 1977), pp. 180–83.
4. On the period in general, see Deno Geanakoplos, "Byzantium and the Crusades, 1354–1453," in *A History of the Crusades*, ed. Kenneth Setton, 2d ed., 4 vols. (Madison: University of Wisconsin Press, 1975), vol. 3: *The Fourteenth and Fifteenth Centuries*, pp. 69–103. See also Halil İnalcık, *The Ottoman Empire: The Classical Age, 1300–1600* (London: Weidenfeld and Nicolson, 1973), chap. 3; Stanford Shaw, *History of the Ottoman Empire and Modern Turkey*, 2 vols. (Cambridge: Cambridge

University Press, 1976), vol. 1: *Empire of the Gazis: The Rise and Decline of the Ottoman Empire, 1280–1808*, chap. 7; and Paul Wittek, "De la défaite d'Ankara à la prise de Constantinople," *Revue des Etudes Islamiques* 12 (1938): 1–34.

5. Christopher de' Buondelmonti, *Description des iles de l'archipel grec*, trans. Emile Legrand (Paris: Leroux, 1897), p. 226.

6. Akın, *Aydın oğulları tarihi*, pp. 63–82 and I. Melikoff, "Aydinoghlu" and "Djunayd," *EI*^{2}.

7. Necmi Ülker, "The Rise of Izmir, 1688–1740" (Ph.D. diss., University of Michigan, 1974), p. 20.

8. BBA, TT 148 and 537.

9. On Bursa, see Haim Gerber, *Economy and Society in an Ottoman City: Bursa, 1600-1700* (Jerusalem: Hebrew University Press, 1988), pp. 3–4. On Istanbul's boat traffic, see Cengiz Orhonlu, "Istanbul'da kayıkçılık ve kayık işletmeciliği," *Tarih Dergisi* 21(1966): 109–34; rpt. *Osmanlı imparatorluğunda şehircilik ve ulaşım üzerine araştırmalar*, ed. Salih Özbaran (Izmir: Ticaret Matbaacılık T.A.Ş, 1984), pp. 83–103.

10. Halil İnalcık, "Bursa and the Commerce of the Levant," *Journal of the Economic and Social History of the Orient* 3(1960): 131–47; and "Bursa: XV. asır sanayi ve ticaret tarihine dair vesikalar," *Belleten* 24 (1960): 47 and 50.

11. BBA, TT 148, p. 12; and TT 537, p. 14.

12. Ömer-Lûtfi Barkan, "Price Revolution of the Sixteenth Century: A Turning Point in the Economic History of the Near East," *International Journal of Middle East Studies* 6 (1975): 4–5.

13. H. Lewis, "Anadolu," *EI*^{2}.

14. For a discussion of the protection model in the European context, see Douglass C. North and Robert Paul Thomas, *The Rise of the Western World: A New Economic History* (Cambridge: Cambridge University Press, 1973), chap. 1.

15. BBA, TT 148, p. 10. The remainder of this chapter is largely a distillation and interpretation of TT 148 and TT 537. See also Appendix 2. On this series of registers, see Atillâ Çetin, *Başbakanlık arşivi kılavuzu* (Istanbul: Enderun Kitabevi, 1979), pp. 83–111; and Heath Lowry, "The Ottoman Liva Kanunnames contained in the Defter-i Hakanî," *Journal of Ottoman Studies* 2 (1981): 43–74. On the knotty problem of household multipliers, see Géza Dávid, "The Age of Unmarried Male Children in the *Tahrir-Defters* (Notes on the Coefficient)," *Acta Orientalie Academiae Scientiarum Hung.* 31 (1977): 347–57; and Leila Erder, "Measurement of Preindustrial Population Changes: The Ottoman Empire from the 15th to the 17th Century," *Middle Eastern Studies* 11 (1975): 294–99. Heath Lowry provocatively questions the methodologies behind all of these works in "The Ottoman Tahrir-Defterleri as a Source for Social and Economic History: Pitfalls and Limitations," (pa-

per presented at the Fourth International Congress on the Social and Economic History of Turkey [1071–1922], Munich, 4–8 August 1986). The brief synthesis that follows tries to keep these limitations in mind. A more detailed analysis and methodological discussion of BBA, TT 148 and 537, dealing with the *kaza* of Izmir, is in Daniel Goffman, "Izmir as a Commercial Center: The Impact of Western Trade on an Ottoman Port, 1570–1650" (Ph.D. diss., University of Chicago, 1985), pp. 15–78.

16. This quarter alone was named a *cemaat* rather than a *mahalle*. It has been suggested that such a designation indicates a recently established area that has not been fully integrated into the municipality. Yet, it should not be used indiscriminately in this way. In 1575–76, the non-Muslim district in Izmir still was "cemaat-i gebran" despite at least fifty years of habitation.

17. BBA, TT 148, p. 12.

18. BBA, TT 148, p. 12. Suraiya Faroqhi in her "Sixteenth Century Periodic Markets in Various Anatolian Sancaks: İcel, Hamid, Karahisar-i Sahib, Kütahya, Aydın, and Menteşe," *Journal of the Economic and Social History of the Orient* 22 (1979): 38–39 traces the existence and growth of market economies through the presence of market dues (*bac-i pazar*) and taxes on superintendants of markets (*ihtisabiye*). See also Faroqhi's *Towns and Townsmen of Ottoman Anatolia: Trade, Crafts and Food Production in an Urban Setting, 1520–1650* (Cambridge: Cambridge University Press, 1984), pp. 69–71.

19. BBA, TT 148, p. 12.

20. On Izmir's customs, see BBA, TT 148, p. 12.

21. Andrew Hess, "The Battle of Lepanto and Its Place in Mediterranean History," *Past and Present* 57 (1972): 54–57.

22. Faroqhi, *Towns and Townsmen*, p. 13.

23. It is possible, although unlikely, that a larger Greek, or Armenian or Jewish, populations did exist, but were administered by religious foundations (*evkaf*) and thus not included in the *tahrir* registrations.

24. The word in the document that I have translated as "mariner" is عرب, could mean either *arab* (Arab) or *azeb* (mariner). Since Izmir is a seaport, it is natural to assume the laborers were mariners. Some doubt exists, however, because of the presence of transplanted Arab camel-drivers in the *kaza* of Izmir. On the Ottoman salt monopoly and its role in the economy, see Lütfi Güçer, "XV–XVII asırlarda Osmanlı imparatorluğunda tuz inhisarı ve tuzlaların işletme nizamı," *Istanbul Üniversitesi İktisat Fakültesi Mecmuası* 23 (1962–63): 97–143; on the organization of the workers, the *tuzcular*, see pp. 101–6 in particular. A table on pp. 130–31 of Güçer's work lists revenue from various salt pans and shows the importance to this industry of the Aydın region. The existence of a *şaphane* or alum house indicates the presence of

leather tanning, while a sesame oil factory in the port produced an annual revenue of 26,500 *akçes*. See BBA, TT 537, pp. 11 and 15.

25. See Appendix 2. Only two of the establishments are designated flour mills. Since flour spoils rapidly and was a staple, more than two such mills must have existed in the *kaza*. It is reasonable to suppose that the 133 unlabeled mills were devoted to the grinding of grains.

26. On luxury goods, see BBA, TT 537, p. 14.

27. On urban expansion, see especially Barkan, "Essai sur les données statistiques," pp. 9–36; Fernand Braudel, *The Mediterranean and the Mediterranean World in the Age of Philip II*, trans. Siân Reynolds, 2 vols. (New York: Harper and Row, 1972), vol. 1, pp. 394–418; and Halil İnalcık, "Impact of the *Annales* School on Ottoman Studies and New Findings," *Review* 1 (1978): 71–77.

28. On the rise of small ports, see Faroqhi, *Towns and Townsmen*, pp. 10–11 and 114–21.

29. Michael A. Cook in *Population Pressure in Rural Anatolia: 1450–1600* (London: Oxford University Press, 1972), analyzes a number of *tahrir* registers and concludes that they cannot reveal the occurrence and effects of population pressure (see especially p. 9).

30. In the *kaza* of Izmir in 1575–76, the farm (*çift*) paid 33 *akçes* annually, the half farm (*nim-çift*) paid 16.5 *akçes*, the landless farmer (*bennak*) paid 12 *akçes*, and the bachelor (*mücerred*) paid 6 *akçes*. On these terms and variations in the *çift* system, see Halil İnalcık, "Osmanlılar'da raiyyet rüsûmu," *Belleten* 23 (1959): 575–610.

31. On France, see Emmanuel Le Roy Ladurie, *The Peasants of Langue-doc*, trans. John Day (Urbana, Illinois: University of Illinois Press, 1974); and on Anatolia, see Mustafa Akdağ, *Celâli isyanları (1550–1603)* (Ankara: Ankara Üniversitesi, 1963); and Akdağ, "Celâli isyan-larından büyük kaçgunluk, 1603–1606," *Tarih Araştırmalar Dergisi* 2 (1966): 1–49.

32. On peasant mobility through migrations, see Faroqhi, *Towns and Towns-men*, chap. 11.

33. Suraiya Faroqhi, "Rural Society in Anatolia and the Balkans during the Sixteenth Century, I," *Turcica* 9 (1977): 169–70; and Bruce McGowan, "Food Supply and Taxation on the Middle Danube (1568–1579)," *Archivum Ottomanicum* 1 (1969): 150.

34. Censuses suggest that relatively little cotton was exported through Izmir until the seventeenth century (see Appendix 2). On the Vene-tian commerce in cotton, see Eliyahu Ashtor, "The Venetian Cotton Trade in Syria in the Later Middle Ages," *Studi Medievali*, ser. 3, 17 (1976): 675–715. On cotton in the Ottoman empire, see Halil İnalcık, "Osmanlı pamuklu pazarı, Hindistan ve İngiltere: Pazar rekabetinde emek maliyetinin rolü," *ODTÜ Gelişme Dergisi/METU Studies in De-*

velopment, special issue 2 (1979–80): 1–65; and Halil İnalcık, "Kutn," *EI²*.

35. BBA, TT 148, p. 5.
36. On the expense of grain transport, see Lütfi Güçer, *XVI–XVII asırlarda Osmanlı imparatorluğunda hububat meselesi ve hububattan alınan vergiler* (Istanbul: Sermet Matbaası, 1964), pp. 28–30.
37. BBA, MD 40, no. 471.
38. Richard Pococke, "Dr. Pococke's Travels in the East," in *Pinkerton's Voyages and Travels*, ed. John Pinkerton, vol. 10 (London: Longman, 1811), p. 644.
39. The presence of such a network limits the usefulness of the concept of surplus. How can one accurately determine it in a diversified market economy? The term is most profitably applied to monocultural regions (see Douglass C. North and Robert Paul Thomas, "Comment," *Journal of Economic History* 35 [1975]: 18–19).
40. BBA, TT 537, p. 57.
41. In the *tahrir* register dealing with the *kaza* of Izmir, while sheep taxes in the average village generated less than 1.5 percent of revenue, almost every village includes a tax called *resm-i kışlak ve resm-i otlak-i yürükan-i kışlakçıyan*. The 1528–29 law code (*kanunname*) of Aydın also stipulates dues for sheep on the hoof and butchered sheep and cites a special category for sheep brought from outside a village to be butchered (see BBA, TT 148, pp. 4–5). On transhumance, see Douglas L. Johnson, *The Nature of Nomadism: A Comparative Study of Pastoral Migrations in Southwestern Asia and Northern Africa* (Chicago: Department of Geography, University of Chicago, 1969), pp. 11–12 and 20–25.
42. BBA, TT 537, p. 70. The "extraordinary taxes" were the *avarız-i divaniyye* and *tekâlif-i örfiyye* (see Güçer, *Hububat meselesi*, pp. 69–92). On mountain-pass guards (*derbendcis*) in the Balkans, see Nicolai Todorov, *The Balkan City, 1400–1900* (Seattle: University of Washington Press, 1983), pp. 34–43.
43. See İnalcık, "Raiyyet rüsûmu," pp. 598–99.
44. See Halil İnalcık, "'Arab' Camel Drivers in Western Anatolia in the Fifteenth Century," *Revue d'Histoire Maghrebine* 31–32 (1983): 256–70.
45. See Suraiya Faroqhi, "Camels, Wagons, and the Ottoman State in the Sixteenth and Seventeenth Centuries," *International Journal of Middle East Studies* 14 (1982): 523–39. On Anatolian caravan routes, see Fr. Taeschner "Anadolu," *EI²*; and Ülker, "Rise of Izmir," pp. 71–76.
46. See Halil İnalcık, "Rice Cultivation and the *Çeltükçi-Reâyâ* System in the Ottoman Empire," *Turcica* 14 (1982): 69–141.
47. BBA, TT 537, pp. 44, 70–71, and 78–80.

CHAPTER TWO

1. On these *levends*, see Mustafa Akdağ, *Celâli isyanları*, chap. 3; and Mustafa Cezar, *Osmanlı tarihinde leventler* (Istanbul: Çelikcilt Matbaası, 1965).

2. On the endemic nature of the uprisings, see Suraiya Faroqhi, "Political Tensions in the Anatolian Countryside Around 1600: An Attempt at Interpretation," in *Türkische Miszellen: Robert Anhegger Festschrift*, ed. Jean-Louis Bacqué-Grammont, Barbara Flemming, Macit Gökberk, and İlber Ortaylı (Istanbul: Editions Divit Press, n.d.), p. 120.

3. BBA, MD 81, no. 367.

4. The literature on these transformations is extensive. For a general survey of the phenomena, see İnalcık, *Ottoman Empire*, pp. 46–51. The classic study on the *celâli* rebellions is Akdağ, *Celâli isyanları* and on the "great flight" that followed, his "Celâli isyanlarından büyük kaçgunluk," pp. 1–49. William James Griswold has published in English an account of the rebellions entitled *The Great Anatolian Rebellion, 1000–1020/1591–1611* (Berlin: Klaus Schwarz, 1983) and İnalcık has produced several studies on Ottoman society during this period. Recently, İnalcık has challenged Akdağ's conclusions concerning the social origins of the *celâli* rebellions and sketched out the problems of Ottoman decline in the seventeenth century in "Military and Fiscal Transformation in the Ottoman Empire, 1600–1700," *Archivum Ottomanicum* 6 (1980): 283–337. He has attacked the theory of Ottoman decline in his "Centralization and Decentralization in Ottoman Administration," in *Studies in Eighteenth-Century Islamic History*, eds. Thomas Naff and Roger Owens (Carbondale, Illinois: Southern Illinois University Press, 1977), pp. 27–52. Both the decline and the decentralization models currently are being challenged. See for instance Suraiya Faroqhi, "Political Initiatives 'From the Bottom Up' in the Sixteenth- and Seventeenth-Century Ottoman Empire: Some Evidence for Their Existence," in *Sonderdruck aus Osmanistische Studien zur Wirtschafts- und Sozialgeschichte in memoriam Vančo Boškov*, ed. Hans Georg Majer (Wiesbaden: Otto Harrassowitz, 1986), pp. 24–33; Douglas A. Howard, "Ottoman Historiography and the Literature of 'Decline' of the Sixteenth and Seventeenth Centuries," *Journal of Asian Studies* 22 (1988): 52–77; and Karen Barkey, Linda T. Darling, Daniel Goffman, and Fariba Zarinebaf-Shahr, "Centralization Versus Autonomy: Was the Ottoman State Really in Control?" (panel presented at the Twenty-First Annual Meeting of The Middle East Studies Association of North America, Baltimore, 14–17 November 1987). It can even be argued that seventeenth-century transformations helped *preserve* the empire. Just as England contemporaneously survived by learning a 'give and take' between capital and county, so might Ottoman re-

siliency during the subsequent two centuries have rested upon a vigorous provincial self-reliance (see Daniel Goffman, "The Ottoman Role in Patterns of Commerce in Aleppo, Chios, Dubrovnik, and Istanbul, 1600–1650," *Proceedings of the Eighth Symposium of the Comité International d'Etudes Pre-Ottomanes et Ottomanes*, Minneapolis, August 1988 [forthcoming]).

5. BBA, MD 30, p. 40.
6. BBA, MD 70, p. 144, no. 283.
7. BBA, MD 71, p. 39, no. 77. He called himself a *sekban*, on which see Akdağ, *Celâli isyanları*, pp. 125–27.
8. BBA, MD 71, p. 346, no. 645.
9. BBA, MD 74, p. 81, no. 237.
10. BBA, MD 81, no. 113. The village of Boynuzsekiz (Boynuzseküsü) administratively was attached to Izmir.
11. For official rates in the province of Aydın in 1575–76, see BBA, TT 148, pp. 3–4.
12. BBA, MD 70, p. 144, no. 283. Özer Ergenç, in his "Osmanlı klâsik dönemindeki 'Eşraf ve A'yan' üzerine bazı bilgiler," *Journal of Ottoman Studies* 3 (1982): 105–18, analyzes the phrase *ayan ve eşraf*, which is usually translated as "notables."
13. Akdağ analyzes the mass dispersal of the *reâyâ* between 1603 and 1606 in his "Celâli isyanlarından büyük kaçgunluk."
14. BBA, MD 75, p. 164, no. 302. This is the government's reply to the villagers' complaint; its response to the notables is almost identical. The *piyade taifesi* was a military organization that recently had been abolished.
15. BBA, MD 75, p. 216 relates a similar incident in Seferihisar in 1605.
16. On *ayan* power structures at the end of the seventeenth and in the eighteenth centuries, see İnalcık, "Centralization and Decentralization," pp. 31–52.
17. BBA, MD 76, p. 67, no. 167.
18. See, in order of mention, BBA, MD 67, p. 27; MD 73, p. 150, no. 348; MD 78, pp. 340 and 392; MZD 8, p. 16; MD 78, p. 86, no. 226; MD 78, p. 863, no. 3050; MD 78, p. 258, no. 481; MD 78, p. 553; MD 80, no. 792; and MD 85, no. 328.
19. In 1607–8, the government charged a collector of firearms around Izmir with arresting brigandage in the district (see BBA, MD 78, p. 86, no. 226).
20. In 1607 and 1608 the grand vezir, Murat Paşa, released from the Austrian wars, brought an army against Anatolian rebels (see Griswold, *Rebellions*), and in 1619 Istanbul dispatched Hüseyin Paşa to destroy the brigand Cennetoğlu (see Çağatay Uluçay, *XVII. asırda Saruhan'da eşkiyalık ve halk hareketleri* [Istanbul: Manisa Halkevi Yayınlarından, 1944], pp. 31–36).

21. İnalcık, "Socio-Political Effects," pp. 195–201.
22. Jennings, "Firearms, Bandits, and Gun-Control," pp. 353–57. The author bases his analysis on the fact that guns rarely were involved in violent crime. Other factors, however, may explain the preference for alternative weapons, particularly in urban crimes when stealth was an important element. A musket is noisy and, unlike a handgun, unwieldy and difficult to conceal. Outside of organized military forces, firearms may simply have been more trouble than they were worth.
23. BBA, MD 7, p. 847.
24. BBA, MD 69, p. 386, no. 568.
25. On the accessibility of firearms, see İnalcık, "Socio-Political Effects," p. 197; and Jennings, "Firearms, Bandits, and Gun-Control," pp. 343–45. Jennings estimates that in Kayseri a musket cost less than a donkey.
26. Documents ordering firearms delivered from western Anatolia to armories include BBA, MD 69, p. 386, no. 568; MD 71, p. 351, no. 653; MD 72, p. 205, no. 395; MD 78, p. 84, no. 221; and MD 78, p. 86, no. 226.
27. BBA, MD 64, p. 95 and MD 65, p. 229.
28. See especially BBA, MD 78, p. 86, no. 226.
29. See as examples BBA, ED 13/1, p. 57 and ED 26/1, p. 7.
30. Kayseri *sicils*, vol. 14, p. 92, item 1, partially translated in Jennings' "Firearms, Bandits, and Gun-Control," p. 348. The author cites this source along with several others as evidence of governmental insistence "upon maintaining its rules . . . regarding the disarming of the *reaya*," even though this document partially contradicts his statement.
31. BBA, MD 71, p. 351, no. 653.
32. BBA, MD 3, p. 163.
33. BBA, MD 3, p. 163, no. 2.
34. BBA, MD 5, p. 10.
35. BBA, MD 7, p. 530.
36. BBA, MD 69, p. 308.
37. Other documents on control of firearms in western Anatolia are BBA, MD 72, p. 205, no. 395; MD 74, p. 148, no. 148; and MD 78, p. 84, no. 221.
38. See Braudel, *Mediterranean and Mediterranean World*, vol. 1, pp. 312–18 and 576–94; and, on cities as regulators of trade, John Hicks, *A Theory of Economic History* (Oxford: Clarendon Press, 1969), pp. 81ff.
39. See Ömer-Lûtfi Barkan, "Quelques observations sur l'organisation économique et sociale des villes Ottomanes des XVIe et XVIIe siècles," *Recueils de la Société Jean Bodin* 7 (1955): 297. On the population of Istanbul in particular, see İnalcık, "Istanbul," *EI*².
40. BBA, MD 5, p. 492.
41. BBA, MD 6, p. 489.

42. Topkapı Sarayı Defteri 8702. Rhoads Murphey analyzes and summarizes this document in his "Functioning of the Ottoman Army," pp. 63–64 and 348–52. He does not cite the document's date.
43. Çağatay Uluçay includes this document in his *XVIIinci yüzyılda Manisa'da ziraat, ticaret ve esnaf teşkilâtı* (Istanbul: Manisa Halkevi Yayınlarından, 1942), pp. 129–31. A similar decree is extant for the year 1626–27, in which the government demands 1,500 *kantar*s of raisins, 150 of almonds, 150 of beeswax, 200 of olive oil, 100 of soap, 150 of pressed and spiced meat, 300 of figs, 200 of wild apricots, 200 of honey, 100 of dried pears, 40,000 sweet pomegranates, 100 boxes of figs, and 100 boxes of honeycombs (see BBA, MM 3457, p. 14). The exact weights of *kantar*s and *kile*s are uncertain. If a *kile* was 12 kilograms (a low estimate), in 1609 the imperial larder alone required 6,000 kilograms of black-eyed peas every year. On the inconsistencies of Ottoman weights and measures, see Halil İnalcık, "Introduction to Ottoman Metrology," *Turcica* 15 (1983): 329–37. On the *kile*, see İnalcık's "Rice Cultivation," Appendix III, pp. 119–20.
44. BBA, MD 6, p. 767.
45. BBA, MD 5, p. 123.
46. BBA, MD 7, pp. 66 and 121.
47. See BBA, MD 26, no. 428; MD 28, no. 462; MD 40, no. 509; and MD 66, no. 119.
48. See, in order of mention, BBA, MD 3, p. 158; MD 5, p. 212; MD 7, p. 137; and MD 7, p. 687.
49. See Braudel, *Mediterranean and Mediterranean World*, vol. 1, pp. 599–602, who emphasizes imbalances in production and prices more than population pressure in explaining these fluctuations and points out that the Venetians again turned to the Levant for grain in 1600–1601 and 1628–29. On the grain trade during this period, see Maurice Aymard, *Venise, Raguse et le commerce du blé pendant la seconde moitié du XVIe siècle* (Paris: S.E.V.P.E.N., 1966), pp. 125–71; and Güçer, *Hububat meselesi*, chap. 1.
50. Le Roy Ladurie examines the relationships between population, subsistence, production, and income in southern France in his *Peasants of Languedoc*, pp. 51–83.
51. CSP, Venice, vol. 9, no. 20.
52. See CSP, Venice, vol. 9, nos. 115, 116, 123, and 127.
53. See İnalcık, "Impact of the *Annales* School," p. 81.
54. BBA, MD 78, p. 745. I have translated *harbi kefere* as "enemy infidel." On this term and the capitulations, see Halil İnalcık, "İmtiyâzât," *EI²*.
55. On Ottoman-Ragusan relations, see Nicolaas H. Biegman, *The Turco-Ragusan Relationship according to the Firmâns of Murâd III (1575–95) Extant in the State Archives of Dubrovnik* (The Hague: Mouton, 1967), pp. 29–45, and also BBA, ED 14/2 and 15/3 and BBA,

HD 2, which are devoted to complaints submitted by the city-state. On Franco-Ottoman relations, see Paul Masson, *Histoire du commerce français dans le Levant au XVIIe* (Paris: Hachette, 1911), pp. xxii–xxvii and xxxi–xxxiii. The Anglo-French commercial struggle is analyzed in Arthur Leon Horniker, "Anglo-French Rivalry in the Levant from 1583 to 1612," *Journal of Modern History* 18 (1946): 289–305 and the Dutch role is discussed in A. H. de Groot, *Ottoman Empire and Dutch Republic: A History of the Earliest Diplomatic Relations, 1610–1630* (Istanbul: Nederlands Historisch-Archaeologisch Instituut, 1978), pp. 102–20.

56. BBA, MZD 8, p. 68.
57. During the *celâli* rebellions, government efforts to arrest movement of foodstuffs from Rumeli to Anatolia indicate a price differential favoring the European provinces (see Akdağ, "Celâli isyanlarından büyük kaçgunluk," p. 2; and İnalcık's "Impact of the *Annales* School," pp. 58–60).
58. On the complexity and involvement of officials in the Istanbul grain trade, see Halil İnalcık, "Capital Formation in the Ottoman Empire," *Journal of Economic History* 19 (1969): 119–20. On the involvement of Halil Paşa, intermittently admiral of the Ottoman navy and grand vezir during the first decades of the seventeenth century, see de Groot, *The Ottoman Empire and the Dutch Republic*, pp. 61–67.
59. BBA, MD 69, p. 75. The "small boats" mentioned in the document were *sandals*, two-oared rowboats of the type commonly found on western sailing ships, and *kara mürsels*, small coastal vessels often used for transporting foodstuffs (see Mehmet Zaki Pakalın, "Karamürsel," *Osmanlı tarih deyimleri ve terimleri sözlüğü*, 2d ed., 3 vols. [Istanbul: Millî Eğitim Basımevi, 1971]). On Ottoman maritime terminology, see Svat Soucek, "On Certain Types of Ships in Ottoman-Turkish Terminology," *Turcica* 7 (1975): 233–49.
60. On the *bertone*, see Alberto Tenenti, *Piracy and the Decline of Venice, 1580–1615*, trans. Janet and Brian Pullan (Berkeley and Los Angeles: University of California Press, 1967), pp. 64–65. On galley warfare, see John Francis Guilmartin, Jr., *Gunpowder and Galleys: Changing Technology and Mediterranean Warfare at Sea in the Sixteenth Century* (Cambridge: Cambridge University Press, 1974), pp. 253–73.
61. Tenenti, *Piracy and the Decline of Venice*, p. 69.
62. See İnalcık, *Ottoman Empire*, pp. 153–55; and Robert Mantran, "Ḥisba," *EI*².
63. BBA, MZD 6, p. 69.
64. BBA, MD 69, pp. 322 and 324.
65. BBA, MD 71, p. 112.
66. BBA, MD 80, no. 232.
67. BBA, MD 74, p. 107.

68. BBA, MD 78, p. 393. This document refers to Izmir as a *bender*, or commercial port, thereby indicating the town's growing importance.
69. BBA, MD 75, p. 296. The document cites one-hundred *kantar*s, which *probably* is approximately twelve-thousand pounds.
70. On Dutch, see Niels Steensgaard, *The Asian Trade Revolution of the Seventeenth Century* (Chicago: University of Chicago Press, 1974), pp. 154–93.
71. Pakalın, "Kapan" and "Kantar," *Deyimleri ve terimleri sözlüğü*.
72. These safeguards are explained in BBA, MD 71, p. 49.
73. On taverns in Izmir, see BBA, MM 18199. On monopolies over wine exports, see İnalcık, "Capital Formation," pp. 122–23; and Salo Wittmayer Baron, *A Social and Religious History of the Jews*, vol. 18: *The Ottoman Empire, Persia, Ethiopia, India, and China* (New York: Columbia University Press, 1983), pp. 88–89.
74. BBA, MD 45, no. 415.
75. BBA, MD 68, p. 69.
76. BBA, MD 76, p. 66. See Faroqhi "Rural Society, I," p. 175.
77. BBA, MD 71, p. 49.
78. BBA, MD 71, p. 203. On avoidance of weighing stations in Izmir in September and December 1593 and attempts to send black grapes, sultanas, figs, hazelnuts, olive oil, and beeswax elsewhere than Istanbul, see BBA, MD 71, pp. 146 and 198.
79. BBA, MD 71, p. 230. The document, for reasons unclear to me, distinguishes between *siyah* and *kara* grapes.
80. Steensgaard (*Asian Trade Revolution*, chap. 1), proposes an Asian peddling economy similar to this one, arguing that it existed until the Dutch and English trading companies invaded eastern markets at the beginning of the seventeenth century. For a critique of the phrase "peddling trade," see T. Bentley Duncan, "Niels Steensgaard and the Europe-Asia Trade of the Early Seventeenth Century," *Journal of Modern History* 47 (1975): 512–18.
81. On *annual* fluctuations in meat and bread prices, see Akdağ, "Celâli isyanlarından büyük kaçgunluk," pp. 3–10. There are no studies of *seasonal* fluctuations.
82. BBA, MZD 6, p. 81.
83. BBA, MD 71, p. 142.
84. BBA, MD 69, p. 324.
85. BBA, MD 74, p. 226.
86. See İnalcık, "Ottoman Metrology," pp. 329–37.
87. Uluçay, *Manisa'da ziraat*, p. 126, doc. 6.
88. BBA, MD 78, p. 866.
89. This was the *resm-i kantar*, presumably identical to the *resm-i kapan* or *hakk-i kantar* (see Robert Mantran, "Ḥisba").

90. Suraiya Faroqhi, "Istanbul'un iasesi ve Tekirdağ-Rodoscuk limanı (16.–17. yüzyıllar)," *ODTÜ Gelişme Dergisi/METU Studies in Development*, special issue 2 (1979–80): 139–54.
91. BBA, MD 71, p. 220, no. 415.
92. BBA, MD 71, p. 113 (October 1593); MD 71, p. 164 (December 1593); and MD 72, p. 237 (May or June 1594).
93. BBA, MD 74, p. 56.
94. Frederic C. Lane, "The Mediterranean Spice Trade: Further Evidence of Its Revival in the Sixteenth Century," in *Crisis and Change in the Venetian Economy*, ed. Brian Pullan (London: Methuen, 1968), pp. 47–58.
95. BBA, MD 72, p. 202.
96. BBA, MD 78, p. 481.
97. BBA, MD 5, p. 288. The document, perhaps exaggeratingly, orders the purchase of 150,000 sailcloths.
98. BBA, MD 5, p. 293.
99. BBA, MM 7534, p. 1285; MD 45, no. 451; and MD 71, p. 360.
100. BBA, MD 68, p. 13; and MD 79, no. 131.
101. BBA, MD 78, p. 258, no. 681.

CHAPTER THREE

1. This interpretation was propounded most persuasively by Steensgaard, *Asian Trade Revolution*, pp. 185–86 who, although shying away from the "event" as explanatory of economic and social change in favor of structural causality, does not attempt to integrate the phenomenon of Izmir's spectacular growth into his thesis of an international crisis in trade, but simply accepts the idea that the renewed war and fighting around Baghdad explains the port's rise. A more sophisticated discussion of the relationship between Aleppo and Izmir is in Bruce Masters, *The Origins of Western Economic Dominance in the Middle East: Mercantilism and the Islamic Economy in Aleppo, 1600–1750* (New York: New York University Press, 1988), pp. 27–28. Elena Frangakis-Syrett embraces a multi-causal approach in her "Trade between Ottoman Empire and Western Europe: The Case of Izmir in the Eighteenth Century," *New Perspectives on Turkey* 2 (1988): 1–2. See also Necmi Ülker, "The Emergence of Izmir as a Mediterranean Commercial Center for the French and English Interests, 1698–1740," *International Journal of Turkish Studies* 4 (1987): 1–7.
2. Steensgaard, *Asian Trade Revolution*, p. 186.
3. Nicolas de Nicolay, *The Navigations, Peregrinations and Voyages, Made into Turkie by Nicholas Nicholay . . .*, trans. T. Washington the Younger (London: T. Dawson, 1585), pp. 35–37.

4. See Fynes Moryson, *An Itinerary: Containing His Ten Yeeres Travel through the Twelve Dominions of Germany, Bohmerland, Sweitzerland, Netherland, Denmarke, Poland, Itally, Turky, France, England, Scotland and Ireland*, 4 vols. (Glasgow: James MacLehose, 1907), vol. 2, p. 85 and vol. 4, p. 122.

5. James Theodore Bent, ed., *Early Voyages and Travels in the Levant*, I.—*The Diary of Master Thomas Dallam, 1599–1600*, II.—*Extracts from the Diaries of Dr. John Covel, 1670–1679* (London: Hakluyt Society, 1893), pp. 43–46.

6. John Sanderson, *The Travels of John Sanderson in the Levant, 1584–1602*, ed. Sir William Foster, Hakluyt Society, ser. 2, vol. 67 (London: Hakluyt Society, 1931), pp. 124 and 218.

7. Henry de Beauvau, *Relation iournaliere du voyage du Levant* (Nancy: Jacob Garnich, 1615), p. 39.

8. George Sandys, *A Relation of a Journey Begun An: Dom: 1610*, 2d ed. (London: W. Barrett, 1621), p. 12. On Sandys' perception of the Levant, see Jonathan Haynes, *The Humanist as Traveler: George Sandys's 'Relation of a Journey Begun An: Dom: 1610'* (Rutherford: Farleigh Dickinson University Press, 1986), pp. 65–81.

9. Sandys, *Relation*, p. 15.

10. William Lithgow, *The Totall Discourse, of the Rare Adventures, and Painefull Peregrinations of Long Nineteene Yeares Travayles, to the Most Famous Kingdoms in Europe, Asia, and Affrica* (London: J. Okes, 1632), p. 173.

11. Louis Deshayes, baron de Courmenin, *Voiage de Levant fait par le Commandement du Roy en l'année 1621 par le Sr D. C.*, 2d ed. (Paris: A Taupinart, 1632), p. 342.

12. Steensgaard, *Asian Trade Revolution*, pp. 34–35.

13. Lewes Roberts, *The Merchants Mappe of Commerce: Wherein, the Universal Manner and Matter of Trade, Is Compendiously Handled* (London: Ralph Mabb, 1638), pp. 118–19.

14. Steensgaard, *Asian Trade Revolution*, pp. 86 and 187.

15. Jacob Spon and George Wheler, *Voyage d'Italie, de Dalmatie, de Grece, et du Levant, fair aux années 1675 et 1676*, 2 vols. (Amsterdam: H. et T. Boom, 1679), vol. 1, pp. 229–39; Cornelis de Bruyn, *Voyage au Levant . . .* (Paris: Corneille le Brun, 1714), p. 27; and Joseph Pitton de Tournefort, *Relation d'un voyage du Levant*, 3 vols. (Lyon, 1727), vol. 3, pp. 365–76. Late-seventeenth-century travelers to Izmir are discussed in Necmi Ülker, "Batılı gözlemcilere göre XVII. yüzyılın ikinci yarısında Izmir şehri ve ticarîsorunları," *Tarih Enstitüsü Dergisi* 12 (1981–82): 317–54. For a stimulating exploration of the reasons men undertook these dangerous and sometimes fatal journeys, see Nathan Glazebrook, *Journey to Kars: A Modern Traveller in the Ottoman Lands* (New York: Holt, Rinehart, and Winston, 1982).

16. Leila T. Erder and Suraiya Faroqhi, "The Development of the Anatolian Urban Network during the Sixteenth Century," *Journal of the Economic and Social History of the Orient* 23 (1980): 276, 280, and the maps on pp. 273 and 280.

17. On indigenous growth, see Erder and Faroqhi, "Anatolian Urban Network," pp. 279–87. Faroqhi in her more recent *Towns and Townsmen* (p. 76) excepts Izmir from her generalization that little maritime traffic passed through Anatolian ports.

18. Erder and Faroqhi, "Anatolian Urban Network," pp. 273 and 285.

19. BBA, MD 75, p. 296 and MD 78, p. 393.

20. Several editions of these capitulations exist (see for example, Charles Schefer, ed., *Mémoires sur l'ambassade de France en Turquie, 1525–1770 par François Guignard, 1735–1821, Comte de Saint-Priest . . .* [1877; rpt., Paris, 1974], p. 419).

21. Faroqhi, *Towns and Townsmen*, pp. 115–16 and 313.

22. Faroqhi states that between 1609 and 1617 the tax farmer annually paid 6,113,581 *akçes* for this unit (see *Towns and Townsmen*, p. 313).

23. Reflecting their traditional relationship, the Ottomans administered commerce through the ports of Chios and Çeşme as a single unit. I will hereafter refer to them as Chios. Sığacık served as the port for the better known Seferihisar.

24. See Otto F. A. Meinardus, "Testimonies to the Economic Vitality of Balat, the Mediaeval Miletus," *Belleten* 37 (1973): 293–94.

25. Zachariadou, *Trade and Crusade*, p. 167; and Marie Louise Heers, "Les Génois et le commerce de l'alun à la fin du moyen-âge," *Revue d'Histoire Economique et Sociale* 32 (1954): 31–53.

26. Faroqhi discusses alum as a possible indicator of the decline in leather production in Anatolia in *Towns and Townsmen*, pp. 159–60.

27. Foça's increasing role in the seventeenth century as guardian of the gulf is recorded in PRO, SP 97/20, fols. 172a–74b and 235a–35b.

28. In Philip P. Argenti, ed., *Chius Vincta or the Occupation of Chios by the Turks (1566) and Their Administration of the Island (1566–1912)* (Cambridge: Cambridge University Press, 1941), pp. 180–83 is an imprecise and muddled transliteration and translation of this document.

29. See Argenti, *Chius Vincta*, pp. xxvii–xliii; and Şerafettin Turan, "Sakız'ın Türk hâkimiyeti altına alınması," *Tarih Araştırmaları Dergisi* 4 (1966): 173–84.

30. BBA, MD 6, p. 489.

31. Turan, "Sakız'ın Türk hâkimiyeti," p. 185.

32. Argenti, *Chius Vincta*, pp. 208–27.

33. Philip P. Argenti, ed., *The Expedition of the Florentines to Chios (1599), Described in Contemporary Diplomatic Reports and Military Dispatches* (London: John Lane, 1934), pp. xii–xiii.

34. BBA, MZD 7, p. 26.

35. BBA, MD 78, p. 423, no. 1085. See also Philip P. Argenti, *The Religious Minorities of Chios: Jews and Roman Catholics* (Cambridge: Cambridge University Press, 1970), p. 164. Zvi Ankori shows what happened to a Jewish quarter in a city tranferred from Latin to Ottoman rule in his "From Zudecha to Yahudi Mahallesi: The Jewish Quarter of Candia in the Seventeenth Century (A Chapter in the History of Cretan Jewry under Muslim Rule)," in *Salo Wittmayer Baron Jubilee Volume*, vol. 1 (New York: Columbia University Press, 1975), pp. 67–124.

36. BBA, TT 363.

37. On this status, see İnalcık, "İmtiyâzât."

38. See, for instance, BBA, ED 13/1, p. 120, no. 1; BBA, ED 13/1, p. 150, no. 1; BBA, ED 13/1, p. 178; and BBA, MM 6004, p. 51, no. 1.

39. See Pullan, ed., *Crisis and Change*; and Richard T. Rapp, "The Unmaking of the Mediterranean Trade Hegemony," *Journal of Economic History* 35 (1975): 499–525. For a bibliography of work relating to Venetian decline, see Frederic C. Lane, *Venice: A Maritime Republic* (Baltimore: Johns Hopkins University Press, 1973), pp. 473–76. A critique of Lane's work is Eric Cochrane and Julius Kirshner's "Deconstructing Lane's *Venice*," *Journal of Modern History* 45 (1975): 321–34.

40. See Masson, *Commerce français*, pp. xii–xix.

41. CSP, Venice, vol. 9, p. 146.

42. See Abel Rigault, "Savary de Lancosme: un épisode de la ligue à Constantinople (1589–1593)," *Revue d'Histoire Diplomatique* 16 (1902): 522–78; Masson, *Commerce français*, pp. xvi–xviii; CSP, Venice, vol. 9, pp. 291, 394–95, and 428–30; and Horniker, "Anglo-French Rivalry." There is a large literature on the establishment of English trade in the Levant. For published collections of sources, see for English documents Richard Hakluyt, *The Principal Navigations, Voyages, Traffiques and Discoveries of the English Nation*, vols. 5–6 (Glasgow: James MacLehose, 1904); and Sanderson, *Travels*. For Turkish documents, see Susan A. Skilliter, *William Harborne and the Trade with Turkey, 1578–1582: A Documentary Study of the First Anglo-Ottoman Relations* (London: Oxford University Press, 1977). For secondary accounts, see in addition to Alfred C. Wood, *A History of the Levant Company* (Oxford: Oxford University Press, 1935), pp. 1–41; Mordecai Epstein, *The English Levant Company: Its Foundation and Its History to 1640* (London: Routledge, 1908), pp. 1–66; Akdes Nimet Kurat, *Türk-İngiliz münasebetlerinin başlangıcı ve gelişmesi (1553–1610)* (Ankara: Türk Tarih Kurumu Basımevi, 1953); Mübahat Kütükoğlu, *Osmanlı-ingiliz iktisâdî münâsebetleri, I (1580–1838)* (Ankara: Türk Kültürünü Araştırma Enstitüsü, 1974), pp. 6–33; and Arthur Leon Horniker, "William Harborne and the Beginning of Anglo-Turkish Diplomatic and Commercial Relations," *Journal of Modern History* 14 (1942): 289–316.

43. Steensgaard, *Asian Trade Revolution*, pp. 189–90.
44. Skilliter in her *William Harborne* presents a critical edition (pp. 232–39) and translation (pp. 86–89) of the 1591 capitulations. See also Tenenti, *Piracy and the Decline of Venice*, pp. 57–81; Maurice Aymard, "XVI. yüzyılın sonunda Akdeniz'de korsanlık ve Venedik," *Istanbul Üniversitesi İktisat Fakültesi Mecmuası* 23 (1962–63): 227–30; and Wood, *Levant Company*, pp. 25–26.
45. CSP, Venice, vol. 9, pp. 394–95.
46. See CSP, Venice, vol. 9, pp. 299, 310, 319, 334, 348, 394–95, 407, 413, 420, and 432–33.
47. CSP, Venice, vol. 9, p. 291.
48. BBA, MD 72, p. 438, no. 849.
49. CSP, Venice, vol. 10, pp. 311, 318.
50. BBA, ED 13/1, p. 63, no. 5. See also Masters, *Origins*, pp. 15–17.
51. See Wood, *Levant Company*, p. 76. According to Braudel, *Mediterranean and Mediterranean World*, vol. 1, p. 565, Aleppo's port only in 1593 had made the move from Tripoli to Alexandretta.
52. Tenenti, *Piracy and the Decline of Venice*, p. 99.
53. On Canbuladoğlu Ali Paşa, see Griswold, *Rebellions*, chap. 4 and Masters, *Origins*, chap. 1. Ottoman officials were not so much "venal" or "rapacious," as indignant westerners claimed, as caught in a great fiscal crisis (see Halil Sahillioğlu, "*Siviş* Year Crises in the Ottoman Empire," in *Studies in the Economic History of the Middle East from the Rise of Islam to the Present Day*, ed. Michael A. Cook [London: Oxford University Press, 1970], pp. 230–52).
54. Steensgaard, *Asian Trade Revolution*, pp. 175–85. On Aleppo in the late seventeenth and early eighteenth centuries, see Masters, *Origins*. Andras Riedlmayer argues that there is no internal evidence for such a downturn in "Ottoman-Safavid Relations and the Anatolian Trade Routes: 1603–1618," *Turkish Studies Association Bulletin* 5 (1981): 7–10
55. CSP, Venice, vol. 12, pp. 179–80.
56. On the Russian venture, see G. D. Ramsay, *English Overseas Trade during the Centuries of Emergence* (London: Macmillan, 1957), pp. 26–28. On the cape route, see Steensgaard, *Asian Trade Revolution*, pp. 367–97. For an overview of northern trade routes, see Pierre Jeannin, "The Sea-borne and the Overland Trade Routes of Northern Europe in the XVIth and XVIIth Centuries," *Journal of European Economic History* 11 (1975): 5–59.
57. CSP, Venice, vol. 11, p. 477.
58. Charles Issawi, "The Tabriz-Trabzon Trade, 1830–1900: Rise and Decline of a Route," *International Journal of Middle East Studies* 1 (1970): 18–27.

59. On Bedik, see also de Groot, *Ottoman Empire and the Dutch Republic*, pp. 188–89; and Masters, *Origins*, 140–41. Masters cites his alleged execution in 1627. A document dated 25 June–4 July 1636, however, mentions an Armenian customs collector in Aleppo, Bedik, to whom the merchants of Marseilles were heavily indebted (see BBA, ED 26, p. 8, no. 1).

60. BBA, ED 13/1, p. 83, no. 2.

61. BBA, ED 13/1, p. 110, no. 3.

62. BBA, ED 13/1, p. 110, no. 5.

63. De Groot, *Ottoman Empire and the Dutch Republic*, pp. 188–89.

64. See Ülker, "Rise of Izmir," pp. 194 and 210; and Wood, *Levant Company*, p. 72.

65. Seventeenth-century European travelers often journeyed between Manisa and Izmir. Paul Rycaut, in *History of the Turkish Empire from the Year 1623 to the Year 1677* . . . (London: J. Starkey, 1680), pp. 35–36, states that the distance was twenty-three miles, and Monsieur de Thevenot remarks that he left Manisa at five in the morning and arrived in Izmir at noon in *Travels of Monsieur de Thevenot in the Levant*, trans. A. Lovell; (rpt., London: Farnborough, Gregg, 1971), p. 91. The English ambassador to Istanbul, Wyche, wrote home to Lord Dorchester in April 1632, however, that a rebel named Elles Bassa (probably İlyas Paşa, on whom see Uluçay, *Eşkiyalık ve halk hareketleri*, pp. 37–38) had taken Manisa, a "two-day journey" from Izmir.

66. On the structures of this and other guilds in Manisa, see Uluçay, *Manisa'da ziraat*.

67. Uluçay, *Manisa'da ziraat*, pp. 127–28.

68. Uluçay, *Manisa'da ziraat*, pp, 129, 131, and 134.

69. BBA, MD 80, no. 980.

70. BBA, MM 7266, p. 11.

71. Uluçay, *Manisa'da ziraat*, p. 49. He found this document in the *Manisa mahkeme-i şeriye sicilleri*, 1051/1641–42, but does not provide a catalogue number.

72. Pococke remarks that Urla was a port where European vessels loaded raisins and olive oil ("Travels," p. 652).

73. BBA, MD 71, p. 148, no. 296. Another ingredient in the soap was suet. For the suggestion that a decline in animal husbandry might account for the decrease in the soap's quality, see Faroqhi, *Towns and Townsmen*, pp. 224–25.

74. BBA, MD 79, no. 397.

75. A passage in Bent, ed., *Early Voyages and Travels* (p. 49) written by Dallam in 1599 describes a gift of tobacco and pipe requested by and delivered to a captain of an Ottoman galley at the mouth of the Dardanelles straits. Kâtib Çelebi, writing in the 1660s, states that

tobacco first appeared in Istanbul in 1601 (*Balance of Truth*, trans. Geoffrey L. Lewis [London: George Allen and Unwin, 1957], p. 51).

76. On tobacco suppression in Manisa, see Uluçay, *Manisa'da ziraat*, p. 42.

77. Kâtib Çelebi, *Balance of Truth*, p. 51.

78. BBA, MD 80, no. 582.

79. Uluçay, *Manisa'da ziraat*, p. 42.

80. On coffee and the Ottoman administration, see Suraiya Faroqhi, "Coffee and Spices: Official Ottoman Reactions to Egyptian Trade in the Later Sixteenth Century," *Festschrift für Andreas Tietze, 76. Band, Wiener Zeitschrift für die Kunde des Morgenlandes* (Vienna: Institutes für Orientalistik, 1986), pp. 87–93. On the coffeehouse in the Ottoman empire, see Ralph S. Hattox, *Coffee and Coffeehouses: The Origins of a Social Beverage in the Medieval Near East* (Seattle: Near Eastern Publications, University of Washington, 1985), pp. 72–111.

81. Walter Edward Minchinton, "Introduction," in *The Growth of English Overseas Trade in the Seventeenth Century*, ed. Walter Edward Minchinton (London: Newton, 1969), p. 6.

82. K. N. Chaudhuri, "The World System East of Longitude 20°: The European Role in Asia, 1500–1750," *Review* 5 (1981): 242.

83. BBA, MD 62, p. 133, cited by Suraiya Faroqhi, "Textile Production and the Arab Provinces: Geographic Distribution and Internal Trade (1560–1650)," *Journal of Ottoman Studies* 1 (1980): 72. See also Faroqhi, "Notes on the Production of Cotton and Cotton Cloth in XVIth and XVIIth Century Anatolia," *Journal of European Economic History* 8 (1972): 405–17.

84. See Ralph Davis, *Aleppo and Devonshire Square: English Trade in the Levant in the Eighteenth Century* (London: Macmillan, 1967); Ülker, "Rise of Izmir," p. 116; and Frangakis-Syrett, "Trade," pp. 10–12.

CHAPTER FOUR

1. On the Armenians in Izmir, see Steensgaard, *Asian Trade Revolution*, pp. 186–87. On the Armenian "trading diaspora," see Philip D. Curtin, *Cross-Cultural Trade in World History* (Cambridge: Cambridge University Press, 1984), pp. 179–206; Keram Kevonian, "Marchands arméniens au XVIIe siècle: A propose d'un livre arménien publié à Amsterdam en 1699," *Cahiers du Monde Russe et Soviétique* 16 (1975): 199–244; and R. W. Ferrier, "The Armenians and the East India Company in Persia in the Seventeenth and Early Eighteenth Centuries," *Economic History Review*, 2d ser., 26 (1973): 38–62. On the Jews in the sixteenth-century Ottoman empire, see Mark Alan Epstein, *The Ottoman Jewish Communities and Their Role in the Fifteenth and Sixteenth Centuries* (Freiburg: Klaus Schwarz, 1980); and Bernard Lewis,

The Jews of Islam (Princeton: Princeton University Press, 1984), pp. 114–48.

2. See İnalcık, "'Arab' Camel Drivers," pp. 255–70.

3. İnalcık shows the importance of Muslim traders in Bursa in his "Bursa and the Commerce of the Levant" and Masters in his *Origins* makes this point one of his central theses.

4. See Ellis Rivkin, *The Shaping of Jewish History: A Radical New Interpretation* (New York: Charles Scribner's, 1971), pp. 140–58; Epstein, *Ottoman Jewish Communities*, preface; and Baron, *Ottoman Empire*, pp. 43–121.

5. On *sürgün*, see Ömer Lûtfi Barkan, "Les déportations comme méthode de peuplement et de colonisation dans l'empire Ottoman," *Istanbul Üniversitesi İktisat Fakültesi Mecmuası* 11 (1949–50): 67–131; and İnalcık, "Istanbul" and "Ottoman Methods of Conquest," *Studia Islamica* 2 (1954): 122–23. See also Lowry's discussion of the forced movement of Greeks from Trabzon to Istanbul in "Ottoman *Tahrir Defters*," p. 146; and the literature on attempts to move Jews from Safed to Cyprus, particularly Bernard Lewis, *Notes and Documents from the Turkish Archives: A Contribution to the History of the Jews in the Ottoman Empire* (Jerusalem: Israel Oriental Society, 1952), pp. 28–35; and Uriel Heyd, "Turkish Documents Concerning the Jews of Safed in the Sixteenth Century," in *Studies on Palestine during the Ottoman Period*, ed. Moshe Mo'az (Jerusalem: Magnes Press, 1975), pp. 111–19.

6. Steven B. Bowman, *The Jews of Byzantium, 1204–1453* (University, Alabama: University of Alabama Press, 1985), pp. 171–200.

7. Mark Alan Epstein, "Leadership of the Ottoman Jews in the Fifteenth and Sixteenth Centuries," in *Christians and Jews in the Ottoman Empire: The Functioning of a Plural Society*, ed. Benjamin Braude and Bernard Lewis, 2 vols. (New York: Holmes and Meier, 1982), vol. 1: *The Central Lands*, pp. 101–15.

8. There are many examples of vicious disputes between rival factions within the community. See Aryeh Shmuelevitz, *Jews of the Ottoman Empire in the Late Fifteenth and Sixteenth Centuries: Administrative, Economic, Legal, and Social Relations as Reflected in the Responsa* (Leiden: E.J. Brill, 1984); and Jacob Barnai and Haim Gerber, *The Jews in Izmir in the Nineteenth Century: Ottoman Documents from the Shar'i Court* (in Hebrew) (Jerusalem: Institute for Research on the Sephardi and Oriental Jewish Heritage, 1984). Here the focus is on the community's role in Ottoman administration, economy, and society.

9. On immigration, see Joseph R. Hacker, "The Impact of the "Sürgün"-System on Jewish Society in the Ottoman Empire in the 15th–17th Centuries," (paper presented at the Fourth International Congress for

the Economic and Social History of Turkey [1071–1922], Munich, 4–8 August 1986).

10. BBA, MD 45, no. 415 and MD 71, p. 299.

11. See most recently Baron, *Ottoman Empire*, pp. 88–89. Because there were no prominent rabbis in sixteenth-century western Anatolia, few rabbinic sources exist for this period. See Jacob Barnai, "The Settlement of the Jewish Community in Izmir in the Ottoman Period" (in Hebrew), *Pa'anim* 12 (1982): 53, who provides some information about when and from where Jews settled in Izmir. For the period post-dating Izmir's rise, the responsa are more useful. See Jacob Barnai's three articles "On the Jewish Community of Izmir in the Late Eighteenth and Early Nineteenth Centuries" (in Hebrew), *Tsiyyon* 47 (1982): 56–76; "The Jewish Community of Izmir in the Seventeenth Century" (in Hebrew), *Proceedings of the Eighth World Congress of Jewish Studies*, Division B, *The Period of the Bible* (Jerusalem: n.p., 1982): 65–88; and "The Development of the Links between the Jews of Izmir and the Jews of Eretz Israel in the 17th–18th Centuries" (in Hebrew), *Shalem, Studies in the History of the Jews in Eretz-Israel* 5 (1987): 95–114.

12. Jacob Leveen, "An Eyewitness Account of the Expedition of the Florentines against Chios in 1599," *Bulletin of the School of Oriental and African Studies* 12 (1948): 542–54.

13. Sanderson, *Travels*, p. 120. On the tombstone, see Abraham Galanté, *Histoire des Juifs d'Anatolie*, 2 vols., vol. 1: *Les Juifs d'Izmir (Smyrne)* (Istanbul: M. Babok, 1937), p. 80.

14. Galanté, *Juifs d'Anatolie*, vol. 1, pp. 9–10. The author, under the mistaken impression that Izmir long had been an important entrepôt, expresses surprise that a community structure was established so late. He ascribes the seemingly inexplicable pattern to earthquake, cholera, and war.

15. Two extensive lists of population estimates by European travelers are M. Çınar Atay, *Tarih içinde Izmir* (Izmir: Tifset Basım ve Yayın Sanayii, 1978), pp. 114–16; and Frangakis-Syrett, "Commerce of Izmir," p. 59.

16. On population, see BBA, MM 14672. A facsimile of the section of this census dealing with the Jews is in Goffman, "Izmir as a Commercial Center," pp. 391–92.

17. See Murat Çizakça, "Price History and the Bursa Silk Industry: A Study in Ottoman Industrial Decline, 1550–1650," *Journal of Economic History* 40 (1980): 533–50; Faroqhi, "Textile Production"; Pullan, ed., *Crisis and Change*; Benjamin Braude, "International Competition and Domestic Cloth in the Ottoman Empire, 1500–1650, a Study of Undevelopment," *Review* 1 (1979): 437–54; and Rapp, "Mediterranean Trade Hegemony," pp. 499–525.

18. On the Jews of Salonica, see Joseph Nehama, *Histoire des Israélites de Salonique*, 5 vols. (Salonica: Emmanuel Sfakianakis, 1935–59).

19. Faroqhi, "Textile Production," p. 69.

20. BBA, MD 79, no. 4. See also Faroqhi, "Textile Production," p. 69.

21. On the Jews in Manisa, see Galanté, *Juifs d'Anatolie*, vol. 2, pp. 70–100. On its textile industry, see Uluçay, *Manisa*, pp. 622–68. On Manisa as a court of an Ottoman prince, see İbrahim Gökçen and M. Çağatay Uluçay, *Manisa tarihi* (Istanbul: Manisa Halkevi Yayınlarından, 1939), pp. 50–55.

22. Amnon Cohen and Bernard Lewis, *Population and Revenue in the Towns of Palestine in the Sixteenth Century* (Princeton: Princeton University Press, 1978), p. 30; and Simon Schwarzfuchs, "La décadence de la Galilée juive de XVIe siècle et la crise du textile au Proche Orient," *Revue du Etudes Juives* 121 (1962): 169–79.

23. BBA, MD 80, no. 980.

24. See BBA, MM 7266, p. 11.

25. BBA, MM 14672, p. 20. On the reliability of such surveys, see Bruce McGowan, *Economic Life in Ottoman Europe* (Cambridge: Cambridge University Press, 1981), pp. 81–83. On Jewish evasion of Ottoman censuses, see Shmuelevitz, *Jews of the Ottoman Empire*, pp. 89–92.

26. On sixteenth-century Kuşadası, see Galanté, *Juifs d'Anatolie*, vol. 2, p. 64.

27. Livio Missir Reggio Mamachi di Lusignano, *Epitaphier des grandes familles Latines de Smyrne*, vol. 2: *Les pierres tombales de l'église française Saint-Polycarpe* (Brussels: Dembla, 1985), p. 22.

28. Daniel Goffman, "The *Maktu'* System and the Jewish Community of Sixteenth-Century Safed: A Study of Two Documents from the Ottoman Archives," *Journal of Ottoman Studies* 3 (1982): 81–90.

29. BBA, MM 15169.

30. BBA, MM 15169, p. A.

31. The document refers to some of the Armenians as *tüccar*, which means important trader. See İnalcık, "Capital Formation," p. 98.

32. Solomon Schechter, "Safed in the Sixteenth-Century—A City of Legists and Mystics," in *Studies in Judaism*, 2d ser. (Philadelphia: Jewish Publication Society, 1908), p. 251.

33. De Groot, *Ottoman Empire and Dutch Republic*, pp. 216–17.

34. BBA, MM 6004, p. 15.

35. İnalcık, "Military and Fiscal Transformation," pp. 313–27.

36. On Joseph Mendes of Nasi, see Baron, *Ottoman Empire*, pp. 84–118.

37. Herbert I. Bloom, *The Economic Activities of the Jews of Amsterdam in the Seventeenth and Eighteenth Centuries* (Port Washington, New York: Bayard Press, 1937), pp. 82–86.

38. Haim Gerber, "Jewish Tax-Farmers in the Ottoman Empire in the 16th and 17th Centuries," *Journal of Turkish Studies* 10 (1986): 143–54.

39. Ülker, "Rise of Izmir," p. 34.
40. BBA, ED 26, p. 143, no. 1.
41. Halil Sahillioğlu, "XVII. yüzyılın ortalarında sirmakeşlik ve altın-gümüş, işlemeli kumaşlarımız," *Belgelerle Türk Tarihi Dergisi* 3.16 (1968–69): 48–53; and Sahillioğlu, "Osmanlı para tarihinde dünya para ve maden hareketinin yeri (1300–1750)," *ODTÜ Gelişme Dergisi/Studies in Development*, special issue 1 (1978): 12–16.
42. BBA, ED 13/1, p. 68, no. 2; ED 26/1, p. 65; and ED 26/1, p. 86.
43. BBA, ED 26/1, pp. 116–17.
44. Gershom G. Scholem, *Sabbatai Ṣevi: The Mystical Messiah, 1626–1676*, trans. R. J. Zwi Werblowsky (Princeton: Princeton University Press, 1973), pp. 106–8. While discussing in detail the ideology and personality of Zvi, Scholem virtually ignores the Ottoman milieu in which the mystic lived.
45. Traian Stoianovich, "The Conquering Balkan Orthodox Merchants," *Journal of Economic History* 20 (1960): 245–46.

CHAPTER FIVE

1. On town autonomy, see Fernand Braudel, *Capitalism and Material Life, 1400–1800*, trans. Miriam Kochan (New York: Harper and Row, 1973), p. 396.
2. Niels Steensgaard, "Consuls and Nations in the Levant from 1570 to 1650," *Scandinavian Economic History Review* 15 (1967): 13–55. The comparison that follows relies heavily on this article. Suraiya Faroqhi looks at the Venetian crisis from a different perspective in "The Venetian Presence in the Ottoman Empire (1600–1630)," *Journal of European Economic History* 22 (1986): 345–84.
3. Dorothy M. Vaughan, *Europe and the Turk: A Pattern of Alliances, 1350–1700* (Liverpool: University Press, 1954), chap. 3.
4. Daniel Goffman, "The Capitulations and the Question of Authority in Levantine Trade," *Journal of Turkish Studies* 10 (1986): 158–59.
5. BBA, MM 6004, p. 124.
6. Uluçay, *Eşkiyalık ve halk hareketleri*, pp. 31–36.
7. On Orlando and the Dutch policy regarding appointment of consuls, see de Groot, *Ottoman Empire and Dutch Republic*, pp. 216–17.
8. On protection money, see Frederic C. Lane, "The Economic Consequences of Organized Violence," *Journal of Economic History* 18 (1958): 401–17.
9. İnalcık, "Centralization and Decentralization," pp. 27–29.
10. On Hüseyin Paşa, see Uluçay, *Eşkiyalık ve halk hareketleri*, documents 46, 47, and 48.
11. On French policies, see Steensgaard, "Consuls and Nations," pp. 29–30.
12. Wood, *Levant Company*, pp. 209–10.

13. Wood, *Levant Company*, pp. 89–92; and Kütükoğlu, *Osmanlı-ingiliz iktisâdî münâsebetleri*, pp. 24–28.
14. PRO, SP 97/16, fols. 88a–89a.
15. Mark Charles Fissel and Daniel Goffman, "Viewing the Scaffold from Istanbul: The Bendysh-Hyde Affair, 1647–1651" (paper presented at the Fourteenth Annual Meeting of the Western Conference on British Studies, Lincoln, Nebraska, 29–31 October 1987).
16. Masson, *Commerce français*, chap. 4.
17. BBA, ED 13/1, p. 20; ED 13/1, p. 124; and MM 6004, p. 28, no. 3.
18. Fernand Braudel and Ruggiero Romano, *Navires et marchandises à l'entrée du port de Livourne, 1547–1611* (Paris: A. Colin, 1951).
19. Lane, *Venice*, pp. 400–401.
20. BBA, ED 13/1, p. 55, no. 2.
21. BBA, MM 6004, p. 6, no. 4. MM 6004, p. 9, no. 1 is a second decree on the same subject. *Eagle* was a common name. Epstein (*English Levant Company*, p. 221) mentions a ship named *Eagle* of 150 tons burden maintained by the English Levant Company in 1590; and Wood refers to another *Eagle* of 500 tons burden that sailed for Scanderoon in 1664 (*Levant Company*, pp. 210–11).
22. Wood, *Levant Company*, pp. 71–73.
23. Lane, *Venice*, p. 298.
24. Sanderson, *Travels*, p. 285.
25. BBA, MM 6004, p. 9, no. 1. See also MM 6004, p. 10, no. 1.
26. CSP, Venice, vol. 21, p. 83, no. 116.
27. CSP, Venice, vol. 21, p. 117, no. 159.
28. BBA, MM 6004, p. 8. Each piece was fifty cubits in length (see Pakalın, "Pastav," *Deyimleri ve terimleri sözlüğü*).
29. BBA, MD 76, p. 141.
30. BBA, ED 13/1, p. 26, no. 1.
31. On these privileges, see BBA, ED 13/1, p. 77; MM 6004, p. 5; and MM 6004, p. 15.
32. BBA, ED 13/1, p. 54.
33. BBA, ED 13/1, p. 56.
34. BBA, ED 13/1, p. 102, no. 6 and MM 6004, p. 10, no. 1.
35. BBA, MM 6004, p. 25, no. 2.
36. BBA, MM 6004, p. 27, no. 1 and MM 6004, p. 43. Ten or fifteen *guruş* was approximately eight-hundred to twelve-hundred *akçes*.
37. BBA, MM 6004, p. 10, no. 3.
38. On fluctuations in the worth of species, see Andrew A. Watson, "Back to Gold–and Silver," *Economic History Review*, 2d ser., 22 (1976): 1–34. On the Ottoman context, see Barkan, "Price Revolution"; İnalcık, "Impact of *Annales* School," pp. 91–96; and Sahillioğlu, "Dünya para ve maden hareketinin yeri."
39. BBA, ED 13/1, p. 27.

40. BBA, ED 13/1, p. 67, no. 6.

41. BBA, ED 13/1, p. 92, no. 5.

42. BBA, ED 13/1, p. 109, no. 5 and ED 13/1, p. 152, no. 1.

43. BBA, ED 13/1, p. 70 and ED 13/1, p. 57, no. 1.

44. BBA, ED 13/1, p. 93, no. 1.

45. Ashtor, "Venetian Cotton Trade," pp. 687–89.

46. Annie Mary Millard, "The Import Trade of London, 1600–1640" (Ph.D. diss., University of London, 1956), p. 185.

47. BBA, ED 13/1, p. 30.

48. BBA, ED 13/1, p. 57, no. 2. See also BBA, ED 13/1 (1618), p. 185.

49. BBA, MM 6004, p. 47, no. 2.

50. BBA, MM 6004, p. 30, no. 2. This complaint had been voiced as early as 1617 and was repeated as late as 1623 (see BBA, ED 13/1, p. 189, no. 2 and MM 6004, p. 50).

51. BBA, MM 6004, p. 34.

52. BBA, MM 6004, p. 47, no. 1.

53. Schefer, *Ambassade de France*, p. 419.

54. BBA, ED 13/1, p. 74.

55. BBA, MM 6004, p. 12.

56. BBA, MM 6004, p. 54, no. 2. BBA, MM 6004, p. 36 and MM 6004, p. 117 also pertain to the case.

57. Lane, *Venice*, pp. 401–2.

58. BBA, ED 13/1, p. 93, no. 2.

59. BBA, ED 13/1, p. 28 and MM 6004, p. 49, no. 2.

60. BBA 6004, p. 49, no. 2.

61. BBA, ED 13/1, p. 36.

62. BBA, ED 13/1, p. 38. Other decrees dealing with the lending of money are BBA, ED 13/1, p. 68, no. 1 (1609); ED 13/1, p. 81, no. 1 (1612); ED 13/1, p. 185, no. 1 (1618); MM 6004, p. 29, no. 1 (1622); and MM 6004, p. 48, no. 1 (1623).

63. BBA, ED 13/1, p. 94.

64. BBA, ED 13/1, p. 140.

65. BBA, ED 13/1, p. 151.

66. BBA, ED 13/1, p. 60.

67. BBA, MM 6004, p. 29, no. 2 and MM 6004, p. 49, no. 1.

68. BBA, MM 6004, p. 51, no. 2.

69. BBA, ED 13/1, p. 42.

70. BBA, ED 13/1, p. 73.

71. CSP, Venice, vol. 9, p. 457, no. 983.

72. CSP, Venice, vol. 9, pp. 463–66.

73. BBA, ED 13/1, p. 49 and ED 13/1, p. 184, no. 2 (1618).

74. On French attempts to pass "hollowed out" coins in Izmir in 1690, see BBA, MD 99, pp. 80 and 144.

75. BBA, MM 6004, p. 53, no. 3. See also BBA, MM 6004, p. 54, no. 1.

76. Halil Sahillioğlu, "1763 de Izmir limanı ihracaat gümrüğü ve tarifesi," *Belgelerle Türk Tarihi Dergisi* 2.8 (1968): 53.
77. On this *iltizam* system, see İnalcık, "Military and Fiscal Transformation," pp. 327–33.
78. BBA, ED 13/1, p. 26, no. 2 and ED 13/1, p. 68, no. 3.
79. BBA, MM 6004, p. 28, no. 1.
80. See also BBA, MM 6004, p. 30, no. 2 and MM 6004, p. 35.
81. Lane, *Venice*, pp. 400–402.

CHAPTER SIX

1. On these difficulties, see Robert Paris, ed., *Commerce de Marseilles*, vol. 4: *De 1599 à 1660, de 1660 à 1789*, Louis Bergasse and Gaston Rambert (Paris: Librarie Plon, 1954), pp. 39–41; and Masson, *Commerce française*, chap. 3.
2. Bergasse and Rambert, *De 1599 à 1660*, pp. 57–61; and Steensgaard, "Consuls and Nations," pp. 25–30.
3. Missir, *Grands familles Latines de Smyrne*, p. 307; and Ülker, "Rise of Izmir," p. 314.
4. This right was written into the commercial agreement of 1569 between the French and the Ottomans and was confirmed in 1604 in the following phrase: "Should a murder or other impropriety occur among the French merchants and factors, the ambassadors and consuls of that nation are empowered to judge it according to their own laws and customs, without any of our officers hindering them" (Schefer, *Ambassade de France*, p. 424).
5. BBA, ED 26/1, p. 143, no. 1.
6. BBA, ED 26/1, p. 5, no. 1.
7. BBA, ED 26/1, pp. 47–48 and 48, no. 2. On indiscipline within the French merchant community, see also Masson, *Commerce français*, pp. 1–23.
8. BBA, ED 26/1, p. 70, no. 3.
9. BBA, ED 26/1, p. 42.
10. BBA, ED 26/1, p. 146, nos. 1 and 2.
11. BBA, ED 26/1, p. 54, no. 2.
12. Masson, *Commerce français*, p. 53. On this ambassador, see Gerard Tongas, *Les relations de la France avec l'empire Ottoman durant la première moitié du XVIIe siècle et l'ambassade à Constantinople de Philippe de Harlay, Comte de Césy (1619–1640)* (Toulouse: F. Boisseau, 1942), pp. 12–21.
13. BBA, ED 26/1, pp. 12–13. See also Masson, *Commerce français*, pp. 56–57.
14. BBA, ED 26/1, p. 16.
15. BBA, ED 26/1, p. 22.

16. Masson, *Commerce français*, pp. 51–62.
17. BBA, ED 26/1, pp. 6 and 7, no. 2. On tax farming in France during this period, see Roland Mousnier, *La vénalité des offices sous Henri IV et Louis XIII* (Rouen: Editions Maugard, 1945).
18. On trading diasporas, see Curtin, *Cross-Cultural Trade*, pp. 1–14; and Bruce Masters, "Trading Diasporas and 'Nations': The Genesis of National Identities in Ottoman Aleppo," *International History Review* 9 (1987): 345–67.
19. BBA, ED 26/1, p. 70, no. 4. On de la Haye's relations with his merchants, see Masson, *Commerce français*, p. 61.
20. Steensgaard, "Consuls and Nations," p. 25.
21. On the capitulations, see Schefer, *Ambassade de France*, p. 424.
22. BBA, ED 26/1, p. 5 no. 1. He also supervised construction of the Capuchin church, St. Polycarpe, which (since rebuilt at least twice) still stands (see Missir, *Grands familles Latines de Smyrne*, p. 33).
23. BBA, ED 13/1, p. 151.
24. BBA, ED 26/1, p. 38, no. 4.
25. BBA, ED 26/1, p. 49.
26. BBA, ED 26/1, p. 39.
27. BBA, ED 26/1, p. 19, no. 1.
28. BBA, ED 26/1, p. 17, no. 1.
29. This case unfolds in BBA, ED 26/1, p. 17, no. 2; ED 26/1, p. 18, no. 1; ED 26/1, p. 18, no. 2; and ED 26/1, p. 19, no. 1.
30. BBA, ED 26/1, p. 20, no. 1.
31. BBA, ED 26/1, p. 7, no. 1.
32. BBA, ED 26/1, p. 36.
33. BBA, ED 26/1, p. 56.
34. On this term, see İnalcık, "İmtiyâzât."
35. BBA, ED 26/1, pp. 60, no. 2 and 60–61.
36. Vaughan, *Europe and the Turk*, p. 244.
37. BBA, ED 26/1, p. 50, no. 2.
38. BBA, ED 26/1, p. 68, no. 1.
39. BBA, ED 26/1, p. 50, no. 1.
40. See Wood, *Levant Company*, pp. 92–93; and CSP, Venice, vol. 28, p. 167, no. 448, where the bailo Niccolo Sagredo reported on 10 October 1650 that "from these actions [of the Bendysh-Hyde affair] it is quite apparent that this ambassador is for the parliament, as I have reported on several occasions, although to the foreign representatives he has sometimes represented himself as being for the royal party."
41. On this incident, difficulties confronting English trade in these years, and the Ottoman response to the political crisis in England, see Fissel and Goffman, "Viewing the Scaffold from Istanbul."
42. PRO, SP 97/17, fol. 57b.
43. PRO, SP 97/16, fols. 53a–b.

44. PRO, SP 97/16, fols. 53a–b.
45. PRO, SP 97/15, fols. 111b–12b.
46. See, in order of mention, BBA, ED 26/1, pp. 121–22; PRO, SP 97/18, fol. 1a; and PRO, SP 97/20, fols. 167a–68b.
47. Courmenin, *Voiage de Levant*, p. 342.
48. BBA, MZD, p. 201. On Ottoman construction, see Cengiz Orhonlu, "Şehir mimarları," *Journal of Ottoman Studies* 2 (1981): 1–30; and Suraiya Faroqhi, "Long-term Change and the Ottoman Construction Site: A Study of Builders' Wages and Iron Prices," *Journal of Turkish Studies* 10 (1986): 111–25.
49. BBA, ED 13/1, p. 55.
50. Atay, *Izmir*, pp. 71–72.
51. BBA, ED 13/1, p. 97.
52. BBA, ED 28/3, p. 20, no. 1. On this earthquake, see Ülker, "Rise of Izmir," pp. 43–54; and on tombstones in St. Polycarpe, see Missir, *Grands familles Latines de Smyrne*.
53. BBA, ED 13/1, p. 20, no. 5.
54. BBA, ED 13/1, p. 90; ED 13/1, p. 186, no. 2.
55. BBA, MM 6004, p. 33, no. 1; MM 6004, p. 33, no. 2; MM 6004, p. 48, no. 2; and MM 6004, p. 48, no. 3.
56. Tournefort, *Voyage into the Levant*, vol. 2, pp. 375 and 377.

CHAPTER SEVEN

1. On the clash between "Islamic" and "mercantilistic" economies, see Masters, *Origins*, pp. 186–213.
2. Braudel, *Capitalism and Material Life*, p. 21.
3. Halil İnalcık, "The Question of the Closing of the Black Sea Under the Ottomans," *Archeion Pontou* 35 (1979): 107–10.
4. On the eighteenth century, see Frangakis-Syrett, "Commerce of Izmir," pp. 84–123. On the nineteenth century, see Reşat Kasaba, *The Ottoman Empire and the World Economy: The Nineteenth Century* (Albany: State University of New York Press, 1988), pp. 87–112.
5. Such adaptations occurred in the nineteenth century (see Donald Quataert, "Ottoman Handicrafts and Industry, 1800–1914: A Reappraisal," in *Osmanistische Studien zur Wirtschafts- und Sozialgeschichte*, pp. 128–34).
6. On western-Anatolian agriculture and the world-economy, see Reşat Kasaba, "Incorporation of the Ottoman Empire, 1750–1820," *Review* 10 (1987): 805–47; and Şevket Pamuk, "Commodity Production for World-Markets and Relations of Production in Ottoman Agriculture, 1840–1913," in *The Ottoman Empire and the World-Economy*, ed. Huri İslamoğlu-İnan (Cambridge: Cambridge University Press, 1987), pp. 181–82 and 195–98.
7. Braudel, *Capitalism and Material Life*, pp. 396ff.

APPENDIX I

1. Sonia Anderson, *An English Consul in Turkey: Paul Rycaut at Smyrna, 1667–1678* (Oxford: Clarendon Press, 1989); Masson, *Commerce français*; Steensgaard, *Asian Trade Revolution*; Tenenti, *Piracy and the Decline of Venice*; and Wood, *Levant Company*.
2. On this series, see Çetin, *Başbakanlık arşivi kılavuzu*, pp. 68–72. The only other studies that have systematically exploited registers from this series are Faroqhi, "Venetian Presence;" Suraiya Faroqhi, "Sie Osmanische Handelspolitik des Frühen 17. Jahrhunderts zwischen Dubrovnik und Venedik," in *Das Osmanische Reich und Europa 1683 bis 1789: Konflikt, Entspannung und Austausch* (Vienna: Verlag für Geschichte und Politik, 1983), pp. 207–22; and Goffman "Capitulations."
3. Gunther E. Rothenberg, "Venice and the Uskoks of Senj: 1537–1618," *Journal of Modern History* 33 (1961): 148–56.
4. Wood, *Levant Company*, p. 89.
5. Christine Woodhead looks at European and Ottoman perceptions of each other in " 'The Present Terrour of the World'? Contemporary Views of the Ottoman Empire c1600," *History* 72 (1987): 20–37.

GLOSSARY

âcir: someone who is hired, an employee; in Izmir, sometimes refers to Ottoman subjects assisting western merchants in the movement of contraband goods.

akçe: a silver coin, also known as an asper; basic monetary unit in the Ottoman empire.

altın: a gold coin.

baylaç hakkı: "the rights of the bailo"; a surcharge, usually of 2 or 3 percent that Levant companies imposed on shipped goods for the upkeep and expenses of the ambassador in Istanbul.

beylerbeyi: governor of the largest administrative unit in the Ottoman empire.

beylerbeyilik: an administrative unit presided over by a *beylerbeyi* (q.v.).

bid'at: innovation; often but not exclusively used to criticize, as contrary to Islamic law, economic or social changes of which the state disapproved.

celâli: a rebel; often refers to the widespread rebellions in late-sixteenth- and early-seventeenth-century Anatolia.

cemaat-i gebran: a community of Christians; often refers to a recently settled, autonomous group.

cizye: head tax collected from non-Muslims; in seventeenth-century Izmir, collected from non-Muslim heads of households.

ecnebi defterleri: registers of foreigners; rescripts responding to the petitions of foreigners living and working in the Ottoman empire.

evkaf: see *vakıf*.

guruş: a piastre; a large silver coin.

gümrük: customs; tariff.

hamal: porter; day laborer; in seventeenth-century Izmir, often refers to the dock workers who carried goods to and from ships.

hane: household; taxable unit.

harbi: non-Muslim enemy; a non-Muslim foreigner who was not legally visiting the empire.

kadı: religious judge; head of a *kaza* (q.v.); because there was no comparable military authority in seventeenth-century Izmir, the official to whom imperial decrees were addressed.

kantar: a measure used for weighing bulky goods; it was not standardized, but equaled approximately fifty-six kilograms.

kapıcı: "gatekeeper"; stationed at the palace, sometimes served as a messenger.

kapudan paşa: commander of the Ottoman fleet.

kayık: similar, but not identical, to the rowboat found on European vessels; often used to ferry contraband aboard ships.

kaymakam: often a substitute for or representative of an Ottoman official.

kaza: the administrative district, or more rarely the responsibilities, of a *kadı* (q.v.).

kile: a measure for grain, usually thirty-seven cubic decimeters in Istanbul, but not standardized.

konsolos/konsolosluk hakkı: "the rights of consulage"; a surcharge similar to and at times interchangeable with the *baylaç hakkı* (q.v.) except that the income from it went to the consul rather than the ambassador.

kotimo: customs; probably the equivalent of *gümrük* (q.v.).

mahalle: quarter or district in a town or city.

menzil: a halting place; inn; hotel.

mukataa: a tax farm, usually bought for a three-year period.

mültezim: holder of an *iltizam*, auctioned off public source of revenue.

nefer: taxable adult male.

osmanî: silver coin introduced by Osman II in 1618 and initially worth ten *akçe*s (q.v.).

piyade taifesi: "class of infantrymen"; a group in the Ottoman army disbanded in the late sixteenth century.

reâyâ: those Ottoman subjects, as distinguished from the military class, who paid taxes.

sancak: an administrative subdivision of a *beylerbeyilik* (q.v.).

sancakbeyi: the governor of a *sancak* (q.v.).

sicil: a judicial register; often refers to the records kept by a *kadı* (q.v.).

sipahi: an Ottoman cavalryman who held a *timar* (q.v.) in return for military service.

sürgün: officially imposed migration.

tarhana: a wheat and curdled milk preparation used because it did not spoil.

timar: an Ottoman military fief that brought in less than twenty-thousand *akçe*s (q.v.) annually.

vakıf: (pl. *evkaf*), a pious or charitable foundation consisting of land or some other source of revenue.

yasakçı: a guard, especially a janissary guarding an ambassador or consul; in Izmir, often refers to janissaries responsible for guarding goods on the wharf.

zimmi: a non-Muslim *reâyâ* (q.v.).

BIBLIOGRAPHY

ARCHIVAL SOURCES

Istanbul

Başbakanlık Arşivi
    Cevdet Tasnifi 28/23776, 28/23787
    Ecnebi Defterleri 13/1, 16, 22, 26/1, 27, 28, 35
    Hadariye Defterleri 2
    İbnülemin Tasnifi (Maliye) 640, 762, 1189, 1924, 2854, 2969, 3797, 5659
    Kâmil Kepeci Tasnifi 2866
    Maliyeden Müdevver 76, 1459, 1522, 2772, 2825, 2947, 3457, 6004, 7028, 7266, 7534, 9842, 9848, 12809, 14556, 14672, 15169, 17901, 18199, 23308
    Mühimme Defterleri 3–7, 26, 28–30. 38, 40, 44–45, 63–88, 99–100
    Mühimme Zeyli Defterleri 6–11
    Tapu-Tahrir Defterleri 148, 363, 366, 537

London
    Public Record Office

    State Papers 97/13–21, 105/209, 105/332, 105/334–35

PUBLISHED SOURCES

Ahrweiler, Helene. "L'histoire et la géographie de la région de Smyrne entre les deux occupations Turques." *Traveaux et Mémoires* 1 (1965): 1–204.
———. "Istanbul, Carrefour des routes continentales et maritimes aux XVe—XIXe siècles." In *Istanbul à la jonction des cultures balkaniques,*

méditerranéennes, slaves et orientales, aux XVIe—XIXe siècles, pp. 9–
26. Bucarest: Association Internationale d'Etudes du Sud-est Européen,
1977.

Akdağ, Mustafa. *Celâli isyanları (1550—1603)*. Ankara: Ankara Üniversitesi, 1963.

———. "Celâli isyanlarından büyük kaçgunluk, 1603–1606." *Tarih Araştırmalar Dergisi* 2 (1966): 1–49.

Akın, Himmet. *Aydın oğulları tarihi hakkında bir araştırma*. Ankara: Ankara Üniversitesi, 1946.

Aktepe, M. Münir. "1727–1728 Izmir isyanına dair bazı vesikalar." *Tarih
Dergisi* 11 (1955): 71–98.

———. "Izmir hanları ve çarşıları hakkında ön bilgi." *Tarih Dergisi* 25
(1971): 105–54.

———. "Izmir şehri Osmanlı devri medreseleri hakkında ön bilgi." *Tarih
Dergisi* 26 (1972): 97–118.

———. "Izmir'in hisar veya Yakub-Bey câmi'i." *Tarih Dergisi* 27 (1973):
84–98.

———. "Osmanlı devri Izmir câmi'leri hakkında ön bilgi—I." *Tarih Enstitüsü Dergisi* 3 (1973): 177–212.

———. "Osmanlı devri Izmir câmi'leri hakkında ön bilgi—II." *Tarih Enstitüsü Dergisi* 4 (1973): 91–152.

———. "Izmir suları çeşme ve sebilleri ile şadırvanları hakkında bir araştırma." *Tarih Dergisi* 30 (1976): 135–78.

Alberi, Eugenio, ed. *Relazione degli ambasciatori Veneti al Senato*. 3d ser.,
vol. 3. Florence: Società Editrice Fiorentina, 1838–63.

Alexandrescu-Dersca, M. "Contribution à l'étude de l'approvisionnement en
blé de Constantinople au XVIIIe siècle." *Studia et Acta Orientalia* 1
(1957): 13–37.

Ambrose, Gwylim. "English Traders at Aleppo (1658–1756)." *Economic
History Review*, o.s. 3 (1931–32): 246–67.

Anderson, Roger Charles. *Naval Wars in the Levant, 1559–1853*. Liverpool:
University Press, 1952.

Anderson, Sonia. *An English Consul in Turkey: Paul Rycaut at Smyrna,
1667–1678*. Oxford: Clarendon Press, 1989.

Andreasyan, Hrand D. "Ermeni seyyahı Polonyalı Simeon'un seyahatnâmesi
(1608–1619)." *Türkiyat Mecmuası* 10 (1951–53): 269–76.

———. "Bir ermeni kaynağına göre celâli isyanları." *Tarih Dergisi* 13
(1963): 27–42.

———. *Polonyalı Simeon'un seyahatnâmesi, 1608–1619*. Istanbul: Baha
Matbaası, 1964.

Ankori, Zvi. *Karaites in Byzantium: The Formation Years, 970–1100*. New
York: Columbia University Press, 1959.

————. "From Zudecha to Yahudi Mahallesi: The Jewish Quarter of Candia in the Seventeenth Century (A Chapter in the History of Cretan Jewry under Muslim Rule)." In *Salo Wittmayer Baron Jubilee Volume*. Vol. 1, pp. 63–127. New York: Columbia University Press, 1975

Argenti, Philip P. *Chius Vincta or the Occupation of Chios by the Turks (1566) and Their Administration of the Island (1566–1912)*. Cambridge: Cambridge University Press, 1941.

————. *The Religious Minorities of Chios: Jews and Roman Catholics*. Cambridge: Cambridge University Press, 1970.

————, ed. *The Expedition of the Florentines to Chios (1599), Described in Contemporary Diplomatic Reports and Military Dispatches*. London: John Lane, 1934.

Arkin, Marcus. "West European Jewry in the Age of Mercantilism: An Economic Interpretation." *Historia Judaica* 22 (1960): 85–103.

Arundell, Francis V. J. *Discoveries in Asia Minor*. London: R. Bently, 1834.

Asdrachas, Sp. I. "Aux Balkans du XVe siècle: Producteurs directs et marché." *Etudes Balkaniques* 6 (1970): 36–69.

Ashtor, Eliyahu. "The Venetian Cotton Trade in Syria in the Latter Middle Ages." *Studi Medievali*. 3d ser., 17 (1976): 675–715.

Atay, M. Çınar. *Tarih içinde Izmir*. Izmir: Tifset Basım ve Yayın Sanayii, 1978.

Aymard, Maurice. "XVI. yüzyılın sonunda Akdeniz'de korsanlık ve Venedik." *Istanbul Üniversitesi İktisat Fakültesi Mecmuası* 23 (1962–63): 219–38.

————. *Venise, Raguse et le commerce du blé pendant la seconde moitié du XVIe siècle*. Paris: S.E.V.P.E.N., 1966.

Baer, Gabriel. "The Administrative, Economic and Social Functions of Turkish Guilds." *International Journal of Middle East Studies* 1 (1970): 28–50.

Bakhit, M. A. "Sidon in Mamluk and Early Ottoman Times." *Journal of Ottoman Studies* 3 (1982): 53–68.

Barkan, Ömer-Lûtfi. "Türkiye'de imparatorluk devirlerinin büyük nüfus ve arazi tahrirler ve hâkana mahsus istatistik defterleri." *Istanbul Üniversitesi İktisat Fakültesi Mecmuası* 2 (1940–41): 20–59, 214–47.

————. "İstilâ devirlerinin kolonizotör Türk dervişleri ve zaviyeler." *Vakıflar Dergisi* 2 (1942): 279–386.

————. *XV. ve XVI. asırlarda Osmanlı imparatorluğunda ziraî ekonominin hukukî ve malî esasları (kanunlar)*. Istanbul: Bürhaneddin Matbaası, 1943.

————. "Les déportations comme méthode de peuplement et de colonisation dans l'empire Ottoman." *Istanbul Üniversitesi İktisat Fakültesi Mecmuası* 11 (1949–50): 67–131.

———. " 'Tarihi Demografi' araştırmaları ve Osmanlı tarihi." *Türkiyat Mecmuası* 10 (1951–52): 1–26.

———. "Quelques observations sur l'organisation économique et sociale des villes Ottomanes des XVIe et XVIIe siècles." *Recueils de la Société Jean Bodin* 7 (1955): 289–310.

———. "Essai sur les données statistiques des registres de recensement dans l'empire Ottoman au XVe et XVIe siècles." *Journal of the Economic and Social History of the Orient* 1 (1957): 9–36.

———. "Price Revolution of the Sixteenth Century: A Turning Point in the Economic History of the Near East." *International Journal of Middle East Studies* 6 (1975): 3–28.

Barkey, Karen; Linda T. Darling; Daniel Goffman; and Fariba Zarinebaf-Shahr. "Centralization Versus Autonomy: Was the Ottoman State Really in Control?" Panel presented at the Twenty-First Annual Meeting of the Middle East Studies Association of North America. Baltimore, 14–17 November 1987.

Barnai, Jacob. "The Settlement of the Jewish Community in Izmir in the Ottoman Period" (in Hebrew). *Pa'amin* 12 (1982): 47–58.

———. "On the Jewish Community of Izmir in the Late Eighteenth and Early Nineteenth Century" (in Hebrew). *Tsiyyon* 47 (1982): 56–76.

———. "The Jewish Community of Izmir in the Seventeenth Century" (in Hebrew). *Proceedings of the Eighth World Congress of Jewish Studies*. Division B: *The Period of the Bible*, pp. 85–88. Jerusalem: n.p., 1982.

———. "The Development of the Links between the Jews of Izmir and the Jews of Eretz Israel in the 17th–18th Centuries" (in Hebrew). *Shalem, Studies in the History of the Jews in Eretz-Israel* 5 (1987): 95–114.

Barnai, Jacob, and Haim Gerber. *The Jews in Izmir in the Nineteenth Century: Ottoman Documents from the Shar'i Court* (in Hebrew). Jerusalem: Institute for Research on the Sephardi and Oriental Jewish Heritage, 1984.

Baron, Salo Wittmayer. *A Social and Religious History of the Jews.* Vol. 18: *The Ottoman Empire, Persia, Ethiopia, India, and China.* New York: Columbia University Press, 1983.

Baron, Salo Wittmayer; Arcadius Kahan; et al. *Economic History of the Jews.* Edited by Nachum Gross. New York: Schocken Books, 1975.

Baulant, Micheline. *Lettres de négociants marseillais: Les frères Hermite (1570–1612).* Paris: A. Colin, 1953.

Bausani, Alessandro. *The Persians from the Earliest Days to the Twentieth Century.* Translated by J. B. Donne. London: Elek, 1971.

Baykara, Tuncer. "Kökboya." *Istanbul Üniversitesi Enstitüsü Dergisi* 14 (1964): 221–26.

———. *Izmir şehri ve tarihi.* Istanbul: Ege Üniversitesi Matbaası, 1974.

Beauvau, Henry de. *Relation iournaliere du voyage du Levant*. Nancy: Iacob Garnich, 1615.

Bediz, D. *Izmir (Smyrna)*. Würzburg: Inaugural diss., Munich, 1935.

Beldiceanu, Nicoara. "Structures socio-économiques à Lemnos à la fin du XVe siècle." *Turcica* 15 (1983): 247–66.

Bent, James Theodore, ed. *Early Voyages and Travels in the Levant*. I.— *The Diary of Master Thomas Dallam, 1599–1600*. II.—*Extracts from the Diaries of Dr. John Covel, 1670–1679*. London: Hakluyt Society, 1893.

Bergasse, Louis, and G. Rambert *Histoire du commerce de Marseilles*. Vol. 4: *De 1599 à 1660, de 1660 à 1789*. Paris: Librairie Plon, 1954.

Biegman, Nicolaas H. *The Turco-Ragusan Relationship according to the Firmâns of Murâd III (1575–1595) Extant in the State Archives of Dubrovnik*. The Hague: Mouton, 1967.

Bloom, Herbert I. *The Economic Activities of the Jews of Amsterdam in the Seventeenth and Eighteenth Centuries*. Port Washington, New York: Bayard Press, 1937.

Blount, Henry. *A Voyage into the Levant*. 2d ed. London: Andrew Crooke, 1636.

Bowen, Harold, and Hamilton Gibb. *Islamic Society and the West*. 2 vols. New York: Oxford University Press, 1950.

Bowman, Steven B. *The Jews of Byzantium, 1204–1453*. University, Alabama: University of Alabama Press, 1985.

Braude, Benjamin. "International Competition and Domestic Cloth in the Ottoman Empire, 1500–1650, A Study in Undevelopment." *Review* 1 (1979): 437–54.

———. "Foundation Myths of the *Millet* System." In *Christians and Jews in the Ottoman Empire*. Edited by Benjamin Braude and Bernard Lewis. Vol. 1: *The Central Lands*, pp. 69–88. New York: Holmes and Meier, 1982.

Braudel, Fernand. *The Mediterranean and the Mediterranean World in the Age of Philip II*. Translated by Siân Reynolds. 2 vols. New York: Harper and Row, 1972.

———. *Capitalism and Material Life, 1400–1800*. Translated by Miriam Kochan. New York: Harper and Row, 1973.

———. *Civilization and Capitalism, 15th–18th Century*. Translated by Siân Reynolds. Vol. 3: *The Perspective of the World*. New York: William Collins, 1984.

Braudel, Fernand, and Ruggiero Romano. *Navires et marchandises à l'entrée du port de Livourne, 1547–1611*. Paris: A. Conlin, 1951.

Braudel, Fernand; Pierre Jeannin; Jean Meuvret; and Ruggiero Romano. "Le déclin de Venise au XVIIème siècle." In *Aspetti e cause della decadenza economica Veneziana nel secolo XVII atti del convegno 27*

Guigno–2 Luglio 1957 Venezia, isola di San Giorgio Maggiore, pp. 23–86. Venice-Rome: Istituto per la collaborazione culturale, 1961.

Bruyn, Cornelis de. *Voyage au Levant.* . . . Paris: Corneille Le Brun, 1714.

Buondelmonti, Christopher de. *Description des iles de l'archipel grec*. Translation and commentary by Emile Legrand. Paris: Leroux, 1897.

Burian, Orhan. "Türkiye hakkında dört ingiliz seyahatnâmesi." *Belleten* 15 (1951): 223–45.

———. "Interest of the English in Turkey as Reflected in English Literature of the Renaissance." *Oriens* 5 (1952): 209–29.

———, ed. *The Report of Lello, Third English Ambassador to the Sublime Porte*. Ankara: Türk Tarih Kurumu Basımevi, 1952.

Cahen, Claude. *Pre-Ottoman Turkey*. London: Sidgwick and Jackson, 1968.

Cahnman, Werner J. "Role and Significance of the Jewish Artisan Class." *Jewish Journal of Sociology* 7 (1965): 207–20.

Calendar of State Papers and Manuscripts Relating to English Affairs Existing in the Archives and Collections of Venice, and in Other Libraries of Northern Italy. London: Longman, 1864–1947.

Carayon, Auguste. *Relations inédites des missions de la Société de Jésus à Constantinople*. Paris: E. Cudin, 1864.

Carter, Charles. *The Western European Powers, 1500–1700*. London: Hodder and Stoughton [for] the Sources of History, 1971.

Carter, Francis W. *Dubrovnik (Ragusa): A Classic City-State*. London: Seminar Press, 1972.

Çetin, Atillâ. *Başbakanlık arşivi kılavuzu*. Istanbul: Enderun Kitabevi, 1979.

Cezar, Mustafa. *Osmanlı tarihinde leventler*. Istanbul: Çelikcilt Matbaası, 1965.

Chandler, Richard. *Travels in Asia Minor*. London: J. Dodsley, 1776.

Chaudhuri, K. N. "The World-System East of Longitude 20°: The European Role in Asia, 1500–1750." *Review* 5 (1981): 219–45.

Chishull, Edmund. *Travels in Turkey and Back to England*. London: W. Bowyer, 1747.

Cipolla, Carlo. "The Decline of Italy: The Case of a Fully Matured Economy." *Economic History Review*. 2d ser., 5 (1952): 178–87.

Çizakça, Murat. "Price History and the Bursa Silk Industry: A Study in Ottoman Industrial Decline, 1550–1650." *Journal of Economic History* 40 (1980): 533–50.

———. "A Short History of the Bursa Silk Industry (1500–1900)." *Journal of the Economic and Social History of the Orient* 23 (1980): 142–52.

Cochrane, Eric, and Julius Kirschner. "Deconstructing Lane's *Venice*." *Journal of Modern History* 45 (1975): 321–34.

Cohen, Amnon. *Palestine in the Eighteenth Century: Patterns of Government and Administration*. Jerusalem: Magnes Press, Hebrew University, 1973.

————. "New Evidence on Demographic Change: The Jewish Community in 16th Century Jerusalem." In *Memorial Ömer Lûtfi Barkan*. Edited by Robert Mantran, pp. 57–64. Paris: Librairie d'Amberique et d'orient Adrien Maissonneuve, 1980.

————. *Jewish Life under Islam: Jerusalem in the Sixteenth Century*. Cambridge, Massachusetts: Harvard University Press, 1984.

Cohen, Amnon, and Bernard Lewis. *Population and Revenue in the Towns of Palestine in the Sixteenth Century*. Princeton: Princeton University Press, 1978.

Cook, Michael A. *Population Pressure in Rural Anatolia: 1450–1600*. London: Oxford University Press, 1972.

————, ed. *A History of the Ottoman Empire to 1730*. Cambridge: Cambridge University Press, 1976.

Courmenin, Louis Deshayes, baron de. *Voiage de Levant fait par le Commandement du Roy en l'année 1621 par Le Sr D.C.* 2d ed. Paris: A. Taupinart, 1632.

Croix, Chevalier de la [pseud.]. *Mémoires, contenans diverses relations très curieuses de l'empire Othoman*. Paris, 1684.

Cunningham, Allan. "Dragomania: The Dragomans of the British Embassy in Turkey." *Middle Eastern Affairs*, no. 2. Edited by Albert Hourani. *St. Anthony's Papers* 11 (1961): 81–100.

Curtin, Philip D. *Cross-Cultural Trade in World History*. Cambridge: Cambridge University Press, 1984.

Cvetkova, Bistra. "Le service des *celep* et le ravitaillement en bétail dans l'empire Ottoman (XVe–XVIIIes)." *Etudes Historiques* 3 (1966): 145–72.

————. "Vie économique des villes et ports balkaniques aux XVe et XVIe siècles." *Revue des Etudes Islamiques* 38 (1970): 267–355.

————. "Les *celep* et leur rôle dans la vie économique des Balkans a l'époque Ottomane (XVe–XVIIIes)." In *Studies in the Economic History of the Middle East from the Rise of Islam to the Present Day*. Edited by Michael A. Cook, pp. 172–92. London: Oxford University Press, 1970.

————. "Changements intervenus dans la condition de la population des terres bulgares (depuis la fin du XVe jusqu'au milieu du XVIIIe siècle)." *Etudes Historiques* 5 (1970): 291–318.

Dalsar, Fahri. *Türk sanayi ve ticaret tarihinde Bursa'da ipekçilik*. Istanbul: Sermet Matbaası, 1960.

Danişmend, İsmail Hamı. *İzahli Osmanlı tarihi kronolojisi*. 4 vols. Istanbul: Türkiye Yayınevi, 1947–55.

Dávid, Géza. "The Age of Unmarried Male Children in the *Tahrir-Defter*s (Notes on the Coefficient)." *Acta Orientalie Academiae Scientiarum Hung.* 31 (1977): 347–57.

Davis, James C. *Pursuit of Power, Venetian Ambassadors' Reports on Turkey, France and Spain, 1560–1600*. New York: Harper and Row, 1970.

Davis, Ralph. "England and the Mediterranean, 1570–1670." In *Essays in the Economic and Social History of Tudor and Stuart England in Honour of R. H. Tawney*. Edited by Frederick Jack Fisher, pp. 117–37. Cambridge: Cambridge University Press, 1961.

———. "Influence de l'Angleterre sur le déclin de Venise au XVIIème siècle." In *Aspetti e cause della decadenza economica Veneziana nel secolo XVII atti del convegno 27 Guigno–2 Luglio 1957 Venezia, isola di San Giorgio Maggiore*, pp. 185–235. Venice-Rome: Istituto per la collaborazione culturale, 1961.

———. *The Rise of the English Shipping Industry*. London: Macmillan, 1962.

———. *Aleppo and Devonshire Square: English Traders in the Levant in the Eighteenth Century*. London: Macmillan, 1967.

———. "English Imports from the Middle East, 1580–1780." In *Studies in the Economic History of the Middle East from the Rise of Islam to the Present Day*. Edited by Michael A. Cook, pp. 193–206. London: Oxford University Press, 1970.

———. *The Rise of the Atlantic Economies*. London: Weidenfeld and Nicolson, 1973.

Delaville la Roulx, J. M. A. "L'occupation chrétienne à Smyrne, 1344–1402." *Melanges sur l'Ordre de Saint-Jean de Jerusalem*. Paris, 1910.

Dewdney, J. C. *Turkey: An Introductory Geography*. New York: Praeger, 1971.

Duncan, T. Bentley. "Niels Steensgaard and the Europe-Asia Trade of the Early Seventeenth Century." *Journal of Modern History* 47 (1975): 512–18.

Eale, Peter. "The Commercial Development of Ancona, 1479–1551." *Economic History Review* 12 (1959): 28–44.

Emmanuel, Isaac Samuel. *Histoire de l'industrie des tissues des Israélites de Salonique*. Lausanne: Universite de Lausanne, 1935.

———. *Histoire des Israélites de Salonique*. n.p., 1936.

Encyclopaedia of Islam. New ed. Leiden: E. J. Brill, 1960–

Encyclopedia Judaica. Jerusalem: Macmillan, 1971.

Epstein, Mark Alan. *The Ottoman Jewish Communities and Their Role in the Fifteenth and Sixteenth Centuries*. Freiburg: Klaus Schwarz, 1980.

———. "Leadership of the Ottoman Jews in the Fifteenth and Sixteenth Centuries." In *Christians and Jews in the Ottoman Empire*. Edited by Benjamin Braude and Bernard Lewis. Vol. 1: *The Central Lands*, pp. 101–16. New York: Holmes and Meier, 1982.

Epstein, Mortimer. *The English Levant Company: Its Foundation and Its History to 1640*. London: Routledge, 1908.

Erder, Leila T. "Measurement of Preindustrial Population Changes: The Ottoman Empire from the 15th to the 17th Century." *Middle Eastern Studies* 11 (1975): 294–99.

Erder, Leila T., and Suraiya Faroqhi. "The Development of the Anatolian Urban Network during the Sixteenth Century." *Journal of the Economic and Social History of the Orient* 23 (1980): 265–303.

Ergenç, Özer. "Osmanlı klâsik dönemindeki 'Eşraf ve A'yan' üzerine bazı bilgiler." *Journal of Ottoman Studies* 3 (1982): 105–13.

Erinç, Sirri, and Necdet Tunçdilek. "The Agricultural Regions of Turkey." *Geographical Review* 42 (1952): 179–203.

Evliya Çelebî. *Seyahatnâmesi*. 9 vols. Istanbul: Devlet Matbaası, 1935.

Faroqhi, Suraiya. "Notes on the Production of Cotton and Cotton Cloth in XVIth and XVIIth Century Anatolia." *Journal of European Economic History* 8 (1972): 405–17.

———. "Rural Society in Anatolia and the Balkans during the Sixteenth Century, I." *Turcica* 9 (1977): 161–95.

———. "Rural Society in Anatolia and the Balkans during the Sixteenth Century, II." *Turcica* 11 (1979): 103–53.

———. "Sixteenth Century Periodic Markets in Various Anatolian Sancaks: İcel, Hamid, Karahisar-i Sahib, Kütahya, Aydın, and Menteşe." *Journal of the Economic and Social History of the Orient* 22 (1979): 32–80.

———. "Istanbul'un iasesi ve Tekirdağ-Rodoscuk limanı (16.–17. yüzyıllar)." *ODTÜ Gelişme Dergisi/METU Studies in Development*, special issue 2 (1979–80): 139–54.

———. "Textile Production and the Arab Provinces: Geographic Distribution and Internal Trade (1560–1650)." *Journal of Ottoman Studies* 1 (1980): 61–83.

———. "Camels, Wagons, and the Ottoman State in the Sixteenth and Seventeenth Centuries." *International Journal of Middle East Studies* 14 (1982): 523–39.

———. "Die Osmanische Handelspolitik des Frühen 17. Jahrhunderts zwischen Dubrovnik und Venedik." In *Das Osmanische Reich und Europa 1683 bis 1789: Konflikt, Entspannung und Austausch* (Vienna: Verlag für Geschichte und Politik, 1983), pp. 207–22.

———. "'Zaviye' Accounts: The Significance for the Social and Economic History of Rural Anatolia." Paper presented at the annual meeting of the Middle East Studies Association of North America. Chicago, November 1983.

———. *Towns and Townsmen of Ottoman Anatolia: Trade, Crafts and Food Production in an Urban Setting, 1520–1650*. Cambridge: Cambridge University Press, 1984.

———— . "Coffee and Spices: Official Ottoman Reactions to Egyptian Trade in the Later Sixteenth Century." In *Festschrift für Andreas Tietze, 76. Band, Wiener Zeitschrift für die Kunde des Morgenlandes*, pp. 87–93. Vienna: Institutes für Orientalistik, 1986.

———— . "Long-Term Change and the Ottoman Construction Site: A Study of Builders' Wages and Iron Prices." *Journal of Turkish Studies* 10 (1986): 111–25.

———— . "Political Initiatives 'From the Bottom Up' in the Sixteenth- and Seventeenth-Century Ottoman Empire: Some Evidence for Their Existence." In *Sonderdruck aus Osmanistische Studien zur Wirtschafts- und Sozialgeschichte in memoriam Vančo Boškov*. Edited by Hans Georg Majer, pp. 24–33. Wiesbaden: Otto Harrassowitz, 1986.

———— . "The Venetian Presence in the Ottoman Empire (1600–1630)." *Journal of European Economic History* 22 (1986): 345–84.

———— . "Town Officials, *Timar*-Holders, and Taxation: The Late Sixteenth-Century Crisis as Seen from Çorum." *Turcica* 18 (1986): 53–82.

———— . "Agriculture and Rural Life in the Ottoman Empire (ca 1500–1878)." *New Perspectives on Turkey* 1 (1987): 3–34.

———— . "Political Tensions in the Anatolian Countryside Around 1600: An Attempt at Interpretation." In *Türkische Miszellen: Robert Anhegger Festschrift*. Edited by Jean-Louis Bacqué-Grammont, Barbara Fleming, Macit Gökberk, and İlber Ortaylı, pp. 117–30. Istanbul: Editions Divit Press, n.d.

Fekete, Lajos. *Die Siyakat-Schrift in der türkische Finanzverwaltung.* 2 vols. Budapest: Akademiai Kiedo, 1955.

Ferrier, R. W. "The Armenians and the East India Company in Persia in the Seventeenth and Early Eighteenth Centuries." *Economic History Review*, 2d ser., 26 (1973): 38–62

Fisher, Frederick Jack. "London's Export Trade in the Early Seventeenth Century." In *The Growth of English Overseas Trade in the Seventeenth Century*. Edited by Walter Edward Minchinton, pp. 64–77. London: H. M. Stationary Office, 1969.

Fissel, Mark Charles, and Daniel Goffman. "Viewing the Scaffold from Istanbul: The Bendysh-Hyde Affair, 1647–1651." Paper presented at the Fourteenth Annual Meeting of the Western Conference on British Studies. Lincoln, Nebraska, 29–31 October 1987.

Fleischer, Cornell H. *Bureaucrat and Intellectual in the Ottoman Empire: The Historian Mustafa Âli (1541–1600).* Princeton: Princeton University Press, 1986.

Frances, E. "La féodalité byzantine et la conquête turque." *Studia et Acta Orientalia* 4 (1962): 62–90.

Franco, Moïse. *Essai sur l'histoire des Israélites de l'empire Ottoman depuis les origins jusqu'à nos jours.* Paris: A. Durlacher, 1897.

Frangakis-Syrett, Elena. "The Commerce of Izmir in the Eighteenth Century (1695–1820)." Ph.D. diss., London University, 1986.

————. "Trade between Ottoman Empire and Western Europe: The Case of Izmir in the Eighteenth Century." *New Perspectives on Turkey* 2 (1988): 1–18.

Galanté, Abraham. *Turcs et Juifs, Etude historique et politique.* Istanbul: Haim, Rozio, 1932.

————. *Nouveaux documents sur Sabbetai Sevi: Organisation et us et coutumes de ses adeptes.* Istanbul: Société Anonyme de Papeterie et d'Imprimerie (Fratelli Haim), 1935.

————. *Histoire des Juifs de Rhodes, Chio, Cos etc.* Istanbul: Société Anonyme de Papeterie et d'Imprimerie (Fratelli Haim), 1935.

————. *Histoire des Juifs d'Anatolie.* Vol. 1: *Les Juifs d'Izmir (Smyrne).* Istanbul: M. Babok, 1937.

————. *Histoire des Juifs d'Anatolie.* Vol. 2. Istanbul: M. Babok, 1939.

————. *Histoire des Juifs d'Istanbul, depuis la prise de cette ville, en 1453, par Fatih Mehmet jusqu'à nos jours.* 2 vols. Istanbul: Hüsnütabiat, 1941.

Geanakoplos, Deno. "Byzantium and the Crusades, 1354–1453." In *A History of the Crusades.* Edited by Kenneth Setton. Vol. 3: *The Fourteenth and Fifteenth Centuries.* Edited by Harry W. Hazard, pp. 69–103. Madison: University of Wisconsin Press, 1975.

Georgiades, Demetrius. *Smyrne et l'Asie Mineure au point de vue économie et commercial.* Paris: Chaix, 1885.

Gerber, Haim. "*Sharia, Kanun,* and Custom in the Ottoman Law: The Court Records of Seventeenth-Century Bursa." *International Journal of Turkish Studies* 2 (1981): 131–47.

————. "Jewish Tax-Farmers in the Ottoman Empire in the 16th and 17th Centuries." *Journal of Turkish Studies* 10 (1986): 143–54.

————. *Economy and Society in an Ottoman City: Bursa, 1600-1700.* Jerusalem: Hebrew University, 1988.

Glamann, Kristof. "European Trade, 1500–1750." In *The Fontana Economic History of Europe.* Edited by Carlo Cipolla. Vol. 3: *The Sixteenth and Seventeenth Centuries,* pp. 427–526. London: Collins, 1974.

Glazebrook, Nathan. *Journey to Kars: A Modern Traveller in the Ottoman Lands.* New York: Holt, Rinehart, and Winston, 1982.

Goffman, Daniel. "The Jews of Safed and the *Maktu'* System in the Sixteenth Century: A Study of Two Documents from the Ottoman Archives." *Journal of Ottoman Studies* 3 (1982): 81–90.

————. "Izmir as a Commercial Center: The Impact of Western Trade on an Ottoman Port, 1570–1650." Ph.D. diss., University of Chicago, 1985.

————. "The Capitulations and the Question of Authority in Levantine Trade." *Journal of Turkish Studies* 10 (1986): 155–61.

────── . "The Ottoman Role in Patterns of Commerce in Aleppo, Chios, Dubrovnik, and Istanbul (1600–1650)." *Proceedings of the Eighth Symposium of the Comité International d'Etudes Pre-Ottomanes et Ottomanes*. Minneapolis, August 1988. (Forthcoming).

Gökçen, İbrahim, and Çağatay Uluçay. *Manisa tarihi*. Istanbul: Manisa Halkevi Yayınlarından, 1939.

Goldman, Israel M. *The Life and Times of Rabbi ibn Abi Zimra: A Social, Economic and Cultural Study of Jewish Life in the Ottoman Empire in the 15th and 16th Centuries as Reflected in the Responsa of the RDBZ*. New York: Jewish Theological Seminary of America, 1970.

Göllner, Charles. *Turcica, Die Europäschen Türkendrucke des XVI Jahrhunderts*. Vol. 2: *1551–1600*. Bucharest-Baden: Editura Academiei, 1968.

Goodblatt, Morris S. *Jewish Life in Turkey in the XVIth Century as Reflected in the Legal Writings of Samuel De Medina*. New York: Jewish Theological Seminary of America, 1952.

Gözenç, Selami. "Küçük Menderes havzasında arazi kullanılışının tarihi temelleri ve halihazır arazinin değer bakımından sınıflandırılması." *Istanbul Üniversitesi Coğrafya Enstitüsü Dergisi* 22 (1977): 127–41.

Grassby, R. "Social Status and Commercial Enterprise under Louis XIV." *Economic History Review* 2.13 (1960): 19–38.

Griswold, William James. *The Great Anatolian Rebellion, 1000–1020/1591–1611*. Berlin: Klaus Schwarz, 1983.

Groot, A. H. de. *The Ottoman Empire and the Dutch Republic: A History of the Earliest Diplomatic Relations, 1610–1630*. Leiden: Nederlands Historisch-Archaeologisch Instituut, 1978.

────── . "The Dutch Nation in Istanbul, 1600–1985: A Contribution to the Social History of Beyoğlu." *Anatolica* 14(1987): 131–50.

Grunebaum-Ballin, P. *Joseph Naci, duc de Naxos*. The Hague: Mouton, 1968.

Güçer, Lütfi. "Le commerce interieur des céréales dans l'empire Ottoman pendant la seconde moitié du XVIème siècle." *Istanbul Üniversitesi İktisat Fakültesi Mecmuası* 11 (1949–50): 163–88.

────── . "Le probleme de l'approvisionnement d'Istanbul en céréales vers le milieu du XVIIème siècle." *Istanbul Üniversitesi İktisat Fakültesi Mecmuası* 11 (1949–50): 153–62.

────── . "XVI yüzyıl sonlarında Osmanlı imparatorluğun dahilinde hububat ticaretinin tabi olduğu kayıtlar." *Istanbul Üniversitesi İktisat Fakültesi Mecmuası* 13 (1951–52): 79–98.

────── . "XV–XVII asırlarda Osmanlı imparatorluğunda tuz inhisarı ve tuzların işletme nizamı." *Istanbul Üniversitesi İktisat Fakültesi Mecmuası* 23 (1962–63): 97–143.

────── . *XVI–XVII asırlarda Osmanlı imparatorluğunda hububat meselesi ve hububattan alınan vergiler*. Istanbul: Sermet Matbaası, 1964.

Guilmartin, John Francis, Jr. *Gunpowder and Galleys: Changing Technology and Mediterranean Warfare at Sea in the Sixteenth Century*. Cambridge: Cambridge University Press, 1974.

Hacker, Joseph R. "Ottoman Policy toward the Jews and Jewish Attitudes toward the Ottomans during the Fifteenth Century." In *Christians and Jews in the Ottoman Empire*. Edited by Benjamin Braude and Bernard Lewis. Vol. 1: *The Central Lands*, pp. 117–25. New York: Holmes and Meier, 1982.

——. "The Impact of the 'Sürgün'-System on Jewish Society in the Ottoman Empire in the 15th–17th Centuries." Paper presented at the Fourth International Congress for the Economic and Social History of Turkey (1071–1922). Munich, 4–8 August 1986.

Hakluyt, Richard. *The Principal Navigations, Voyages, Traffiques and Discoveries of the English Nation*. 12 vols. Glasgow: James MacLehose, 1904.

Hammer-Purgstall, Joseph von. *Geschichte des Osmanischen Reiches*. 10 vols. Pest: C. A. Hartleben, 1827–35.

Hattox, Ralph S. *Coffee and Coffeehouses: The Origins of a Social Beverage in the Medieval Near East*. Seattle: Near Eastern Publications, University of Washington, 1985.

Hauser, Henri. "The Characteristic Features of French Economic History from the Middle of the Sixteenth to the Middle of the Eighteenth Centuries." *Economic History Review* 1 (1933): 257–72.

Haynes, Jonathan. *The Humanist as Traveler: George Sandys's 'Relation of a Journey begun An: Dom: 1610.'* Rutherford: Farleigh Dickinson University Press, 1986.

Heers, Jacques. *Gênes au XVe siècle: activité économique et problemes sociaux*. Paris: S.E.V.P.E.N., 1961.

Heers, Marie Louise. "Les Génois et le commerce de l'alun à la fin du moyen-âge." *Revue d'Histoire Economique et Sociale* 32 (1954): 31–53.

Hess, Andrew. "The Battle of Lepanto and Its Place in Mediterranean History." *Past and Present* 57 (1972): 53–73.

Hexter, Jack H. "Fernand Braudel and the Monde Braudellian." *Journal of Modern History* 44 (1972): 480–539.

Heyd, Uriel. "The Jewish Communities of Istanbul in the XVIIth Century." *Oriens* 6 (1953): 299–314.

——. *Ottoman Documents on Palestine, 1552–1615*. Oxford: Clarendon Press, 1960.

——. "Moses Hamon, Chief Jewish Physician to Sultan Süleyman the Magnificent." *Oriens* 16 (1963): 152–70.

——. "Turkish Documents Concerning the Jews of Safed in the Sixteenth Century." In *Studies on Palestine during the Ottoman Period*. Edited by Moshe Mo'az, pp. 111–18. Jerusalem: Magnes Press, 1975.

Heyd, Wilhelm von. *Histoire du commerce du Levant au moyen-âge*. Rev. ed. 2 vols. Amsterdam: A. M. Hakkert, 1959.

Hicks, John. *A Theory of Economic History*. Oxford: Clarendon Press, 1969.

Hinz, Walther. *Islamische Masse und Gewichte: Umgerechnet ins Metrische System*. Leiden: E. J. Brill, 1955.

Holt, Peter Malcolm; Ann K. S. Lambton; and Bernard Lewis, eds. *The Cambridge History of Islam*. Cambridge: Cambridge University Press, 1970.

Homsy, Basile. *Les capitulations et la protection des chrétiens au Proche-Orient aux XVIe, XVIIe et XVIIIe siècles*. Paris: Harissa, 1956.

Horniker, Arthur Leon. "William Harborne and the Beginning of Anglo-Turkish Diplomatic and Commercial Relations." *Journal of Modern History* 14 (1942): 289–316.

———. "Anglo-French Rivalry in the Levant from 1583 to 1612." *Journal of Modern History* 18 (1946): 289–305.

Howard, Douglas A. "Ottoman Historiography and the Literature of 'Decline' of the Sixteenth and Seventeenth Centuries." *Journal of Asian History* 22 (1988): 52–77.

İnalcık, Halil. "Ottoman Methods of Conquest." *Studia Islamica* 2 (1954): 112–22.

———. "Osmanlılar'da raiyyet rüsûmu." *Belleten* 23 (1959): 575–610.

———. "Bursa and the Commerce of the Levant." *Journal of the Economic and Social History of the Orient* 3 (1960): 131–47.

———. "Bursa: XV. asır sanayi ve ticaret tarihine dair vesikalar." *Belleten* 24 (1960): 45–102.

———. "Adâletnameler." *Belgeler. Türk Tarih Belgeleri Dergisi* 2 (1965): 49–145.

———. "Capital Formation in the Ottoman Empire." *Journal of Economic History* 19 (1969): 97–140.

———. "Süleyman the Lawgiver." *Archivum Ottomanicum* 1 (1969): 105–38.

———. "The Ottoman Economic Mind and Aspects of the Ottoman Economy." In *Studies in the Economic History of the Ottoman Empire from the Rise of Islam to the Present Day*. Edited by Michael A. Cook, pp. 207–18. London: Oxford University Press, 1970.

———. "The Ottoman Decline and Its Effects upon the *Reaya*." In *Aspects of the Balkans, Continuity and Change. Contributions to the International Balkan Conference held at UCLA, 22–28 October 1969*, pp. 338–54. Edited by Henrik Birnbaum and Speros Vryonis, Jr. Hague: Mouton, 1972. Reprinted in İnalcık, Halil. *The Ottoman Empire: Conquest, Organization and Economy*. London: Variorum Reprints, 1978.

————. *The Ottoman Empire: The Classical Age, 1300–1600*. Translated by Norman Itzkowitz and Colin Imber. London: Weidenfeld and Nicolson, 1973.

————. "The Socio-Political Effects of the Diffusion of Firearms in the Middle East." In *War, Technology, and Society in the Middle East*. Edited by Vernon J. Parry and M. E. Yapp, pp. 195–217. London: Oxford University Press, 1975. Reprinted in İnalcık, Halil. *The Ottoman Empire: Conquest, Organization and Economy*. London: Variorum Reprints, 1978.

————. "Centralization and Decentralization in Ottoman Administration." In *Studies in Eighteenth-Century Islamic History*. Edited by Thomas Naff and Roger Owens, pp. 27–52. Carbondale, Illinois: Southern Illinois University Press, 1977.

————. "Impact of the *Annales* School on Ottoman Studies and New Findings." *Review* 1 (1978): 69–96.

————. "Ottoman Policy and Administration in Cyprus after the Conquest." Reprinted in İnalcık, Halil. *The Ottoman Empire: Conquest, Organization and Economy*. London: Variorum Reprints, 1978.

————. "The Question of the Closing of the Black Sea Under the Ottomans." *Archeion Pontou* 35 (1979): 74–110.

————. "Osmanlı pamuklu pazarı, Hindistan ve İngiltere: Pazar rekabetinde emek maliyetinin rolü." *ODTÜ Gelişme Dergisi/METU Studies in Development*, special issue 2 (1979–80): 1–65

————. "Military and Fiscal Transformation in the Ottoman Empire, 1600–1700." *Archivum Ottomanicum* 6 (1980): 283–337.

————. "Rice Cultivation and the *Çeltükçi-Re'âyâ* System in the Ottoman Empire." *Turcica* 14 (1982): 69–141.

————. "'Arab' Camel Drivers in Western Anatolia in the Fifteenth Century." *Revue d'Histoire Maghrebine* 31–32 (1983): 255–70.

————. "Introduction to Ottoman Metrology." *Turcica* 15 (1983): 311–48.

————. "Yük (Himl) in Ottoman Silk Trade, Mining, and Agriculture." *Turcica* 16 (1984): 131–53.

————, ed. *Hicrî 835 tarihli sûret-i defter-i sancak-i Arvanid*. Ankara: Türk Tarih Kurumu Basımevi, 1954.

İnalcık, Halil, and Mevlûd Oğuz. *Gazavât-i Sultân Murâd b. Mehemmed Hân: İzlâdi ve Varna savaşları (1443–1444) üzerinde anonim 'Gazavât-nâme'*. Ankara: Türk Tarih Kurumu Basımevi, 1978.

İnan, Afet. "Tarih boyunca Izmir şehri ve halkı hakkında kısa biligler." In *Tarih üzerine İnceleme ve Makaleler*, pp. 256–65. Ankara, 1960.

İslamoğlu, Huri, and Suraiya Faroqhi. "Crop Patterns and Agricultural Production Trends in Sixteenth-Century Anatolia." *Review* 3 (1979): 401–36.

İslamoğlu, Huri, and Çağlar Keyder. "Agenda for Ottoman History." *Review* 1 (1977): 31–55.

Issawi, Charles. "The Tabriz-Trabzon Trade, 1830–1900: Rise and Decline of a Route." *International Journal of Middle East Studies* 1 (1970): 18–27.

Izmir şehir rehberi. Izmir: Harita Genel Müdürlüğü Matbaası, 1981.

Jacoby, D. "The Jews in Chios under Genoese Rule (1346–1566)." *Zion* 26 (1961): 180–97.

Jeannin, Pierre. "The Sea-borne and the Overland Trade Routes of Northern Europe in the XVIth and XVIIth Centuries." *Journal of European Economic History* 11 (1975): 5–59.

Jennings, Ronald C. "Loans and Credit in Early 17th Century Ottoman Judicial Records: The Sharia Court of Anatolian Kayseri." *Journal of the Economic and Social History of the Orient* 16 (1973): 168–216.

———. "The Office of Vekil (Wakil) in 17th Century Sharia Courts." *Studia Islamica* 42 (1975): 147–69.

———. "Urban Population in Anatolia in the Sixteenth Century: A Study of Kayseri, Karaman, Amasya, Trabzon, and Erzerum." *International Journal of Middle East Studies* 7 (1976): 21–57.

———. "Firearms, Bandits, and Gun-Control: Some Evidence on Ottoman Policy towards Firearms in the Possession of *Reaya*, from Judicial Records of Kayseri, 1600–1627." *Archivum Ottomanicum* 6 (1976): 229–58.

———. "Kadi, Court and Legal Procedure in Seventeenth-Century Ottoman Kayseri." *Studia Islamica* 48 (1978): 133–72.

———. "Limitations of the Judicial Powers of the Kadi in Seventeenth-Century Ottoman Kayseri." *Studia Islamica* 50 (1979): 151–84.

Johnson, Douglas L. *The Nature of Nomadism: A Comparative Study of Pastoral Migrations in Southwestern Asia and Northern Africa*. Chicago: Department of Geography, University of Chicago, 1969.

Kahane, Henry R., and Renée and Andreas Tietze. *The Lingua Franca in the Levant*. Urbana, Illinois: University of Illinois Press, 1958.

Káldy-Nagy, J. "Names of Merchandises in a Mediterranean Turkish Customs Register." *Acta Orientalie Academiae Scientiarum Hung.* 18 (1965): 299–304.

———. "The Administration of the Sanjaq Registrations in Hungary." *Acta Orientali Academiae Scientiarum Hung.* 21 (1968): 181–223.

———. "The First Centuries of the Ottoman Military Organization." *Acta Orientalie Academiae Scientiarum Hung.* 31 (1977): 147–83.

Kampman, Arie Abraham. "XVII. ve XVIII. yüzyıllarda Osmanlı imparatorluğunda Hollandalılar." *Belleten* 23 (1959): 513–23.

Kasaba, Reşat. "Incorporation of the Ottoman Empire, 1750–1820." *Review* 10 (1987): 805–47.

————. *The Ottoman Empire and the World Economy: The Nineteenth Century*. Albany: State University of New York Press, 1988.

————. "Was There a Compradore Bourgeoisie in Mid-Nineteenth-Century Western Anatolia?" *Review* 11 (1988): 215–28.

Kâtib Çelebi. *The Balance of Truth*. Translated by G. L. Lewis. London: George Allen and Unwin, 1957.

Keleş, Ruşen. *Izmir mahalleleri (bir tipleştirme örneği)*. Ankara: Sosyal Bilimler Derneği Yayınları, 1972.

Kenaani, Y. "Economic Life in Safed and Its Surroundings during the Sixteenth and the First Half of the Seventeenth Centuries" (in Hebrew). *Tsiyyon* 6 (1933–34): 172–217.

Kevonian, Keram. "Marchands arméniens au XVIIe siècle: A propose d'un livre arménien publié à Amsterdam en 1699." *Cahiers du Monde Russe et Soviétique* 16 (1975): 199–244.

Keyder, Çağlar. "The Dissolution of the Asiatic Mode of Production." *Economy and Society* 5 (1976): 178–95.

Korkut, Cevat, and Erol Tümertekin. "Izmir şehrinde nüfus dağılışı." *Istanbul Üniversitesi Enstitüsü Dergisi* 14 (1964): 123–31.

Kunt, İ. Metin. "Transformation of *Zimmi* into *Askeri*." In *Christians and Jews in the Ottoman Empire*. Edited by Benjamin Braude and Bernard Lewis. Vol. 1: *The Central Lands*, pp. 55–67. New York: Holmes and Meier, 1982.

————. *The Sultan's Servants: The Transformation of Ottoman Provincial Government, 1550–1650*. New York: Columbia University Press, 1983.

Kurat, Akdes Nimet. *Türk-İngiliz münasebetlerinin başlangıcı ve gelişmesi (1553–1610)*. Ankara: Türk Tarih Kurumu Basımevi, 1953.

Kütükoğlu, Mübahat S. "XVIII. yüzyılda İngiliz ve Fransız korsanlık hareketlerinin Akdeniz ticareti üzerinde etkileri." *Belgelerle Türk Tarihi Dergisi* 2.12 (1968): 57–71.

————. *Osmanlı-ingiliz iktisâdî münâsebetleri, I (1580–1838)*. Ankara: Türk Kültürünü Araştırma Enstitüsü, 1974.

Lane, Frederic C. "Economic Consequences of Organized Violence." *Journal of Economic History* 18 (1958): 401–17.

————. "The Mediterranean Spice Trade: Further Evidence of Its Revival in the Sixteenth Century." In *Crisis and Change in the Venetian Economy*. Edited by Brian Pullan, pp. 47–58. London: Methuen, 1968.

————. *Venice: A Maritime Republic*. Baltimore: Johns Hopkins University Press, 1973.

Le Roy Ladurie, Emmanuel. *The Peasants of Languedoc*. Translated by John Day. Urbana, Illinois: University of Illinois Press, 1974.

Lemerle, Paul. *L'émirat d'Aydın, Byzance et l'Occident: Recherches sur 'La Geste d'Umur Pacha'*. Paris: Presses Universitaires de France, 1957.

Leveen, Jacob. "An Eyewitness Account of the Expedition of the Florentines against Chios in 1599." *Bulletin of the School of Oriental and African Studies* 12 (1948): 542–54.

Lewis, Bernard. *Notes and Documents from the Turkish Archives: A Contribution to the History of the Jews in the Ottoman Empire.* Jerusalem: Israel Oriental Society, 1952.

———. "Studies in the Ottoman Archives I." *Bulletin of the School of Oriental and African Studies* 16 (1954): 469–501.

———. *The Jews of Islam.* Princeton: Princeton University Press, 1984.

Lithgow, William. *The Totall Discourse, of the Rare Adventures, and Painefull Peregrinations of Long Nineteene Yeares Travayles, to the Most Famous Kingdoms in Europe, Asia, and Affrica.* London: J. Okes, 1632.

Lopes, R. "Market Expansion: The Case of Genoa." *Journal of Economic History* 24 (1964): 445–64.

Lowry, Heath. "The Ottoman *Tahrir Defter*s as a Source for Urban Demographic History: The Case Study of Trabzon (ca. 1486–1583)." Ph.D. diss., University of California at Los Angeles, 1977.

———. "The Ottoman Liva Kanunnames Contained in the Defter-i Hakanî." *Journal of Ottoman Studies* 2 (1981): 43–74.

———. "The Ottoman Tahrir-Defterleri as a Source for Social and Economic History: Pitfalls and Limitations." Paper presented at the Fourth International Congress on the Social and Economic History of Turkey (1071–1922). Munich, 4–8 August 1986.

Mantran, Robert. *Istanbul dans la seconde moitié du XVIIe siècle.* Paris: Librairie d'Amberique et d'Orient Adrien Maisonneuve, 1962.

———. "Centralisation administrative et financière. Problèmes du ravitaillement d'Istanbul aux XVIIe et XVIIIes." In *Istanbul à la jonction des cultures balkaniques, méditerranéennes, slaves et orientales, aux XVIe–XIXe siècles*, pp. 59–68. Bucharest: Association Internationale d'Etudes du Sud-est Européen, 1977.

———. "Foreign Merchants and the Minorities in Istanbul during the Sixteenth and Seventeenth Centuries." In *Christians and Jews in the Ottoman Empire.* Edited by Benjamin Braude and Bernard Lewis. Vol. 1: *The Central Lands*, pp. 127–37. New York: Holmes and Meier, 1982.

Masson, Paul. *Histoire du commerce français dans le Levant au XVIIe.* Paris: Hachette, 1911.

Masters, Bruce. "Trading Diasporas and 'Nations': The Genesis of National Identities in Ottoman Aleppo." *International History Review* 9 (1987): 345–67.

———. *The Origins of Western Economic Dominance in the Middle East: Mercantilism and the Islamic Economy in Aleppo, 1600–1750.* New York: New York University Press, 1988.

McGowan, Bruce. "Food Supply and Taxation on the Middle Danube (1568–1579)." *Archivum Ottomanicum* 1 (1969): 139–96.

———. "The Study of Land and Agriculture in the Ottoman Provinces within the Context of an Expanding World Economy in the 17th and 18th Centuries." *International Journal of Turkish Studies* 2 (1981): 57–63.

———. *Economic Life in Ottoman Europe*. Cambridge: Cambridge University Press, 1981.

Meinardus, Otto F. A. "Testimonies to the Economic Vitality of Balat, the Mediaeval Miletus." *Belleten* 37 (1973): 289–309.

Ménage, V. L. "The English Capitulations of 1580: A Review Article." *International Journal of Middle East Studies* 12 (1980): 373–83.

Millard, Annie Mary. "The Import Trade of London, 1600–1640." Ph.D. diss., University of London, 1956.

Minchinton, Walter Edward, ed. *The Growth of English Overseas Trade in the Seventeenth Century*. London: Newton, 1969.

Mirkovich, Nicholas. "Ragusa and the Portuguese Spice Trade." *Slavonic and East European Review* 21 (1943): 174–87.

Missir Reggio Mamchi di Lusignano, Livio. *Epitaphier des grandes familles Latines de Smyrne*. Vol. 2: *Les pierres tombales de l'église française Saint-Polycarpe*. Brussels: Dembla, 1985.

Mousnier, Roland. *La vénalité des offices sous Henri IV et Louis XIII*. Rouen: Editions Maugard, 1945.

Moryson, Fynes. *An Itinerary: Containing His Ten Yeeres Travell through the Twelve Dominions of Germany, Bohmerland, Sweitzerland, Netherlands, Denmarke, Poland, Itally, Turky, France, England, Scotland and Ireland*. 4 vols. Glasgow: J. MacLehose, 1907.

Murphey, Rhoads. "Functioning of the Ottoman Army under Murad IV (1623–1639/1032–1049): Key to the Understanding of the Relationship between Center and Periphery in Seventeenth-Century Turkey." Ph.D. diss., University of Chicago, 1979.

Nehama, Joseph. *Histoire des Israélites de Salonique*. 5 vols. Salonica: Emmanuel Sfakianakis, 1935–59.

Nezihi, Raif. *Izmir'in tarihi*. Izmir: n.p., 1926.

Nicolay, Nicolas de. *The Navigations, Peregrinations and Voyages, Made into Turkie by Nicholas Nicholay*. Translated by T. Washington the Younger. London: T. Dawson, 1585.

North, Douglass C., and Robert Paul Thomas. "An Economic Theory of the Growth of the Western World." *Economic History Review*. 2d ser., 23 (1970): 1–17.

———. *The Rise of the Western World: A New Economic History*. Cambridge: Cambridge University Press, 1973.

———. "Comment." *Journal of Economic History* 35 (1975): 18–19.

Oikonomos, Konstantin S. *Etude sur Smyrne*. Translated by Bonaventure F. Slaars. Izmir: B. Taitikian, 1868.

Olson, Robert W. "The Sixteenth Century 'Price Revolution' and Its Effect on the Ottoman Empire and on Ottoman-Safavid Relations." *Acta Orientalia* 37 (1976): 45–55.

Orhonlu, Cengiz. "Istanbul'da kayıkçılık ve kayık işletmeciliği." *Tarih Dergisi* 21 (1966): 109–34. Reprinted in *Osmanlı imparatorluğunda şehircilik ve ulaşım üzerine araştırmalar*. Edited by Salih Özbaran, pp. 83–103. Izmir: Ticaret Matbaacılık T.A.Ş., 1984.

———. "Şehir mimarları." *Journal of Ottoman Studies* 2 (1981): 1–30.

Ostrogorsky, George. *History of the Byzantine State*. Translated by Joan Hussey. New Brunswick: Rutgers University Press, 1957.

Pakalın, Mehmet Zaki. *Osmanlı tarih deyinleri ve terimleri sözlüğü*. 2d ed. 3 vols. Istanbul: Millî Eğitim Basımevi, 1971.

Pamuk, Şevket. "Commodity Production for World-Markets and Relations of Production in Ottoman Agriculture, 1840–1913." In *The Ottoman Empire and the World-Economy*. Edited by Huri İslamoğlu-İnan, pp. 178–202. Cambridge: Cambridge University Press, 1987.

———. *The Ottoman Empire and European Capitalism, 1820–1913*. Cambridge: Cambridge University Press, 1987.

Panzac, Daniel. "La peste à Smyrne au XVIIIe siècle." *Annales* 28 (1973): 1071–93.

———. "Activité et diversité d'un grand port Ottoman: Smyrne dans la première moitié du XVIIIe siècle." In *Memorial Ömer Lûtfi Barkan*. Edited by Robert Mantran, pp. 159–64. Paris: Librairie d'Amberique et d'Orient Adrien Maisonneuve, 1980.

Paris, Robert. *Histoire du commerce de Marseilles*. Vol. 5: *De 1660 à 1789, Le Levant*. Paris: Librarie Plon, 1957.

———, ed. *Histoire du commerce de Marseilles*. Vol. 3: *De 1480 à 1599*, Joseph Billioud and Raymond Collier. Paris: Librarie Plon, 1951.

Perjes, Géza. "Army Provisioning, Logistics and Strategy in the Second Half of the 17th Century." *Acta Historica Academiae Scientarium Hung.* 16 (1970): 1–51.

Piri Re'is. *Piri Re'is Bahrije: Das Türkische Segelhandbuch für das Mittellandische Meer vom Jahre 1521*. Edited and translated by Paul Kahle. Berlin: W. de Gruyter, 1926.

Pitcher, Donald Edgar. *An Historical Geography of the Ottoman Empire from Earliest Times to the End of the Sixteenth Century*. Leiden: E. J. Brill, 1972.

Pococke, Richard. "Dr. Pococke's Travels in the East." In *A General Collection of the Best and Most Interesting Voyages and Travels in All Parts of the World*. Edited by John Pinkerton. Vol. 10, pp. 406–770. London: Longman, 1811.

Podea, I. I. "A Contribution to the Study of Queen Elizabeth's Eastern Policy (1590–1593)." In *Mélanges d'Histoire Générale II*. Edited by Constantin Marinescu, pp. 423–76. Bucharest, 1938.

Pullan, Brian, ed. *Crisis and Change in the Venetian Economy*. London: Methuen, 1968.

Purchas, Samuel. *Hakluytus Posthumus or Purchas His Pilgrimes*. 20 vols. Glasgow: MacLahose, 1905.

Quataert, Donald. "Ottoman Handicrafts and Industry, 1800–1914: A Reappraissal." In *Osmanistische Studien zur Wirtschafts- und Sozialgeschichte in memoriam Vančo Boškov*. Edited by Hans Georg Majer, pp. 128–34. Wiesbaden: Otto Harrassowitz, 1986.

Ramsay, G. D. *English Overseas Trade during the Centuries of Emergence*. London: Macmillan, 1957.

Rapp, Richard T. "The Unmaking of the Mediterranean Trade Hegemony." *Journal of Economic History* 35 (1975): 499–525.

Refik, Ahmet (Altınay). *16 asırda Istanbul hayatı, 1553–1591*. 2d ed. Istanbul: Devlet Basımevi, 1935.

Reychman, J. and Zajaczkowski, A. *Handbook of Ottoman-Turkish Diplomatics*. Translated by A. S. Ehrenkreutz. Edited by T. Halasi-Kun. The Hague: Mouton, 1968.

Rhodes, Alexandre de. *Divers voyages et missions du P. Alexandre de Rhodes*. Paris: Chez S. Cramoisy, 1653.

Riedlmayer, Andras. "Ottoman-Safavid Relations and the Anatolian Trade Routes: 1603–1618." *Turkish Studies Association Bulletin* 5 (1981): 7–10.

Riemersma, Jelle C. "Government Influence on Company Organization in Holland and England (1550–1650)." *Journal of Economic History*, supplement 10 (1950): 31–39.

Rigault, Abel. "Savary de Lancosme: Un épisode de la ligue à Constantinople (1589–1593)." *Revue d'Histoire Diplomatique* 16 (1902): 522–78.

Rivkin, Ellis. *The Shaping of Jewish History: A Radical New Interpretation*. New York: Charles Scribner's, 1971.

Roberts, Lewes. *The Merchants Mappe of Commerce: Wherein, the Universall Manner and Matter of Trade, Is Compendiously Handled*. London: Ralph Mabb, 1638.

Roe, Thomas. *The Negotiations of Thomas Roe in His Embassy to the Ottoman Porte from the Year of 1621 to 1628 Inclusive*. London: S. Richardson, 1740.

Rosedale, H. G. *Queen Elizabeth and the Levant Company*. London: H. Frowde, 1904.

Roth, Cecil. *The House of Nasi*. Vol. 1: *The Duke of Naxos*. Philadelphia: Jewish Publication Society of America, 1948.

Rothenberg, Gunther E. "Venice and the Uskoks of Senj: 1537–1618." *Journal of Modern History* 33 (1961): 148–56.

Rozanes, S. *History of the Jews in Turkey* (in Hebrew). Vol. 3: *1575–1640*. Sofia: Amichpat, 1938.

Rycaut, Paul. *History of the Turkish Empire from the Year 1623 to the Year 1677.* . . . London: J. Starkey, 1680.

Sahillioğlu, Halil. "1763 de Izmir limanı ihracaat gümrüğü ve tarifesi." *Belgelerle Türk Tarihi Dergisi* 2.8 (1968): 53–57.

———. "XVII. yüzyılın ortalarında sirmakeşlik ve altın-gümüş işlemeli kumaşlarımız." *Belgelerle Türk Tarihi Dergisi* 3.16 (1968–69): 48–53.

———. "Yabancı gözüyle Türkler, Yahudiler, Ermeniler, Rumlar." *Belgelerle Türk Tarihi Dergisi* 3.15 (1968–69): 44–48.

———. "*Sivis* Year Crises in the Ottoman Empire." In *Studies in the Economic History of the Middle East from the Rise of Islam to the Present Day*. Edited by Michael A. Cook, pp. 230–52. London: Oxford University Press, 1970.

———. "Osmanlı para tarihinde dünya para ve maden hareketinin yeri (1300–1750)." *ODTÜ Gelişme Dergisi/Studies in Development*, special issue 1 (1978): 1–38.

Sanderson, John. *The Travels of John Sanderson in the Levant, 1584–1602*. Edited by Sir William Forster. Hakluyt Society. 2d ser., vol. 67. London: Hakluyt Society, 1931.

Sandys, George. *A Relation of a Journey Begun An: Dom: 1610*. 2d ed. London: W. Barrett, 1621.

Schechter, Solomon. "Safed in the Sixteenth Century—A City of Legists and Mystics." In *Studies in Judaism*. 2d ser., pp. 202–88. Philadelphia: Jewish Publication Society of America, 1908.

Schefer, Charles, ed. *Mémoires sur l'ambassade de France en Turquie, 1525–1770 par François Emmanuel Guignard, 1735–1821, Comte de Saint-Priest*. . . . 1877; rpt., Paris, 1974.

Scholem, Gershom G. *Major Trends in Jewish Mysticism*. 3d rev. ed. New York: Schocken Books, 1954.

———. *Sabbatai Ṣevi: The Mystical Messiah, 1626–1676*. Translated by R. J. Zwi Werblowsky. Princeton: Princeton University Press, 1973.

Schwarzfuchs, Simon. "La décadence de la Galilée juive de XVIe siècle et la crise du textile au Proche Orient." *Revue du Etudes Juives* 121 (1962): 169–79.

Sella, Domenico. "Les mouvements longs de l'industrie lainière à Venise aux XVIe et XVIIe siècles." *Annales* 12 (1957): 29–45.

Sertoğlu, Mithat. "VI. asırda Izmir." *Belgelerle Türk Tarihi Dergisi* 16.16 (1976–77): 72–76.

Shaw, Ezel Kural. "The Double Veil: Travelers' Views of the Ottoman Empire, Sixteenth through Eighteenth Centuries." In *English and Con-*

tinental Views of the Ottoman Empire, 1500–1800, pp. 1–29. Los Angeles: William Andrews Clark Memorial Library, University of California, 1972.

Shaw, Stanford. *History of the Ottoman Empire and Modern Turkey.* Vol. 1: *Empire of the Gazis: The Rise and Decline of the Ottoman Empire, 1280–1808.* Cambridge: Cambridge University Press, 1976.

Sherley, Anthony. *His Relations of His Travels.* London: N. Butter and L. Bagset, 1613.

Shmuelevitz, Aryeh. *The Jews of the Ottoman Empire in the Late Fifteenth and Sixteenth Centuries: Administrative, Economic, Legal and Social Relations as Reflected in the Responsa.* Leiden: E. J. Brill, 1984.

Skilliter, Susan A. *William Harborne and the Trade with Turkey, 1578–1582: A Documentary Study of the First Anglo-Ottoman Relations.* London: Oxford University Press, 1977.

Sokol, Edward D. *Tamerlane.* Lawrence, Kansas: Coronado Press, 1977.

Soucek, Svat. "Certain Types of Ships in Ottoman-Turkish Terminology." *Turcica* 7 (1975): 233–49.

Spon, Jacob, and George Wheler. *Voyage d'Italie, de Dalmatie, de Grece et du Levant, fair aux années 1675. et 1676.* Amsterdam: H. et T. Boom, 1679.

Steensgaard, Niels. "Freight Costs in the English East India Trade, 1601–1657." *Scandinavian Economic History Review* 13 (1965): 143–62.

———. "Consuls and Nations in the Levant from 1570 to 1650." *Scandinavian Economic History Review* 15 (1967): 13–55.

———. "European Shipping to Asia, 1497–1700." *Scandinavian Economic History Review* 18 (1970): 1–11.

———. *The Asian Trade Revolution of the Seventeenth Century.* Chicago: University of Chicago Press, 1974.

———. "Violence and the Rise of Capitalism: Frederic C. Lane's Theory of Protection and Tribute." *Review* 5 (1981): 247–73.

Stoianovich, Traian. "The Conquering Balkan Orthodox Merchants." *Journal of Economic History* 20 (1960): 234–313.

———. "Le maïs dans les Balkans." *Annales* 21 (1966): 1026–40.

———. "Pour un modèle du commerce du Levant: Economie concurrentielle et économie de bazar, 1500–1800." *Istanbul à la jonction des cultures balkaniques, méditerranéenes, slaves et orientales, au XVIe–XIXe siècles*, pp. 189–248. Bucharest: Association Internationale d'Etudes du Sud-est Européen, 1977.

Suceska, Avdo. "Die Entwicklung der Besteurung durch die Avarız-i divaniye und die Tekâlif-i örfiye im Osmanischen Reich wahrend des 17. und 18. Jahrhunderts." *Sud-ost Forschungen* 27 (1968): 89–130.

Svoronos, Nicholas G. *Le commerce de Salonique au XVIIIe siècle.* Paris: Presses Universitaires de France, 1956.

Tavernier, Jean Baptiste. *Six Voyages through Turkey into Asia*. London: 1678.

Tenenti, Alberto. *Piracy and the Decline of Venice, 1580–1615*. Translated by Janet and Brian Pullan. Berkeley and Los Angeles: University of California Press, 1967.

Thevenot, Jean de. *Travels of Monsieur de Thevenot into the Levant*. Translated by A. Lovell. Rpt., London: Farnborough, Gregg, 1971.

Todorov, Nikolai. *The Balkan City, 1400–1900*. Seattle: University of Washington Press, 1983.

Tongas, Gerard. *Les relations de la France avec l'empire Ottoman durant la première moitié du XVIIe siècle et l'ambassade à Constantinople de Philippe de Harlay, Comte de Césy (1614–1640)*. Toulouse: F. Boisseau, 1942.

Tournefort, Joseph Pitton de. *Relation d'un voyage du Levant*. 3 Vols. Lyon, 1727.

Tuncel, Bedrettin. "L'âge des drogmans." In *Istanbul à la jonction des cultures balkaniques, méditerranéennes, slaves et orientales, aux XVIe–XIXe siècles*, pp. 261–70. Bucharest: Association Internationale d'Etudes du Sud-est Européen, 1977.

Turan, Şerafettin. "Sakız'ın Türk hâkimiyeti altına alınması." *Tarih Araştırmaları Dergisi* 4 (1966): 173–99.

Ülker, Necmi. "The Rise of Izmir, 1688–1740." Ph.D. diss., University of Michigan, 1974.

———. "Batılı gözlemcilere göre XVII. yüzyılın ikinci yarısında Izmir şehri ve ticarî sorunları." *Tarih Enstitüsü Dergisi* 12 (1981–82): 317–54.

———. "The Emergence of Izmir as a Mediterranean Commercial Center for the French and English Interests, 1698–1740." *International Journal of Turkish Studies* 4 (1987): 1–37.

Uluçay, M. Çağatay. *XVIInci yüzyılda Manisa'da ziraat, ticaret ve esnaf teşkilâtı*. Istanbul: Manisa Halkevi Yayınlarından, 1942.

———. *XVII. asırda Saruhan'da eşkiyalık ve halk hareketleri*. Istanbul: Manisa Halkevi Yayınlarından, 1944.

Unat, Faik Reşit. *Hicrî tarihleri Milâdî tarihe çevirme kılavuzu*. Ankara: Türk Tarih Kurumu Basımevi, 1974.

Uzunçarşılı, İsmail Hakkı. "Kıbrıs fethi ile Lepant (İnebahtı) muharebesi sırasında Türk devletile Venedik ve müttefiklerinin faaliyetine dâir bazı Hazine-i Evrak kayıtlar." *Türkiyat Mecmuası* 3 (1926–33): 257–92.

Vaughan, Dorothy M. *Europe and the Turk: A Pattern of Alliances, 1350–1700*. Liverpool: University Press, 1954.

Veinstein, Gilles. "'Âyân' de la région d'Izmir et commerce du Levant (deuxième moitié du XVIIIe siècle)." *Etudes Balkaniques* 12 (1976): 71–83.

Vryonis, Speros, Jr. *The Decline of Medieval Hellenism in Asia Minor and the Process of Islamization from the Eleventh through the Fifteenth Century*. Berkeley and Los Angeles: University of California Press, 1971.

Wallerstein, Immanuel. *The Modern World-System: Capitalist Agriculture and the Origins of the European World-Economy in the Sixteenth Century*. New York: Academic Press, 1974.

Watson, Andrew A. "Back to Gold—and Silver." *Economic History Review*. 2d ser., 22 (1967): 1–34.

Weber, Shirley Howard. *Voyages and Travels in Greece, the Near East and Adjacent Regions Made Previous to the Year 1801*. Princeton: American School of Classical Studies at Athens, 1953.

Weinryb, Bernard D. *The Jews of Poland: A Social and Economic History of the Jewish Community in Poland from 1100 to 1800*. Philadelphia: Jewish Publication Society of America, 1973.

Werblowsky, Raphael Jehudah Zwi. *Joseph Karo: Lawyer and Mystic*. Philadelphia: Jewish Publication Society of America, 1977.

Willan, Thomas Stuart. "Some Aspects of English Trade with the Levant in the Sixteenth Century." *English Historical Review* 70 (1955): 399–410.

Wilson, Charles. "Cloth Production and International Competition in the Seventeenth Century." *Economic History Review*. 2d ser., 18 (1960): 209–21.

Wittek, Paul. "De la défaite d'Ankara à la prise de Constantinople." *Revue des Etudes Islamiques* 12 (1938): 1–34.

———. "The Turkish Documents in Hakluyt's 'Voyages'." *Bulletin of the Institute for Historical Research* 19 (1941–43): 121–39.

Wood, Alfred C. "The English Embassy at Constantinople, 1660–1762." *English Historical Review* 40 (1925): 533–61.

———. *A History of the Levant Company*. Oxford: Oxford University Press, 1935.

Woodhead, Christine. "'The Present Terrour of the World'? Contemporary Views of the Ottoman Empire c1600." *History* 72 (1987): 20–37.

Zachariadou, Elizabeth A. *Trade and Crusade: Venetian Crete and the Emirates of Menteshe and Aydın (1300–1415)*. Venice: Library of the Hellenic Institute of Byzantine and Post-Byzantine Studies, 1983.

Zeller, Gaston. "Une légende qui à la vie duré: Les capitulations de 1535." *Revue d'Histoire Moderne et Contemporaine* 2 (1955): 127–32.

INDEX

Library of Congress Cataloging-in-Publication Data

Goffman, Daniel, 1954–
    Izmir and the Levantine World, 1550–1650 / Daniel Goffman.
       p. cm. – (Publications on the Near East, University of
  Washington ; no. 5)
    Includes bibliographical references.
    ISBN 0-295-96932-6
    1. Izmir (Turkey)—Commerce—Middle East—History—17th century.
2. Middle East—Commerce—Turkey—Izmir—History—17th century.
3. Izmir (Turkey)—Economic conditions. 4. Izmir (Turkey)—Ethnic
relations.   I. Title.   II. Series.
HF3736.5.Z7M6284   1990
382.09562–dc20   89-39759
                                       CIP

DISCARD